Crafting Labor Policy

Techniques and Lessons from Latin America

Cover design by Patricia Hord Graphik Design.
Photos provided by (front cover, left to right) Curt Carnemark/World Bank Photo Library,
Photodisc, and Truman Packard; (back cover, left to right) Thomas Sennett/World Bank
Photo Library, Corbis, and Curt Carnemark/World Bank Photo Library.

Crafting Labor Policy

Techniques and Lessons from Latin America

Edited by
Indermit S. Gill
Claudio E. Montenegro
and
Dörte Dömeland

A copublication of the World Bank and Oxford University Press

A copublication of the World Bank and Oxford University Press.

Oxford University Press
198 Madison Avenue
New York, NY 10016

The findings, interpretations, and conclusions expressed here are those of the author(s) and do not necessarily reflect the views of the Board of Executive Directors of the World Bank or the governments they represent.

The World Bank cannot guarantee the accuracy of the data included in this work. The boundaries, colors, denominations, and other information shown on any map in this work do not imply on the part of the World Bank any judgment of the legal status of any territory or the endorsement or acceptance of such boundaries.

ISBN 0-8213-5112-5 hardcover
ISBN 0-8213-5111-7 paperback

Library of Congress Cataloging-in-Publication Data
Crafting labor policy : techniques and lessons from Latin America / edited by Indermit S. Gill, Claudio E. Montenegro, Dörte Dömeland.
  p. cm.
Includes bibliographical references and index.
ISBN 0-8213-5112-5 — ISBN 0-8213-5111-7 (pbk.)
  1. Labor policy—Latin America.   I. Gill, Indermit Singh, 1961–   II. Montenegro, Claudio.   III. Dömeland, Dörte, 1971–

HD8110.5 .C73 2002
331.12'042'098—dc21   2002019991

Contents

Tables and Figures

Tables

Foreword

THIS VOLUME PRESENTS a set of papers on labor market issues in Argentina, Brazil, and Chile, based on work sponsored by the World Bank. Some of the leading labor economists in the three countries covered here have coauthored these papers with the editors. An introductory chapter provides the context, summarizing labor market reforms in Latin America since the late 1980s. A concluding chapter summarizes the main results and policy implications for these and other countries.

The papers attempt to answer important labor policy questions in a quantitative manner. They have two features in common: each uses an estimation technique—sometimes one that is fairly complex—to do this, and the papers all have a strong policy focus. Thus,

- For Argentina, we use a labor force participation model to see if the structure of the labor market is such that the labor force grows during periods of economic slowdown and leads to exaggerated unemployment fluctuations, and wage and output elasticities of demand for labor to determine whether unemployment can be reduced substantially without labor market reforms to lower the price of labor relative to capital.
- For Brazil, we calculate public-private compensation differentials to determine the public employment reforms that would lower the fiscal deficit in Brazil in a sustainable manner, and identify specific labor laws that influence earnings and employment conditions by using statistical techniques to identify the pressure points in labor legislation.

- For Chile, we use a labor flow model to determine if employment has become more precarious even as unemployment has fallen, and quantile regression techniques to examine if the labor market rewards to skills and effort differ for workers from different socioeconomic groups.

We study labor issues in these countries during 1995–98. In macro-economic terms, of course, they were at very different stages of structural adjustment:

- Argentina's experience was analyzed during a stage of moderate growth and high unemployment, having undergone stabilization in the early 1990s and when it was midway through a fiscal adjustment.
- Brazil was examined during a stage of sluggish growth and low but rising unemployment, while still struggling to affect a fiscal adjustment and sustain the stabilization begun in 1994.
- Chile was studied during a stage of sustained growth and low unemployment, having completed its stabilization and fiscal adjustment in the mid-1980s.

The book looks at labor policy from three different angles:

- In the case of Argentina, the focus is structural: that is, labor demand and labor supply.
- In the case of Brazil, the approach is sectoral: that is, public and private employment and earnings.
- In the case of Chile, we focus on the main labor market outcomes: earnings and employment.

Finally, the study contains material at three levels of technical sophistication:

- Readable, nontechnical, and policymaker-friendly introductory and concluding chapters, written with the broadest audience in mind: policymakers, researchers beginning work on Latin America, and those with a temporary or casual interest in labor market issues in developing countries.
- Readable but somewhat more technical policy chapters on each country, written with a narrower target audience: policymakers who have a deeper interest in labor market issues and labor market specialists.
- Technical annexes that summarize the main techniques and models used in the empirical analysis in some of the policy chapters which

serve as a brief introduction to these techniques, aimed at researchers interested in empirical labor market issues and students of economic policy in developing countries.

We hope this book advances labor market reform—which has correctly been referred to as the "unfinished" economic reform in Latin America—in this and other parts of the world through quantification of some important issues, so that the debate is increasingly based on objective arguments instead of rhetoric. We will consider this and similar ventures worth the effort if and when labor reforms in emerging markets are upgraded in status from mostly unfinished to merely tardy.

Acknowledgments

WE WOULD LIKE TO THANK Homi Kharas, Danny Leipziger, and John Underwood who, as lead economists during the time that this work was initiated, provided valuable guidance in identifying labor market issues for closer scrutiny and determining policy-focused treatment of these subjects. We are also grateful to José Luis Guasch, Alberto Valdés, and Gautam Datta for their help in carrying out these ideas; as task managers of World Bank reports for which the studies collected here were commissioned, they encouraged analytical rigor in our inquiry even when time was short and budgets tight. Of course, all errors remain ours.

We would like to express our gratitude to Gobind Nankani and Suman Bery for encouraging us to write this book even when other tasks could have had priority. We would also like to thank Ana-Maria Arriagada, Amit Dar, Robert Holzmann, and Zafiris Tzannatos for financial support for the participation of Dörte Dömeland and Claudio E. Montenegro. The comments of Norman Hicks and three anonymous referees have helped us improve the contents of this book, and Diane Stamm has improved its form. Finally, we would like to thank Thaisa Tiglao of the World Bank's Office of the Publisher for her balanced advice and encouragement, and Cindy Fisher for shepherding the book through the final stages.

Acronyms
and Abbreviations

AR1	First-order autoregressive
AR2	Second-order autoregressive
BCRA	Banco Central de la República Argentina (Central Bank of the Republic of Argentina), Argentina
CAGED	Cadastro Geral de Empregados e Desempregados (Official Register of Employment and Unemployment), Brazil
CASEN	Encuesta de Caracterización Socioeconomica Nacional (National Socioeconomic Population Survey), Chile
CES	Constant elasticity of substitution
CIEPLAN	Corporación de Investigaciones Económicas para América Latina (Latin American Economic Research Corporation), Chile
CPI	Consumer price index
CLT	Consolidação das Leis do Trabalho (Consolidated Labor Code), Brazil
CRS	Constant returns to scale
EC	European Community
ECLAC	Economic Commission for Latin America and the Caribbean
EFTA	European Free Trade Association

EPH   Encuesta Permanente de Hogares (Continuing Household Survey)

FAT   Fundo de Aparelho de Trabalhadores (Fund for Work Assistance Programs and Unemployment Insurance), Brazil

FGTS   Fundo de Garantia do Tempo de Serviço (Severance Fund)

FIEL   Fundación de Investigaciones Económicas Latinoamericanas (Latin American Economic Research Foundation), Argentina

GBA   Greater Buenos Aires

GDP   Gross domestic product

GNP   Gross national product

IADB   Inter-American Development Bank

IDB   International Development Bank

ILO   International Labour Organization

INCRA   Instituto Nacional de Colonização e Reforma Agraria (Federal Land Reform Agency), Brazil

INDEC   Instituto Nacional de Estadística y Census (National Statistics and Census Institute), Argentina

EPH   Encuesta Permanente de Hogares (Permanent Household Survey), Argentina

INPC   Índice Nacional de Preços ao Consumidor (National Index of Consumer Prices), Brazil

INSS   Instituto Nacional de Seguridade Social (National Institute of Social Security), Brazil

IPEA   Instituto de Pesquisa Económica Aplicada (Institute for Applied Economic Research), Brazil

IPI   Industrial production index

IV   Instrumental variable

JSA   Job search assistance

KLEM   Capital, labor, energy, materials (short for an estimation model that includes these four variables)

LF   Labor force

LFP	Labor force participation
MARE	Ministerio da Administração Federal e Reforma do Estado (Ministry of Federal Administration and State Reform), Brazil
OECD	Organisation for Economic Co-operation and Development
OLS	Ordinary least squares
PASEP	Programa de Formação de Patrimônio do Servidor Público (Program of Assistance to Civil Servants), Brazil
PDV	Programa de demissão voluntaria (Voluntary Dismissal Program), Brazil
PIS	Programa de Integração Social (Social Integration Program), Brazil
PK	Price of capital
PL	Price of labor
PME	Pesquisa Mensal de Emprego (Monthly Employment Survey), Brazil
PNAD	Pesquisa Nacional por Amostra de Domicilios (National Household Survey), Brazil
PUC	Pontificada Universidade Católica (Catholic Pontifical University), Brazil
QLM	Quantile regression method
QRM	Quintile regression method
R$	Reals—Brazilian national currency
RAIS	Relação Annual de Informações Sociais (Annual Report of Social Indicators), Brazil
RGPS	Regime Geral da Previdencia Social (General Regime for Social Security), Brazil
RJU	Regime Jurídico Único (Pension Regime of Government Workers), Brazil
SEBRAE	Serviço de Apoioàs Pequenas Empresas (Assistance Program for Small Enterprises), Brazil
SENAC	Serviço Nacional de Aprendizagem Comercial (National Apprenticeship Program in Commerce), Brazil

SENAI	Serviço Nacional de Aprendizagem Industrial (National Apprenticeship Program in Industry), Brazil
SENCE	Serviço Nacional de Capacitación y Empleo (National Formation and Employment Program), Chile
SESC	Serviço Social do Comércio (Social Service Program for Industrial Workers in Commerce), Brazil
SESI	Serviço Social da Industria (Social Service Program for Workers in Industry), Brazil
SIMCE	Sistema de Medición de la Calidad de la Educación (Educational Quality Measurement System), Chile
SINE	Sistema Nacional de Emprego (National Employment System), Brazil
SURE	Seemingly unrelated regression estimator
TFP	Total factor productivity
UI	Unemployment insurance
V-T	Technical and vocational
WPI	Wholesale price index
WTO	World Trade Organization

1 Labor Reform in Latin America during the 1990s

DÖRTE DÖMELAND AND INDERMIT S. GILL

AFTER THE 1980s, a period characterized by high economic volatility and stagnation combined with worsening income inequality, the 1990s promised better days for Latin American workers. Indeed, macroeconomic indicators did improve during the decade, despite the Tequila Crisis during 1994–95 and the financial turmoil following the East Asia and Russia crisis during 1997–98. Gross domestic product (GDP) growth increased from less than 3 percent in the second half of the 1980s to more than 4 percent during 1991–97 before falling again. Inflation rates fell to single digits in many countries. Fiscal deficits fell. Even the rising trend in aggregate volatility in Latin America as measured by volatility in GDP growth, wages, and consumption was reversed during the 1990s. It was expected that economic growth induced by macroeconomic stabilization and structural reforms would generate new employment.

But this did not happen. Wages grew, but real wage levels in some countries still do not exceed the levels workers had attained in the early 1980s. In some countries, the increase in the supply of skilled labor did not keep up with the demand for skilled labor, leading to increases in the real wages of highly skilled, wealthier workers relative to those of the less skilled. Again, while the gains from the macroeconomic reforms did translate into productivity increases in most countries, they did not appear to generate the sort of jobs people had in mind. Argentina, Brazil, Mexico, and Uruguay experienced periods of growth, but little job creation in the formal, or regulated, sector. Compared with the second half of the 1980s, the rate of job creation in these four countries, particularly in the formal sector, actually fell.

1

The supply side of the labor market featured high labor force growth, largely due to increasing labor force participation of women. This, combined with the low job creation rate in the formal sector, implied both an increase in the share of the informal employment sector and in unemployment rates. The regional unemployment rate rose to about 10 percent by the end of the decade. In more than half the countries studied by de Ferranti and others (2000), unemployment rates remained above the levels of the 1970s. In Argentina, Paraguay, Peru, and the República Bolivariana de Venezuela unemployment rates increased to levels that are high even in absolute terms.

Colombia and Uruguay faced decreases in unemployment in the early 1990s, which were sharply reversed by the end of the decade. These high recorded rates of unemployment are worrisome. Given the large informal sector and the absence of widespread formal unemployment insurance, even low unemployment rates do not necessarily imply the absence of employment problems in most Latin American countries. Informal sector employment in Latin America and the Caribbean region increased from 52 percent in 1990 to more than 57 percent in 1996, and is likely to be close to 60 percent today. So understanding Latin American earnings and employment clearly requires a careful look at the informal sector, even more so now than a decade ago. During the first half of the 1990s, rates of informality increased in every Latin American country (Lora and Márquez 1998), and according to the International Labour Organization and the Inter-American Development Bank, 80 out of 100 jobs in the 1990s were created in the informal sector.[1]

However, informal firms show high rates of mortality and income variance (Levenson and Maloney 1998). Hence, it is not surprising that the jobs they offer are usually of "low quality" in the sense that they imply low salaries, long working hours, low job stability, and no pension benefits.[2]

Given these problems, it is not surprising that many Latin Americans harshly judge the developments during the last decade, and view the future somewhat pessimistically. Using data from the *Latinobarometro* survey, Lora and Márquez (1998) find that most Latin Americans considered unemployment to be the number one problem. At the time of the survey, 7 out of 10 Latin Americans were concerned about becoming unemployed within the next year. Even in countries with relatively low unemployment rates, such as Chile and Uruguay, this number was 5 out of 10. This concern may have increased since the Asian and Russian crises. Workers consider education and low wages the next two most important issues.[3] On the other hand, employers worry more about the deficiencies in labor supply and inadequate worker training, fearing that the educational system does not meet the needs of a more competitive economy. A strikingly large percentage of Latin Americans now call for more government action: 88 percent of respondents in the Latinobarometro survey believe it is government's responsibility to give work to everyone, and 85 percent believe governments have to provide a decent standard of living for the unemployed.

The design of labor laws in many Latin American countries shares some of the responsibility for these poor outcomes. Labor legislation in Latin America was originally enacted and designed to "protect" male household heads who worked for the government and other large- and medium-size employers. Over time, with the increases in female labor force participation and the size of the informal sector, the proportion of workers not covered by the legislation has increased, thus gradually increasing the tension between legislation and labor market realities. With stabilization and trade liberalization during the late 1980s and the 1990s, labor laws may have come under additional strain as the costs of "protection" of some workers increased. These pressures may have made Latin American labor markets ripe for reform in that the dissatisfaction may be peaking. But the desired direction of change is far from obvious. The aim of this book is to help inform policymakers and others about the most promising directions of change in labor market regulation.

Some Latin American governments have already reacted to these concerns by introducing more or less profound changes in their labor regulations. In most Latin American countries, constitutions or labor codes, which are based on the civil law system, regulate the type and duration of labor contracts and the conditions for their enforcement.[4] For the purposes of this book, we define labor market reforms as changes in labor laws and regulations. In this chapter, we describe the basic labor market reforms that took place during the 1990s, and which are related to the topics that seem to most concern workers in the region—unemployment, job stability, and informality.

The labor laws we focus on in this chapter are those that affect job security while workers are employed, and that provide support—such as severance payments, individual severance funds, and unemployment insurance—during unemployment. We discuss the pros and cons of the measures taken and summarize existing evidence on the effect of these reforms on the welfare of Latin American workers. We survey the reforms that are likely to affect labor turnover in the formal sector, such as temporary contracts, job security legislation, and income support for the unemployed.[5] Public sector reforms may have underlined the pessimism in

Latin America, as some workers who held secure jobs suddenly faced the prospect of joblessness. For this reason we also provide a short summary of the most important public sector reforms. Given the large share of informal workers in the Latin American labor market, we explicitly deal with the issue of coverage and noncompliance. The final section concludes with an introduction to the six country chapters in this book—two each for Argentina, Brazil, and Chile—and a brief discussion of how this book addresses some of the main concerns of Latin American workers.

Reforms in Job Security Legislation

Job security legislation in Latin America varies considerably across countries.[6] Among the few common elements are limitations on temporary hiring and tenure-related severance payments that raise the cost of hiring "permanent" workers. These regulations came under attack during the 1990s, when it became clear that economic growth by itself would not be enough to increase job creation and job quality.[7]

The trade, financial, and fiscal reforms that were introduced during the 1990s reduced inflation and increased competition. Inflation had been an important instrument for adjusting wages during the 1980s. Proponents of labor market reform claim that the decrease in inflation exacerbated the rigidity in real wages, and forced an adjustment through formal employment instead. Further, it is argued that increased competition aggravated the negative effects of this rigid labor legislation, as firms required increasingly more flexibility to adjust their workforce when economic conditions changed in a competitive environment. Changes in relative prices and more intensive use of machinery in the tradable sectors in the wake of trade reforms and stabilization led to an increased share of employment in the nontradable goods sectors. This reallocation of labor among the sectors reflected changes in the size and composition of the workforce at the plant level. The restrictions on the firing of workers increased the costs of these adjustments, and may have prolonged the transitional phase and hindered an efficient allocation of workers. They may also have reduced job creation, because high dismissal costs affect the hiring decisions of firms, especially in an environment with intrinsically greater economic uncertainty.

Finally, proponents of reduced job security pointed out that rigid labor legislation was likely to encourage noncompliance, and hence increase the size of the informal sector. For some firms this implies pressures to produce at a smaller (possibly less efficient) scale in order to avoid detection by tax and labor authorities. According to this argument, reducing job security might increase the number of firms that offer formal contracts, and hence the proportion of workers covered by labor legislation. Further, it might increase productivity by not distorting the decision of the optimal size for the firm. To summarize, deregulating the labor market would lower labor costs, which would result in more labor-intensive production and higher job creation in the formal sector and enhanced compliance, leading to a reduction of the informal sector and, hence, an improvement in the quality of jobs.

But this line of argument must answer certain questions. First, if job security legislation is so bad, why was it implemented in the first place? There is some evidence that job security decreases the volatility of employment and improves the welfare of certain groups who are likely to be better represented in the political process. For them, many of the regulations that are considered distortionary actually increase the quality of jobs in terms of wage, work amount, and job stability.[8] Those who suffer from the regulations and who could benefit from deregulation are often politically less well represented.

Second, while it is claimed that job security reduces the level of employment, where is the evidence? Actually, the theoretical and empirical evidence on the net effects of firing costs on employment and unemployment is ambiguous. Hence, benefits of reforms are often not well understood, which may introduce some reluctance on the part of policymakers to undertake reform. However, high labor market flexibility increases the volatility of employment, leading to higher firing relative to hiring during recessions, and increased hiring relative to firing during booms. This may contribute to the fear of workers of introducing labor market flexibility in an environment that is already characterized by great economic volatility. Saavedra (1999) relates a telling anecdote about the popularity of job security in Peru. When the Peruvian public was informed in 1996 that a draft law reducing mandatory severance payments was being considered, it created such an uproar that the Peruvian government quickly recanted, claiming that the purported reduction in benefits was in fact a typographical error. It ended up *increasing* mandated severance payments instead!

The fact that deregulation of labor market reforms is difficult to implement might be reflected in the low number of countries in Latin America that actually undertook serious reforms. While 23 out of 26 countries in the region carried out profound trade reform and 24 notably liberalized their financial sectors, only 6 have introduced substantial changes to their labor legislation since the late 1980s: Argentina (1991, 1995, 1999); Brazil

(1988); Colombia (1990); Guatemala (1990); Panama (1995); and Peru (1991). And while it is generally believed that macroeconomic, financial sector, and trade reforms have been steps in the right direction, it is far from obvious whether changes in labor laws qualify as improvements.

Temporary Contracts

To promote stable employment, 14 out of 26 countries in Latin America restrict the use of temporary contracts or fixed-term contracts. Until the 1990s, legislation either explicitly prohibited the use of temporary contracts for permanent activities, or restricted the duration and number of times these contracts could be renewed. Temporary contracts were usually allowed only for work temporary in nature, such as harvesting or construction. During the 1990s, Argentina, Brazil, Colombia, Ecuador, and Peru introduced new rules for contracts, especially temporary contracts. Essentially, the duration of periods during which the work relationship was legally classified as "temporary" was extended. During this time these contracts have lower dismissal costs. In addition, the employers are sometimes required to pay lower payroll taxes for such workers, making them "special" as well as temporary.

Advocates of the more extensive use of temporary contracts in Latin America point out that temporary contracts reduce the cost of employment adjustment, especially in an environment characterized by high dismissal costs. Temporary contracts allow firms to hire workers during periods of high labor demand, such as seasonal work or during booms. Using temporary contracts for this purpose was not generally forbidden by legislation in most Latin American countries, but the administrative costs of using temporary contract provision (for example, requiring labor union consent in each case) may have been high. The second argument often put forward is that firms might use temporary contracts as a screening device. This improves the allocation of workers, leading to efficiency gains. A final argument is that temporary contracts might open up new possibilities for workers who traditionally have low employment possibilities, such as women and youths. Women and young workers have the highest unemployment rates in Latin America. Permanent contracts may induce discrimination against women if there are higher implicit costs of hiring women due to maternity leave and allowance. Temporary contracts might help young workers gain experience, and thus facilitate their incorporation into the workforce.

Opponents of temporary contracts claim that they reduce job stability. Although temporary contracts facilitate adjustment of a firm's workforce, these contracts might imply that the workers subject to them bear the entire brunt of adjustment, further increasing the rents of workers with permanent contracts. Screening good workers from bad is unlikely to be the primary objective of temporary contracts in Latin America, since most Latin American countries have probationary periods, ranging from 2 months in Colombia to 12 months in Brazil and Chile, even for regular contracts. Whether young workers really benefit from temporary contracts is also not clear, because the short time temporary workers are in the firm reduces incentives for the firm to invest in their human capital. A last critical argument regarding the use of temporary contracts in Latin America concerns the unstable political environment. If employers fear that the existing labor regime might change, they might use temporary contracts extensively, because they would not incur new, unpredictable obligations if the law were changed.

Argentina, Brazil, Colombia, Ecuador, and Peru introduced new formulas for temporary contracts. The most important changes were probably introduced in Argentina, Colombia, and Peru (see Table 1-1). In Argentina, temporary contracts were illegal in all cases, except where explicitly allowed before the 1991 reform.[9] Temporary contracts could not

TABLE 1-1

Changes in Temporary Contract Legislation

Country	Year	Change
Argentina	1991	Introduction of fixed-term and training contracts to promote employment and training with lower mandatory severance payment and payroll taxes.
	1995	Introduction of trial period provision. Special employment promotion contracts, special conditions for small firms streamlining use of temporary contracts.
	1998	Abolition of most of the exemptions from severance payments and payroll taxes and reduction of probation period to one year.
Colombia	1990	Reduction of minimum duration of temporary (fixed-term) contracts.
Peru	1991	Introduction of different forms for temporary contracts. Extension of eligibility criteria. Reduction of administrative costs of implementing temporary contracts.

exceed five years in duration and required a severance payment. The 1991 reform introduced new types of contracts, called *modalidades promovidas*, with the explicit objective of promoting reemployment of former public sector workers who had lost their jobs during public sector reform in Argentina. To facilitate the incorporation of young workers in the labor market, contracts were created that aimed at providing training and work experience for those with previous training. Each contract was applicable only to specific workers (unemployed, laid off as a consequence of public sector cutback, or less than 24 years of age) or firms (new firms, new lines of production, or services in existing establishments). Duration of these new types of contracts ranged from six months to a maximum of two years. The contracts, however, applied only if trade unions approved them, and were required to be registered at the employment office. This may have severely reduced their expansion. Hopenhayn (2001) finds that less than 5,000 new employment contracts were registered every month for the entire country. Guasch (2000) points out that only the largest companies with the greatest turnover rates actually took advantage of the law.

In 1995, a special employment promotion contract for workers over 40 years of age was introduced that did not require payment of severance at termination of contract, and lowered the labor taxes that employers had to pay. Labor taxes and severance payments of the training promotion contract increased. A new provision introduced a three-month trial period for all new contracts, during which time no severance payments for termination had to be paid. This provision applied to all new contracts. Small firms were allowed to use the previous employment promotion contracts, without the requirements of the approval of trade unions, the need to register the contract in the government employment agency, and to pay severance. This new reform contributed to a more extensive use of temporary contracts. While at the beginning of 1996 the contracts did not surpass 5 percent of total employment, toward the beginning of 1998, 12 percent of formal employment were covered by them. Forty percent of the total net formal jobs that were generated between January 1996 and January 1998 were subject to these new contracts (Guasch 2000).

Using the labor-cost elasticities presented in Chapter 5, "Increasing Labor Demand in Argentina," Guasch (2000) calculates that 13 percent fewer jobs would have been created in the absence of the new contractual forms. Hopenhayn (2001) shows that the probability of exiting employment (that is, becoming unemployed or leaving the labor force) increased during the trial period by about 40 percent. Hopenhayn does not find sizeable effects for small firms and young workers. This may be explained by the fact that temporary contracts implied lower taxes, which induced an increase in hiring, but at the same time replaced longer-term employment with short-term employment. Despite the economic benefits of such contracts, this reform was not politically popular. In May 1998, the Argentine Congress passed a law abolishing most of the exemption from severance payments and payroll taxes, and reduced the probation period to one year.

In Peru temporary contracts were introduced in the 1970s. Many provided social benefits but did not have an employment protection clause. Consequently, even before the reform in 1991, about 20 percent of workers in formal firms were subject to a temporary contract. However, the administrative costs of implementing temporary contracts were high, since they required the prior authorization of the Ministry of Labor. The 1991 reform reduced these costs and extended the reasons for hiring workers under temporary contracts. This resulted in a substantial increase in the use of temporary contracts from 1991 to 1996, cutting formal permanent wage employment from 80 percent in 1991 to 39 percent in 1997 (Pagés 1999; Saavedra and Torero 2000). This example highlights something that employers and policymakers know well but economists need to be reminded of: when assessing changes in job security legislation, the implied changes in administrative costs should not be ignored.

In Colombia, temporary contracts—which did not require severance payment if they ended on the agreed date—were limited to a year's duration. The reform of 1990 relaxed this minimum duration. At the same time, permanent contracts also became more flexible, as we will discuss below. For Colombia, Kugler (2000) finds that the labor legislation reform substantially increased the exit rates out of employment. After the reform the probability of exiting employment was 7 percent higher for temporary formal sector workers than for temporary informal sector workers, but only about 6 percent higher for permanent formal workers than for permanent informal workers. This suggests that temporary contracts partially increased turnover of formal workers, but their effect on the increase in exit rates out of unemployment was relatively small.

Given that permanent contracts have high dismissal costs, temporary contracts have helped in circumventing rigid labor laws. In the absence of such avenues, firms may evade compliance with labor legislation entirely, for example, by remaining small. Larger firms resort to legal methods of avoiding these restrictions through, for example, subcontracting smaller firms to deliver the services that workers might have provided if these laws were less onerous. Indeed, during the 1990s, subcontracting increased in most countries. The International Labour Organization (1999) argues that the economic reforms increased the pressure on big firms to improve their productivity, leading to an increased tendency to subcontract for certain activities. But this might also be due to new (unrelated) policies of restructured firms to subcontract to, for example, firms that might themselves subcontract cleaning and security services to smaller firms that hire employees informally (de Ferranti and others 2000).

Temporary contracts have been an attractive instrument for introducing labor market flexibility at the margin, and thus avoiding more pronounced labor reforms. While these contracts are beneficial to employers because they reduce adjustment costs, they do not necessarily increase worker welfare. Temporary contracts in Latin America might introduce an intermediate layer of job security regulation that lies between the formal and informal sectors. Their design will determine whether they place potentially formal workers into a category that lies between the formal and informal in terms of employment security and nonwage benefits, or whether they draw informal employees into the realm of regulated workers. This points to the fact that understanding the impact of labor legislation on the informal sector is an important task in assessing the effect of labor market reforms on worker welfare. Chapter 3, "Assessing the Impact of Regulations on Informal Workers in Brazil," tries to do this.

Severance Payments

The level of mandated severance payment when a "permanent" contract is ended varies widely among Latin American countries, always increases with tenure, and is related to cause. The basic formula for calculating a severance payment is generally a proportion of monthly wages times years of service. Often a ceiling is imposed, and workers with high tenure usually have additional rights, as will be discussed later. During the 1990s, decreases in the level of severance payment were introduced in Colombia, Guyana, Guatemala, Nicaragua, Peru, and the República Bolivariana de Venezuela, while Brazil (1988), Chile (1991), and the Dominican Republic (1992) increased the amount a firm had to pay upon dismissal of a worker. In Brazil the increase was substantial.

Originally, severance payments were designed to protect workers against "unjust dismissal," not to provide dismissed workers with income support. This was achieved by imposing additional costs on a firm for firing a worker. There is clear evidence that severance payments decrease the probability of a worker losing his or her job. For Brazil, Paes de Barros, Corseuil, and Bahia (1999) find that an increase in severance payments increases the duration of employment spells. The Colombian reform in 1990 reduced severance payments, enlarged the definition of just dismissal, extended the use of temporary contracts, and reduced the advance notice for mass dismissals. For Colombia, Kugler (2000) finds that the average tenure of formal workers (who are covered by the reform), relative to informal workers, decreased. This was largely due to a decrease in the average tenure of formal workers.

Employment protection may have further positive impact on labor productivity. Firms will invest more in training if they expect employees to stay with them longer. Productivity improvements also crucially depend on a cooperative working environment, which is usually not achieved in a hostile atmosphere. Given the high frequency of litigation with respect to severance payments in Latin America, the question arises whether the design of severance payments—which are mandatory, not voluntary—actually increases the potential for conflict rather than contributes to a cooperative environment.

Opponents of high levels of job security point out that mandated severance payments might deter job creation because they not only reduce firing, but also hiring, by firms. Low job creation was one of the major employment problems during the 1990s. However, from an empirical viewpoint this claim is not unambiguously supported. Some empirical evidence for Latin America and the Caribbean indeed suggests a significant adverse effect of job security on unemployment rates (Heckman and Pagés 2000).[10] But using a rank indicator for job security, Márquez (1998a) finds that job security is not significantly associated with lower employment once other factors are controlled for. Nor does empirical analysis for specific countries that changed job security legislation reveal a clear picture (notably Kugler 2000 for Colombia; MacIsaac and Rama 2001 for Peru).

To compound the problem, in Latin America high dismissal costs are combined with weak enforcement institutions. Weak enforcement institutions may imply that (even formal) firms offer job security only to those workers who they expect to stay with the firm in the near future. In that case, having job security is more an indicator of the quality of a worker than a means of protecting workers against unjust dismissal. MacIsaac and Rama (2001) find that in Peru private sector workers who are legally entitled to severance payments earn lower wage rates than workers who are not. But they work longer hours, so their monthly earnings are higher than those of workers who do not receive severance payments. This implies that the objective of protecting workers against unjust dismissal is not served well in the first place.[11]

What is perhaps even more important is the effect of severance payments on informality. As pointed out, most informal firms are actually small.[12] High levels of severance payments are especially difficult to handle for small firms, because they are more likely to be credit constrained and face more uncertain production and sales conditions (Levenson and Maloney 1998). High dismissal costs therefore increase the premium for small firms to stay informal. But most of the jobs during the 1990s were created in these small firms, implying an increase in the number of workers not officially protected by labor legislation.

To reduce the informality premium and thus increase the coverage of job security, one has to either lower the dismissal costs or increase the probability of being detected and fined in case of noncompliance.[13] While some countries opted for a decrease in severance payments, Argentina, Brazil, and Chile tried to strengthen their enforcement institutions during the 1990s. In Argentina a law was introduced in 1991 that established fines for the employer in case a worker is not registered or is registered incorrectly. In 1991 the Chilean government increased the resources devoted to the enforcement of the labor legislation and carried out mass-media campaigns. Regulations that provide more effective access to the legal system for lower-income workers and legislation that allows more appropriate control of compliance were streamlined (Cortázar 1997). Since 1998 Brazil has stepped up efforts to tighten the enforcement of social security legislation and has increased penalties for noncompliance.

While the effect of severance payments on aggregate employment is not unambiguous, design of severance pay legislation leads to a protection of some workers at the expense of others.[14] This is especially true if severance pay is tenure related. MacIsaac and Rama (2001) find, for example, that in Peru only one in five private sector workers and one in three private sector wage-earners is actually entitled to receive severance payments, and these covered workers tend to be wealthier.[15] Entitlement to severance pay is nearly twice as high for the richest quintile group as for the poorest. This gap increases when coverage indicators are used, such as the presence of a written contract, coverage by social security, and employment in unionized or large enterprises. On the other hand, it may segregate the labor market. But this is not the whole story. If high dismissal costs are combined with weak enforcement institutions, this may weaken the effect of high severance payments on aggregate formal employment, but is likely to increase the size of the informal sector.

Severance pay, however, may affect not only the composition of employment with respect to the informal sector, but may increase the formal employment rates of those protected by the legislation relative to those who are excluded. Apart from informal sector workers, these are lower-tenured workers, who are usually younger, less experienced, unskilled, and female. For Colombia, for example, Kugler (1999) finds that average unemployment spells of women, young and middle-aged with incomplete secondary and incomplete university education, decreased. These effects become stronger when severance pay is related to tenure.

Severance pay laws often intend to reward workers for long-term commitment to a firm. Accordingly, severance payments usually increase with tenure. Additionally, workers with certain years of tenure are given special rights. In Brazil, until the institution of individualized severance funds, workers with more than 10 years of tenure could not be fired except on rare disciplinary grounds. Before the 1990 reform in Colombia, workers with more than 10 years of tenure could sue the firm in case of dismissal. If the firm could not prove just cause, it had to rehire the worker. Moreover, it had to pay the total amount of wages that the worker had foregone during the proceedings, and the firm had to take over the worker's pension at the time of his or her retirement (Lora and Henao 1997). Similar rights of reinstatement also existed in Panama and Peru.

As expected, tenure-related severance payments lead to lower employment rates for young relative to older workers in Latin America, because they reduce hiring and increase firing of less-tenured workers relative to more-tenured workers. Using an index for job security, Heckman and Pagés (2000) find that an increase in expected dismissal costs especially affected the employment rates of young workers. For Chile, Pagés and Montenegro (1999) provide evidence that tenure-based job security biases employment and wages in favor of middle-aged and older workers and reduces long-term aggregate employment. They do not find a visible impact on unemployment, because the reduction in youth unemployment coincides with a reduction in labor force participation among the youth. Hence the authors recommend a flat severance payment, because this would have little effect on youth employment or on aggregate employment and unemployment rates. This requires either reducing the maximum amount a worker can receive as severance pay, or reducing the rate at which the severance pay increases with tenure.

Tenured workers are made better off relative to untenured workers or those with lower tenure if the maximum ceiling increases (as in Chile) or if slope of the severance pay–tenure profile increases (as in Colombia, the Dominican Republic, and Peru). Only Argentina seems to have reduced severance costs for higher-tenure workers during the 1990s (see Table 1-2).

TABLE 1-2
Changes in How Severance Pay Increases with Tenure

Country	Year	Change
Argentina	1991	Maximum ceiling imposed.[a] Advance notice of one month independent of tenure. No severance payment for termination within trial period of three months.
Brazil	1988	Employer must contribute every month the equivalent of 8 percent of each employee's current monthly wage, which is accumulated in a government-administered individual account. The penalty for dismissal without just cause was raised from 10 to 40 percent of this accumulated balance.
Chile	1991	Maximum ceiling was raised from 5 to 11 months' wages. Workers with more than six years of tenure could opt out of job security provision and participate in "unemployment fund."
Colombia	1990	Workers with more than 10 years of tenure lost the right to sue for back pay and reinstatement, but cost of dismissing workers with more than 10 years of tenure increased.
Dominican Republic	1992	Severance payment increased for all new employees, but to a larger extent for workers with more than five years of tenure.
Nicaragua	1996	Severance payment for workers with more than three years of tenure increased. Maximum ceiling of five monthly wages was imposed.
Panama	1995	Severance payment converted to 3.4 weeks per year of service if less than 10 years of service. Two additional weeks otherwise. Workers with more then 10 years of tenure receive 1.5 months less than before if fired because of economic cause.
Peru	1991	Job security law eliminated for new contracts. No severance payment for workers with less than one year of service.

Country	Year	Change
	1995	Job security eliminated for all contracts. Severance payment for workers with less than three years decrease compared with 1991.
	1996	Severance payment increased for all workers. Maximum ceiling became available for workers with 8 years of tenure (in 1991, 12 years).
Venezuela, R. B. de	1997	Severance payment increased from one monthly wage per year of service to two monthly wages per year of service.

a. Such that maximum yearly payment cannot exceed the equivalent of the average of three months' salary determined in the collective bargaining agreement that applies to the worker. Note that the maximum ceiling existed until September 1989, when the Economic Emergency Law eliminated it.

The changes may indicate that decreasing the rights to tenure is difficult because this is likely to reduce employment rates for older workers. Older workers exert pressure to maintain their level of job security provisions, and these workers are usually better represented in the political process. Policymakers can either try to pursue broad coalitions of the groups which will be favored by the reform, or apply changes only to new contracts. On the other hand, consideration should be given to the fact that older displaced workers might be especially hurt by layoffs due to their inability to update their skills, or by the unwillingness of firms to employ them for other reasons. In the 1990s, older workers in Peru displayed a higher probability of becoming informal, and in Argentina and Uruguay unemployment spells of older workers became longer (de Ferranti and others 2000).

If the basic idea of introducing severance payments is to protect workers against unjust dismissal—for engaging in union activity, for example—it is understandable that labor legislation in most Latin American countries mandates that workers usually receive severance payments only when dismissal is not justified. Justified dismissal refers to serious misconduct as defined in the labor legislation. Further, consistent with the idea of protecting workers against unjust dismissal is the fact that economic problems of the firm are not considered a reason for just dismissal.

However, it is often claimed that the objective of severance payments is stability. The exclusion of dismissals due to economic reasons from the list of justified reasons is consistent with the idea of worker protection. Where this is not true, as in Chile, it may provide an important loophole for evading job security legislation. Cortázar (1997) points out that in Chile before 1990 about half of the termination of labor contracts was due to economic cause.[16] Further, the fact that access to severance payments depends on cause implies that employees attempt to turn voluntary quits into dismissals in order to receive severance payments, which has led to high litigation costs. For example, Rama and Maloney (2000) point out that most of the complaints registered in Latin American labor courts are related to severance payments.

In most Latin American countries no unemployment insurance system exists. Precautionary savings are low and workers are largely credit constrained. Because severance payments provide funds at the moment of firing, they also help protect workers from income loss in the period immediately following unemployment. Consequently, severance payments play the role of unemployment insurance. But as a means of providing income support for the unemployed, their relation to cause—and the resulting uncertainty about the amount the worker will receive—contributes to their inefficiency. Employment distortions introduced by severance payments could be evaded if workers would forego part of their earnings when employed, which they could use in case of unemployment independent of the cause of job separation. This is the idea underlying compensation funds.

Considering severance payments as a type of unemployment insurance implies then that the uncertainty about obtaining payments should be reduced. Table 1-3 indicates again that no clear trend emerged among Latin American countries. However, as we will see, during the 1990s Chile, Colombia, Panama, Peru, and the República Bolivariana de Venezuela introduced compensation funds, and these were the countries which actually also seemed to increase access to severance payments.

Whether mandated severance payments are likely to be useful tools for unemployment insurance is doubtful. First, coverage may be low and richer workers are more likely to be covered by severance pay legislation, largely because of the exclusion of the informal sector. MacIsaac and Rama (2001) find that in Peru only one in five private sector workers and one in three private sector wage earners is actually entitled to receive severance payments.[17] Wealthier workers are covered by the legislation: eligibility for severance pay is twice as high for the richest quantile compared to the poorest. This gap increases when the authors use coverage indicators. Second, in Latin America unemployment rates are especially high for female, young, and low-skilled workers (Márquez 1998b), and these are the groups whose employment rates are likely to be depressed by the sev-

TABLE 1-3
Changes in Severance Payment Laws and Cause of Dismissal

Country	Year	Change
Argentina	1991	If dismissal is due to just cause, severance payment is half of the payment for unjust cause. Economic reasons now considered just cause.
Bolivia	1990	Access to same severance payment for quits and layoffs after five years on the job.
Brazil	1988	In case of dismissal without just cause, employer has to pay 40 percent of severance fund balance; this was 10 percent until 1988.
Chile	1991	Clause stipulating that economic reasons are a just cause was reinstated. Failure to prove economic cause raises legal severance by 20 percent. Failure to prove just cause raises legal severance by 50 percent. Workers participating in unemployment fund have access to fund independent of cause.
Colombia	1990	Just cause extended to include any dismissal for failure to comply with firm regulation and instructions from one's supervisor.
Nicaragua	1996	Workers who quit receive a severance payment. Severance payment paid in case of economic cause increases. In both cases this accounts to monthly wage times years of service up to the third year, and increases thereafter.
Panama	1995	One-fourth of monthly wage per year of service available for new contracts if worker quits (only after 10 or more years of service). Compensation for dismissal in case of economic causes decreases for all new contracts.
Peru	1991	The definition of "unjustified dismissal" made more restrictive. Access to compensation fund independent of cause.
Venezuela, R. B. de	1997	Access to compensation fund independent of cause.

erance legislation. Further, given the relation of severance to tenure and wages, they also receive relatively low payments. Third, in general severance payments do not link the amount received and unemployment duration, so severance pay may largely serve to bridge short-term unemployment. Again, female, young, and low-skilled workers have the highest unemployment duration and least benefit from severance pay. Fourth, the relation of severance payment to cause limits its ability to ensure against idiosyncratic risk. The fact that the firm does pay them and that often economic cause is excluded does not allow insurance against aggregate risk. De Ferranti and others (2000) point out that before trade reform these risks were effectively pooled over a larger population because higher prices mean that consumers effectively subsidized these firms. Given that more firms sell closer to world prices as trade regimes are liberalized, this is no longer possible. Finally, as pointed out, distortionary effects of severance payments are likely to be large. One way to decrease these effects is to reduce uncertainty and directly link contributions and benefits. This is the basic idea of severance compensation funds.

Compensation Funds

Compensation funds are individualized accounts to which workers regularly transfer a part of their salaries. Workers can draw on their accounts when they are separated from their jobs. Sometimes partial withdrawals from the fund are possible for housing, education, or health expenses. These funds provide a form of forced self-insurance. In contrast to severance payments and unemployment insurance, they provide no net transfers to workers who lose their jobs. Mandatory self-insurance may be welfare-improving if the government cannot credibly state that it will not intervene if individuals become unemployed. It evades the employment distortions introduced by the severance pay regulation because it introduces a direct link between payments and contributions. Compensation funds are not designed to increase job stability; they are created to protect workers against the income loss they face at the moment they become unemployed.

Compensation funds have been introduced in Chile, Panama, Peru, and the República Bolivariana de Venezuela. Colombia reformed its existing compensation fund. This may reflect a higher demand for unemployment insurance and the fact that it is easier to introduce compensation funds than to change severance payment legislation. This is reflected in the fact that in Colombia, Ecuador, Peru, and the República Bolivariana de Venezuela, in the event of dismissal, workers receive both compensation from the fund and severance payments.

The relatively high coverage of the compensation funds is consistent with the evidence that workers do not opt out of them when given the choice. In Colombia 47 percent of urban workers are covered by the compensation fund. Kugler (2000) finds that in 1995 only 1.5 percent of workers in manufacturing and 0.6 percent of workers in commerce preferred a higher salary in exchange for not being covered by the Colombian compensation fund, *Fondo de Cesantia.*

The *Fundo de Garantia do Tempo de Serviço* (FGTS) in Brazil, which was created in 1966 and provides an individualized fund for each worker, is atypical in the sense that it combines the fund with an extra fine which can be assessed only in case of dismissal. Every month the employer contributes 8 percent of his or her employee's current wage to the fund. This implies that the worker's FGTS increases with tenure and that the amount accumulated in the Fund per year corresponds approximately to one monthly wage. In general, the FGTS can be accessed by the worker only upon dismissal (not if he or she quits) or upon retirement.[18] When a worker is dismissed without just cause (*sem justa causa*) the employer must also pay a penalty that is proportional to the FGTS balance of the worker. Thus, when dismissed, the worker gains access to his or her accumulated balance in the FGTS, and additional compensation of 10 percent of the FGTS balance at the time of dismissal if it was judged as being without just cause. In 1988 this fine for unjust dismissal was increased to 40 percent of the FGTS (see Table 1-4 and Chapter 3).

Unemployment Compensation

The purpose of unemployment insurance is to provide short-term financial support to workers if they are laid off from their jobs, and not to change the firing decisions of firms. Unemployment insurance systems may vary in their eligibility criteria, the level and length of benefits, and the way they are administered, depending on country-specific labor market characteristics and national consensus on secondary objectives. The programs may prevent unemployed workers from sliding into poverty, which means that unemployment insurance could provide a safety net. On the other hand, unemployment insurance can provide a worker with the opportunity to search for a job that better corresponds to his or her skills and interests, and may also induce workers to hold out for higher-wage jobs. An unemployment insurance system may also encourage work-

TABLE 1-4

Changes in Severance Compensation Fund Legislation

Country	Year	Change
Brazil	1988	Fine for unjustified dismissal increased from 10 percent to 40 percent of worker's FGTS, which is equivalent to the worker's current monthly wage. Access to fund independent of cause.
Chile	1990	All workers with tenure above six years can opt out of severance payment and participate in fund. Employer deposits 4.11 percent of gross wages in a bank account bearing worker's name.
Colombia	1990	Employer contributes one month of yearly salary to a capitalized fund bearing the worker's name. Access independent of cause.
Panama	1995	Firms are obliged to create a collective fund which is managed by a private entity. Employers contribute to this fund.
Peru	1995	Employer deposits half a month's salary twice a year in a bank account bearing the worker's name. Access independent of cause.
Venezuela, R. B. de	1997	Employer deposits fund in a collective account. Consequently, the severance payment does not equal the accumulated capital, but is last year's salary times years worked times the interest on the accumulated funds. If the firm cannot prove that the cause is justified, it must pay a supplementary severance.

ers to apply for high-wage jobs with high unemployment risk. In response, firms may offer jobs with higher unemployment risk, higher capital-labor ratios, and higher wages, implying that moderate unemployment insurance may not only improve risk-sharing, but also increase output.[19] Finally, an unemployment insurance system may help as a macroeconomic stabilization tool. Countercyclical spending due to unemployment insurance may improve consumption levels and welfare during recessions and thus insure against both idiosyncratic and aggregate risk. To satisfy this objective, the unemployment insurance system requires covering a large part of the population and having high enough fiscal resources that allow paying benefits even during recessions.

Opponents of unemployment insurance systems for Latin America point out its demanding administrative requirements costs and the common moral hazard issue. Building up an unemployment insurance system is admittedly not an easy task. For example, in the early stages of the unemployment insurance system in Brazil, the delivery mechanism did not work very well, so some workers had to wait up to a year to receive their checks (Mazza 1999). But administrative capacity can be built and administrative effort reduced by, for example, relying on already existing infrastructure and keeping the benefit structure simple. Moral hazard—the fact that the unemployed reduce their job search effort in the presence of unemployment insurance—can lead to an increase in the duration of unemployment. This issue can be tackled by keeping benefit levels low and the duration of benefits short, and by imposing certain work search requirements. This issue is discussed in more detail in Chapter 7, in the context of concerns in Chile that employment has become more precarious over the last decade.

The existence of a large informal sector in many Latin American countries introduces further complications concerning implementation of an unemployment insurance system. The most obvious problem is that a large informal sector makes it difficult to determine whether persons are actually unemployed or, rather, working in the informal sector. Argentina, for example, has tried to deal with this problem by increasing the cost of collecting unemployment benefits in terms of time (for example, having to collect payments in person, during peak business hours, and waiting in long queues). The existence of a large informal sector also makes it doubtful that the objectives an unemployment insurance system may fulfill are in fact achieved. First, the high proportion of informal workers who are not covered by unemployment insurance limits the usefulness of unemployment insurance systems as a safety net. Second, if workers do work in the informal sector while receiving unemployment benefits, this may undermine the function of unemployment to improve worker-firm matches. Unemployment insurance then may even contribute to an increase in the informal sector by creating disincentives to finding jobs in the formal sector as long as unemployment benefits are paid. Finally, the existence of a large informal sector reduces the strength of unemployment insurance as a macroeconomic stabilization tool.

A problem unrelated to the design of these schemes is that unemployment insurance systems in Latin America were added on to existing mandated severance laws. With social security also being mostly funded by high taxes on labor income, the tax burden is already high. In Argentina, Brazil, Colombia, and Uruguay the costs of contribution to Social Security exceed 30 percent of wage costs. In Organisation for Economic Co-operation and Development (OECD) countries the costs are between 15 and 30 percent.[20] What is more important is the problem of combining unemployment insurance with severance pay and individualized compensation funds. This lack of coordination and overlapping of different programs may introduce substantial inefficiencies. In some Latin American countries severance payments exceed the amount a worker receives from unemployment insurance. This may introduce the perverse effect that unemployment insurance is converted into a type of unemployment subsidy, rather than a means of cushioning the drop in income. Thus, implementation of an unemployment insurance system must consider the existing mix of termination and severance benefits.

In Latin America, Argentina, Barbados, Brazil, Chile, Ecuador, Mexico, Uruguay, and the República Bolivariana de Venezuela have some kind of special unemployment assistance programs, nearly all of which were implemented during the 1980s and 1990s. Eligibility criteria are rather strict. In Argentina, Barbados, Uruguay, and the República Bolivariana de Venezuela access to unemployment subsidies requires a certain number of months of contributions to social security or the unemployment fund. The worker must be immediately available to work in Argentina, Chile, and the República Bolivariana de Venezuela, and the worker has to be laid off for just or economic cause to have access in Argentina, Brazil, Chile, and Uruguay. Coverage of these programs is rather low. This may be because the benefits are small, as in Chile and Ecuador, or the worker has to prove economic necessity, as in Brazil. Reforms took place from the end of the 1980s in Argentina (1991 and 1995), Brazil (1990), and the República Bolivariana de Venezuela (1989 and 1998).

In Chile, an unemployment insurance bill was introduced by the government in 1993, but not implemented. Mandated individual accounts with some pooling of risks were introduced in Chile in 2001. In the República Bolivariana de Venezuela, the unemployment insurance system was enacted in 1989, reformed in 1999, but not yet implemented. In Argentina, the Employment Law implemented an unemployment insurance system in March 1992.[21] Coverage of the Argentine unemployment insurance system is low. Nationwide, the system covers only 10 percent of the unemployed. The average beneficiary of the Argentina unemployment insurance program is a prime-aged male without family responsibility (Mazza 1999). Fifty-one percent of the applicants earned 300 to 600 pesos per month and 17 percent earned more than 1,000 pesos per month, which was three times more than the maximum unemployment insurance benefit level in the late 1980s. Only 6 percent earn less the 300 pesos per month, which indicates that the unemployment insurance systems does not meet the role of a safety net.[22] The scheme is not integrated with other programs. A person who is laid off can get severance pay and unemployment benefit emergency funds at the same time.

Whether the unemployment insurance system in Argentina meets the role of macroeconomic stabilization is also questionable, given that the government decreased unemployment benefits in times of recession. In the wake of the Tequila Crisis in 1995, the government officially lowered the maximum amount of benefits. In Chapter 4, "Understanding Labor Supply Dynamics in Argentina," female labor force participation in Argentina is shown to exhibit strong procyclical fluctuations. This behavior is explained by the added worker effect, which implies that women enter the labor market when the earnings of their husbands decrease due to a job loss or reduction in work hours. In Argentina this aggravates unemployment rates during recession. Cutting unemployment benefits during this period may even increase the cyclical response of female labor force participation.

In Brazil the current unemployment system was created in 1986. It underwent major changes in 1990 when a larger fund, called the *Fundo do Amparo ao Trabalhador* (FAT), was created. It is the largest in Latin America, with an average of up to 4 million beneficiaries per year. Unemployment insurance is completely financed by the employer, who pays a tax of about 0.65 percent of total business sales to unemployment insurance. Length of benefit duration usually ranges between three and five months. Benefit levels increase only slightly with the duration of work experience. Benefit levels range from the minimum wage to twice the minimum wage. Workers who are laid off by their employer and have a formal contract are eligible for unemployment benefits. The worker must have worked six months during the last three years to receive the minimum benefit. Once a worker has obtained unemployment insurance, he or she is not eligible for additional insurance for another 16 months. The fact that a very short employment period is required may mean that the system is heavily used by young workers, a finding confirmed by Mazza (1999). About 50 percent of the workers are 30 years of age or younger. The average beneficiary receives about 1.5 times the minimum wage, is a male 35 years of age or younger, is in the service or industrial sector, and has an eighth-grade education (Mazza 1999).[23]

Evidence on unemployment insurance in Latin America is still weak. In Argentina and Brazil unemployment insurance systems seem to support middle-income groups and not the poorest workers, due to the fact that poor workers are usually in the informal sector and have low employment spells, which disqualifies them from having access to the system. Severance payments do not seem to be an adequate way of providing unemployment insurance due the distortions they introduce, the uncertainty about the amount transferred, and the high legal costs they imply. Whether compensation funds or unemployment insurance should be used as a means of income support best suited for a country will depend on the frequency and duration of unemployment, and the extent of the informal sector and its administrative capacity. Furthermore, it should be kept in mind that existing instruments do not seem to be adequate measures for insuring low-wage earners and informal workers against long-term unemployment.

Public Sector Employment and Earnings

Proponents of labor market reforms claim that the only reforms that may have a negative effect on aggregate employment in the short term are those related to privatization and public sector downsizing. The 1990s was a decade of privatization for Latin America. Large privatization programs decreased the share of government employment from 15.3 percent in 1990 to 13.2 percent in 1995. Argentina and Mexico privatized about 2 percent of the value of their GDP from 1990 to 1994, and Brazil had equally ambitious privatizations between 1996 and 1999. In terms of value, 43 percent of privatizations in the region occurred in the area of utilities, which were traditionally not open for private participation. The sale of banks and similar institutions contributed a further 23 percent.

Argentina reduced the number of federal administration and railroad workers during 1990–94, reducing public sector employment from 10 percent of the total in 1990 to approximately 5 percent by 1998. Restructuring the workforce was considered an important component of public sector reform, because wages accounted for about 70 percent of federal expenditures, not including interest payments and transfers. Under the federal administration program 400,000 workers lost their jobs. Rehiring was forbidden by law. About 73,000 railroad workers lost their jobs (Haltiwanger and Singh 1999).

Peru performed a large public sector downsizing (of the civil service) that involved more than 225,000 job separations from 1991 to 1993. Both lump-sum severance payments and pension enhancements were used to induce departure. About 112,000 workers received severance packages averaging about $1,000. One of the major issues was that the program was targeted badly. This further aggravated pre-existing shortages in human capital, because many of the most qualified civil servants left the public sector. Furthermore, rehiring of separated workers was significant, implying that reductions of employment in the federal government were offset by increases at the regional level. When the dust settled, 163,000 of the originally dismissed workers had been rehired (Haltiwanger and Singh 1999). Reduction in public sector employment may also have contributed to an increase in the informal sector. Pagés (1999) points out that the public sector reform and the privatization process reduced employment in these sectors by about 12 percent. Workers who lost their jobs due to this process were on average about 50 years of age and had not completed secondary education. Due to difficulties in finding jobs in the formal sector, most of them opted for self-employment, contributing to the growth of informality in Peru.

To summarize, privatization included a reduction in the workforce of the privatized enterprises, but Lora and Pagés (1996) conclude that, with the exception of Argentina, there is little evidence that this had an effect on aggregate employment.

A Road Map for the Book

For Latin America, the decade of the 1990s was largely characterized by economic growth but low formal job creation. Informality and unemployment levels increased. These employment problems triggered discussions on the distortionary effects introduced by existing labor laws that mostly had remained untouched since the 1950s, and moved labor reform into the spotlight. This chapter discussed the principal labor market reforms related to job security and the provision of financial support to the unemployed. The picture that emerges is one in which labor market regulations were generally not characterized by profound changes, but were at best improvements at the margin. In some cases, even this would be a generous characterization.

But the way forward is much less clear. Labor legislation in Latin America is distinguished more by its heterogeneity than by its homogeneity. And even if a law is identical in two countries, its effect on wages and employment may be different due to differences in employment structure (such as changes in the composition of the labor force or the size of the informal sector), political history, administrative capacity and incentives for compliance, and other aspects of each country's labor legislation. This implies that labor markets have to be studied country by country in order to identify the reforms that would most benefit workers, firms, and governments, and that is what this book does for three countries in Latin America.

Chapters 2 and 3 are dedicated to Brazil, which underwent changes in labor legislation in 1988. With the exception of social security reforms, few reforms of the public sector were successful. This is striking since reducing the fiscal burden of public employment was viewed as central to sustaining the stabilization begun in 1994. Public sector employment in Brazil is approximately 10 percent of the total, similar to the percentage Argentina faced before its public sector reform. Large-scale public sector reforms may reduce employment levels in the short term, and are difficult to implement. Hence, identifying the most-needed public sector reforms is important. Difficulties in implementing public sector reforms and the possible negative effect on employment require a thorough analysis of where inefficiencies exist in the public sector, in order to target the reforms. The approach in Chapter 2, "Improving Public Sector Efficiency in Brazil," allows us to identify those sectors within the public sector where the problem was one of excess employment, and where the problem was one of higher-than-market compensation. The chapter finds that while not all government employees earn more than similar private sector employees, public-private pension differentials are large. During 1999–2000, Brazil reformed the social security system for private sector workers, which has increased the existing public-private pension gap even further.

Labor legislation in Brazil requires formal sector employers to sign a standard contract ratified by the Ministry of Labor, which is called the *carteira de trabalho,* or work card. The household dataset we use in our analysis provides information on whether or not a worker has this signed work card. This provides a unique opportunity to identify informal wage earners, who are usually identified from the characteristics of the firm they work for, and allows us to study the effects of labor legislation on informal sector workers. It is usually assumed that labor laws that increase labor costs increase the size of the informal sector, but the direct effect of labor legislation on workers is generally not considered. Chapter 3, "Assessing the Impact of Regulations on Informal Workers in Brazil," examines whether labor market regulations, such as minimum wages and maximum hours worked, distort the wage and hour distribution of informal sector workers as well. The chapter illustrates the pitfalls of making generalizations about informal sector work being precarious or unprotected.

The average unemployment rate in Argentina over the last decade was among the highest in Latin America (aside from Panama and Nicaragua), peaking in 1995 at about 18 percent. At the same time, Argentina faced large increases in the female participation rate. Chapter 4, "Understanding Labor Supply Dynamics in Argentina," examines whether female labor force participation in Argentina exhibits noticeable cyclical patterns, and whether this aggravates or ameliorates unemployment rates during recession. We can then speculate about whether cutting unemployment benefits during recessions, as the Argentine government did during the Tequila Crisis during 1994–95, affects the cyclical response of female labor force participation and hence unemployment rates.

Benefits of reforms are often not well understood, which naturally introduces a reluctance to reform. Hence, understanding the impact of reforms on employment is important. Chapter 5, "Increasing Labor Demand in Argentina," provides numerical estimates of employment growth that would occur if labor costs were reduced due to labor market reform, using the wage elasticity of employment. Argentina introduced substantial changes to labor legislation during the 1990s (relative to most other Latin American countries), but reversed some of them by the end of the decade. It relaxed labor legislation on temporary contracts, introducing labor market flexibility at the margin. It increased the monthly basis for calculating severance payments, but widened the definition of just cause and imposed a maximum ceiling for higher-tenure workers. At the end of the decade, these reforms did not appear to have led to a significant reduction in labor costs.

In much of Latin America, the increase in the supply of skilled workers did not keep up with the demand for skilled labor, leading to increases in real wages in favor of especially highly skilled workers, and widening the differentials among skilled and unskilled workers. Chapter 6, "Responding to Earning Differentials in Chile," provides evidence on returns to education across different quantiles, analyzes whether rewards to education differ by socioeconomic status, and quantifies the effect of policies that improve access and quality of education for poorer sections of Chilean society.

Besides the concern of rising wage inequality, a perceived increase in instability of employment worried observers in Chile in the mid-1990s. Chile had been exceptional in the region because in 1981 it had already introduced significant labor market reforms, which involved fewer job security restrictions. The government not only reformed labor legislation related to individual contracts, but also introduced changes in legislation concerning unions and collective bargaining. In contrast to the other countries in the region, basic labor market indicators since the 1990s were promising. Chile's per capita output grew by about 5 percent, and unemployment rates fell from more than 20 percent in the early 1980s to less than 6 percent. Between 1984 and 1994, average real wages grew by 28 percent. By 1995, poverty fell to about half of what it was in the early 1980s. Chapter 7, "Dealing with Employment Instability in Chile," examines whether, in spite of these favorable developments, the Chilean labor market has become a less reliable source of earnings, because of increased precariousness of employment.

In this book, therefore, we analyze this wide range of different labor market topics for Argentina, Brazil, and Chile. The policy guidance provided takes country-specific conditions into account, but we use standard statistical and econometric tools that can be easily applied to similar problems in other countries. While focused on labor market analysis, the book considers macroeconomic conditions and labor market institutions where relevant. Implementation of labor reforms becomes more likely if—due to changes in macroeconomic and labor market fundamentals—societies become less willing to keep labor market restrictions in place. In Latin America, changes in labor legislation were not profound during the 1990s, but it is encouraging that after several decades of inaction, the first steps have been taken. Perhaps the next decade will see more progress in this area of regulation, and Latin American workers will take home more of the benefits of reform in other areas of economic policy.

Notes

1. Small firms are more likely to be informal both because it is easier to hide from legislation and because they generally do not benefit from formal contracting, risk-pooling, and other programs that may be advantageous for larger firms. According to the definition of the World Trade Organization, firms with less than five employees are considered informal. In this book we follow country-specific definitions of informality. For example, in Brazil informality is defined as wage-earners and self-employed workers who do not have a signed work card, implying that social security and other contributions are not made by them or their employers.

2. Of course, not all small enterprises are dedicated to simple survival. There are also informal firms with relatively high levels of technology and human capital. There is evidence that the proportion of qualified personnel in microenterprises increased during the 1990s, but remains below the levels in larger firms.

"Low-quality" jobs may arise because of a low level of technology, low social protection, or noncompliance with existing norms.

3. Poverty and social diseases such as crime, corruption, and political violence appear to be relatively minor concerns.

4. This does not apply for Caribbean economies, which we will not consider in the analysis that follows.

5. While we recognize that in Chile in the 1990s there were substantial reforms in the areas of union and collective bargaining, we do not address those reforms here.

6. By job security we refer to all those provisions that increase the costs of worker dismissal.

7. A similar debate emerged in Europe during the 1980s after the economic downturn in the wake of oil shocks.

8. For example, full-time, indefinite contracts; mandatory severance payments; notice periods; limits on working hours; surcharges for overtime, night and holiday work; social security contributions; and minimum wages.

9. Temporary contracts were allowed only in the case of force majeure, lack or reduction of work due to seasonal peak in work, organization of congresses and reunions, requirement of urgent security measures, and extraordinary and transitory necessities of firms (Bour 1994).

10. Heckman and Pagés (2000) and Pagés and Montenegro (1999) use a job security index that also includes advance notification and foregone wages during any trial in which a worker contests dismissal. In this sense it is not a pure measure of the effect of severance payments.

11. Furthermore, job turnover may be partially reduced because job search is reduced.

12. See footnote 1.

13. Note that increasing coverage of job security legislation may also imply a reduction in labor demand. A rare study on the extension of job security provision in developing countries was done by Fallon and Lucas (1991), who find a drop in labor demand in Zimbabwe.

14. Groups, for example, that are not covered, are the informal sector, family workers, and workers with low tenure. Domestic workers often receive lower severance pay.

15. Note that in Peru less than two-thirds of private sector workers are wage earners.

16. Severance payments do increase job stability, but they may also reduce the intensity of job searches by employed workers. Furthermore, it creates a potential for conflict, which may induce large liability costs. Dismissals in Peru before 1991 had to be approved by the government, and if considered "unjustified" the worker could opt for being reinstated instead of receiving a severance payment. The need for government approval was abolished by the 1991 reforms, and the right of reinstatement was abolished in the 1995 reform. In 1995 Panama reduced the

wages firms had to pay from the time of firing until the court decision was handed down.

17. Note that in Peru, less than two-thirds of private sector workers are wage earners. Severance payments are rather high. MacIsaac and Rama (2000) find that unemployed workers who receive severance pay have consumption levels about 20 to 30 percent higher than workers who continue to work!

18. Withdrawals are possible for large health expenses or the acquisition of a home.

19. For a theoretical development of this idea see Acemoglu and Shimer (1998).

20. The actual tax burden in a country is difficult to quantify because of issues concerning tax compliance and the role of nontaxable wages.

21. The benefits paid out by the unemployment insurance system in Argentina are financed by a 1.5 percent payroll tax on employers and 1 percent on employees. Except for workers in the construction, agriculture, and domestic service sectors, all workers are eligible for the new unemployment insurance system if they worked a minimum of one year on the last job and were laid off without cause. Payment duration ranges from 4 to 12 months, depending on the length of employment in the previous job. Benefits range from 150 to 300 pesos per month and have a median level of 284 pesos per month. This compares to an average wage rate of 840 pesos in October 1993 for individuals in Greater Buenos Aires working more than 30 hours per week, but at the same time, 30 percent earn less than 400 pesos (Pessino 1997). Compensation decreases over time, a common means of addressing the moral hazard issue.

22. At the same time the informal sector in Argentina increased from approximately 25 in 1988 to 40 percent in 1998 (Mazza 1999).

23. Ramos (1999) finds that households with income between 20 and 30 minimum wages receive 43 percent of unemployment benefit payments, while only 5.5 percent accrue to households with income between 3 and 5 minimum wages. In the case of FGTS accounts, households with income higher than 30 minimum wages make 47 percent of the withdrawals, while only 2.3 percent are made by households with incomes between 2 and 5 minimum wages.

References

Acemoglu, Daron, and Robert Shimer. 1998. "Efficient Unemployment Insurance." Working Paper No. 6686. National Bureau of Economic Research, Cambridge, Mass.

Bour, Juan Luis. 1994. "Regulaciones laborales y funcionamiento del mercado de trabajo en america latina: el caso argentino." In Gustavo Márquez, ed., *Regulación del mercado de trabajo en America Latina*. Coalición Costarricense de Iniciativas de Desarrollo (CINDE).

Cortázar, René. 1997. "Chile: The Evolution and Reform of the Labor Market." In Sebastian Edwards and Nora Lustig, (eds.), *Labor Markets in Latin America. Combining Social Protection with Market Flexibility.* Washington, D.C.: The Brookings Institution.

de Ferranti, David, Guillermo Perry, Indermit Gill, and Luis Servén. 2000. "Securing our Future in a Global Economy." Latin American and Caribbean Studies. World Bank, Washington, D.C.

Fallon, Peter R., and Robert Lucas. 1991. "The Impact of Changes in Job Security Regulations in India and Zimbabwe." *World Bank Economic Review* 5 (3): 395–413.

Guasch, Luis. 2000. *Argentina: Labor Market in the New Millennium.* Washington, D.C: World Bank.

Haltiwanger, John, and Manisha Singh. 1999. "Cross-Country Evidence on Public Sector Downsizing." *World Bank Economic Review* 31 (1): 23–66.

Heckman, James, and Carmen Pagés. 2000. "The Cost of Job Security Regulation: Evidence from Latin American Labor Markets." Working Paper No. 7773. National Bureau of Economic Research, Cambridge, Mass.

Hopenhayn, Hugo. 2001. "Labor Market Policies and Employment Duration: The Effects of Labor Market Reform in Argentina." Working Paper No. 407. Inter-American Development Bank Research Department, Washington, D.C.

International Labour Organization (ILO). 1999. "Decent Work and Protection for All: Priority of the Americas." Report of the Director General. Geneva.

Kugler, Adriana. 1999. "The Impact of Firing Costs on Turnover and Unemployment: Evidence from the Colombian Labour Market Reform." *International Tax and Public Finance* 6 (3): 389–410.

———. 2000. "The Incidence of Job Security Regulations on Labor Market Flexibility and Compliance in Colombia: Evidence from the 1990 Reform." Research Network Working Paper No. R-393. Inter-American Development Bank Research Department, Washington, D.C.

Levenson, Alec R., and William Maloney. 1998. "The Informal Sector, Firm Dynamics, and Institutional Participation." Policy Research Working Paper No. 1988. World Bank, Washington, D.C.

Lora, Eduardo, and Carmen Pagés. 1996. "La legislación laboral en el proceso de reformas estructurales de América Latina y el Caribe." Office of the Chief Economist. Inter-American Development Bank, Washington, D.C.

Lora, Eduardo, and Gustavo Márquez. 1998. "The Employment Problem in Latin America: Perceptions and Stylized Facts." Working Paper No. 371. Inter-American Development Bank Research Department, Washington, D.C.

Lora, Eduardo, and Marta Luz Henao. 1997. "Colombia: The Evolution and Reform of the Labor Market. Labor Markets in Latin America." In Sebastian Edwards and Nora Lustig, (eds.), *Combining Social Protection with Market Flexibility.* Washington, D.C.: The Brookings Institution.

MacIsaac, Donna, and Martin Rama. 2000. "Mandatory Severance Pay in Peru: An Assessment of its Coverage Using Panel Data." Paper prepared for the Regional Study on Economic Insecurity. Office of the Chief Economist. World Bank, Washington, D.C.

———. 2001. "Mandatory Severance Payment: Its Coverage and Effects in Peru." Development Research Group. World Bank, Washington D.C.

Márquez, Gustavo. 1998a. "Protección al empleo y funcionamiento del mercado de trabajo: una aproximación comparativa." Inter-American Development Bank, Washington, D.C. Processed.

———. 1998b. "El Desempleo en América Latina y el Caribe a Mediados de los Años 90." Office of the Chief Economist Working Paper No. 377. Inter-American Development Bank, Washington, D.C.

Mazza, Jacqueline. 1999. "Unemployment Insurance: Case Studies and Lessons for Latin America and the Caribbean." RE2/SO2, Technical Study. Inter-American Development Bank, Washington, D.C.

Paes de Barros, Ricardo, Carlos Corseuil, and Monica Bahia. 1999. "Labor Market Regulations and the Duration of Employment in Brazil." Texto para Discussao No. 676. Institute of Applied Economic Research, Rio de Janeiro.

Pagés, Carmen. 1999. "Apertura, Reforma y Mercado de Trabajo: La experiencia de un década de cambios estructurales en el Perú." Office of the Chief Economist, Working Paper No. 397. Inter-American Development Bank, Washington, D.C.

Pagés, Carmen, and Claudio Montenegro. 1999. "Job Security and the Age-Composition of Employment. Evidence from Chile." Office of the Chief Economist, Working Paper No. 398. Inter-American Development Bank, Washington, D.C.

Pessino, Carola. 1997. "Argentina: The Labor Market During the Economic Transition." In Sebastian Edwards and Nora Lustig, eds., *Labor Markets in Latin America. Combining Social Protection with Market Flexibility.* Washington, D.C.: The Brookings Institution.

Rama, Martin, and William Maloney. 2000. "Income Support Programs for the Unemployed in Latin America." World Bank, Washington, D.C. Draft.

Ramos, Lauro A. 1999. "Impacto Distributivo dos Gastos Sociais no Mercado de Trábalho." Institute of Applied Economic Research, Ministry of Planning and Budget. Brazil.

Saavedra, Jaime. 1999. "Reformas Laborales en un Contexto de Apertura Económica." Unpublished manuscript. Grupo de Análisis para el Desarrollo, Lima.

Saavedra, Jaime, and Máximo Torero. 2000. "Labor Market Reforms and Their Impact on Formal Labor Demand and Job Market Turnover: The Case of Peru." Research Network Working Paper No. R-394, Inter-American Development Bank Research Department, Washington, D.C.

Public and Private Sector Labor Markets in Brazil

CHAPTERS 2 AND 3 diagnose the main imbalances in the functioning of public and private sector labor markets in Brazil, and propose policy remedies.

Fiscal adjustment is required to complete the stabilization begun by Brazil with the Real Plan launched in 1994. Importantly, this involves public employment reform to reduce payroll-related expenses. For public employment reform to be sustainable, and to minimize the probability of reversals, it must be based on the principle of labor market efficiency. The most important rule in this regard is that compensation for government workers should be in line with pay and employment conditions in the private sector. Using a nationally representative household survey, Chapter 2 examines public-private differentials in salaries and pensions. Compared with equally qualified workers in the private sector, salaries of public employees are 30 to 50 percent higher for federal administration, judicial, and legislative workers; 20 to 35 percent higher for employees in federal and state enterprises, and roughly the same for state civil servants; and 5 to 15 percent lower for municipal administrations and education and health sector workers. Compared with their private sector counterparts, pension levels of civil servants are 25 to 50 percent higher, depending on their salary level, gender, and occupation.

These findings imply that efforts to reduce government payroll expenses should focus on lowering salary levels at the federal level, and a mix of salary restraint and reduced employment at the state level. At the municipal level, however, reductions of employment should be combined

with selected pay increases. Reductions in public-private pension differences would significantly reduce the lifetime earnings gap between the two
systems. Moreover, they would eliminate the significant hidden transfers
of pension liability from states and municipalities to the federal social security system that occur when subnational governments reduce employment through voluntary severance programs.

Chapter 3 takes up the issue of labor reform in some detail. Brazil's experience shows that the economic and political history of a country is a
critical determinant of which labor laws influence wages and employment,
and which are not binding. Long periods of high inflation, workforce illiteracy, and biases in the design and enforcement of labor legislation bred
by the country's socioeconomic history are all important in determining
the reach of labor laws. Defying conventional wisdom, these factors are
shown to affect labor market outcomes even in the sector of employment
regarded as unregulated. Following accepted practice in Brazil, the authors
distinguish regulated from unregulated workers by determining whether
or not their contracts have been ratified by the Ministry of Labor. Chapter 3 then examines the degree of adherence to labor laws in the formal
and informal sectors, and finds evidence of effects of the legislation regarding minimum wage and work-hour restrictions in both the formal
and informal sectors of the Brazilian labor market.

The incentives to stay informal are naturally higher for workers who are
assured of protection under labor legislation regardless of the nature of
their contracts, which alters their financial relationship only with the government. The findings of Chapter 3 imply that informality in Brazil is
mainly a fiscal and not a "legal" phenomenon. But the manner in which
these laws have been enforced is also a critical determinant of informality
in Brazil: poor record keeping has strengthened the incentives to stay informal that are already built into the design of the main social security
programs, and ambiguities in the design of labor legislation combined
with slanted enforcement by labor courts have led to workers effectively
being accorded the same labor rights whether or not they have ratified
contracts. Chapter 3 concludes that informality in Brazil will remain high
as long as labor laws remain ambiguous and are enforced with a clear prolabor bias, and social security programs lack tight benefit-contribution
linkages and strong enforcement mechanisms.

In 1999 and 2000, Brazil made some headway in reforming its social
security system, principally by tightening enforcement of pension rules for
government workers and strengthening the linkage between social security
contributions and benefits for private sector workers, and considerably re-

ducing the generosity of these benefits. These changes may help stem the increase in informality, but at the same time they have increased existing public-private pension gaps. No significant reform of labor legislation has been undertaken during the last decade: payroll taxes and mandatory non-wage benefits remain high, rules for dismissals remain contentious, and enforcement of labor laws has changed little, if at all. The most recent change is in fact an increase in employer contribution rates to the individual severance (Fundo de Garantia do Tempo de Serviço—FGTS) accounts and the penalties levied on employers for "unjust dismissal," forced by a judicial decision. Brazil enters the new millennium with a daunting agenda for labor reform.

2 Improving Public Sector Efficiency in Brazil

RICARDO PAES DE BARROS,
MIGUEL N. FOGUEL, INDERMIT S. GILL,
AND ROSANE SILVA PINTO DE MENDONÇA

BRAZIL IS IN THE PROCESS OF consolidating the macro-economic stabilization begun when the Real Plan was launched in July 1994. Tight money and a loose fiscal stance have helped improve poverty rates in the short term, but involve a longer-term compromise in the form of reduced growth. The public sector deficit almost doubled to about 8 percent of GDP between August 1996 and 1998. The financing of the public sector deficit through inflows of volatile foreign capital has made Brazil vulnerable to exogenous shocks, as witnessed by the financial crises of October 1997 and August–September 1998. Since deeper tax reforms involve addressing sensitive fiscal federalism issues, and Brazil's tax collections are already high at about 30 percent of GDP, much of the adjustment must take place on the expenditures side. Given the already squeezed capital budgets at all levels of government, reducing the fiscal burden of public employment is viewed as central to sustaining the successful stabilization.

Alleviating the fiscal burden may be achieved by means of reductions in either public employment and public wages. In general terms, employment in consolidated government (excluding public enterprises) in Brazil is neither extraordinarily high nor low by international standards. The most up-to-date study of public sector employment in 90 countries (Rama 1997) finds that the predicted level of government employment for Brazil is about 9.6 percent for the 1990s. This is close to the actual figures from the nationwide annual household surveys (*Pesquisa Nacional por Amostra de Domicílios*—PNAD), which ranged from 9 percent to 9.4 percent during 1990–95. There is no clear trend in this ratio, indicating that government employment has not risen faster or slower than private employment. Including employment in Brazil's public enterprises, the share of government goes up to about 12 percent, which is also not unusually high by international standards. At the most aggregate level, therefore, the problem of high payroll expenses in Brazil seems due not to excessive government employment, but to excessively high pay, pensions, and perks. However, this does not rule out the possibility of public sector redundancies in particular regions (for example, in some northeastern states), at particular levels of government (for example, at the municipal level) or for particular classes of workers (for example, for judicial and legislative workers). This chapter identifies sectors where public employment is relatively high.

Alternatively, the Brazilian government may reduce public sector wages. To understand whether this policy measure would improve the efficiency of the public sector, we analyze public-private sector differentials in compensation.[1] To detect inefficiency in the public sector labor market, a benchmark has to be specified against which the outcome in the public sector can be compared. The ideal benchmark would be employment and earnings outcomes, which would exist if the decisionmakers in the public sector considered efficiency to be their only objective. In practice, the private sector serves as this benchmark. Furthermore, small differentials between public and private sector compensation are attractive from an equity point of view, which suggests that a worker should not become better or worse off simply by changing sector. Salaries and pensions are the main components of compensation: both labor market efficiency and equity concerns imply that their public-private differences should be small.

Reducing the wage bill for civil servants in Brazil is a difficult task. The 1988 Constitution disallows layoffs of public servants without "just cause" and considerably limits the government's ability to control personnel expenditures. Reductions in employment are constrained by the presence of tenure or near-tenure rights of most public sector workers that, until recently, were guaranteed under the Constitution. The payment of generous pensions paid to civil servants results in their becoming a financial burden for life (or even longer because of generous survivor benefit schemes), but reduction of pensions paid or increases in time of contribution are difficult because these rights are unassailable under the Constitution. Furthermore, the Brazilian government's efforts to reduce the wage bill for civil servants by reducing their real salary levels have become increasingly difficult since 1996 with the decline in inflation to single-digit levels. Nominal reductions are still forbidden by law.

In order to deal with the high burden of public employment, the strategy of the government in the fiscal readjustment process in Brazil has been two pronged: The first is constitutional reform to reduce pension expenditures and allow mass dismissals of tenured civil servants in case of fiscal necessity, through the Social Security reform bill, partially approved by Congress in November 1998, and the Administrative Reform Bill. The Administrative Reform Bill, aimed at revoking job tenure rights for public servants was passed in early 1998, but awaits supporting legislation by states and municipalities. The second is based on inducing tenured public employees to voluntarily leave government employment. As a consequence, a number of redundancy programs, or *programas de demissão voluntaria* (PDVs), were carried out in both federal and state administrations and enterprises especially between 1995 and 1997 (see Carneiro and Gill forthcoming). The size of severance packages required to induce employees to leave depends upon public-private differences in earnings, pensions, and other benefits, and not on the level of public earnings. Much of the discussion surrounding fiscal adjustment in Brazil, however, has focused on the latter.

In this chapter, we present an overview of this issue and focus explicitly on public-private differentials in earnings and pensions:

- Based on nationwide household surveys, we compute public-private differences in monthly earnings, adjusting for worker characteristics such as education, age, tenure, sex, and race.
- Using experience, earnings profiles, and rules for determining pensions, we compute public-private differentials in pensions.

Furthermore, we estimate the severance packages that are sufficient to compensate public servants for possible losses in earnings and pensions and identify their fiscal effects.

We find that the overall public-private wage differential adjusted for hours with respect to the private sector wage is large, and that there is significant heterogeneity among different segments of the public sector. However, differences in the composition of the labor force, with respect to education, race, and gender, explain most of the overall differentials. Once we control for individual worker characteristics, the large positive public-private differentials become smaller, and the absolute value of negative wage differentials for certain types of public sector workers increases. This indicates that not all segments of the public sector have significant wage advantages when compared to similar private sector employees. However, differentials in pension levels are large. Compared to their private sector counterparts, pension levels of civil servants are 25 to 50 percent higher, depending on salary level, gender, and occupation. Combined with the greater job security (another benefit) that public sector workers enjoy, it may not be unreasonable to argue that, in the aggregate, government workers are overcompensated relative to similarly qualified workers in the private sector. This is consistent with the finding discussed earlier that while the share of government employment is not out of line with international benchmarks, the expenditures on government salaries and pensions are clearly higher in Brazil than in countries at similar stages of development.

Employment and Earnings in the Public and Private Sectors

Employment, 1981–95

PNAD surveys indicate that total employment in Brazil was 62.5 million in September 1995. Public employment—other than in state-owned firms—was approximately 5.6 million (2.2 million in public administration, more than half at the municipal level; 0.6 million in the judiciary, legislature, and military; and 2.9 million in the education and health sectors). The private employment sector, including employment in public enterprises, had 56.9 million workers (16.1 million in agriculture, 8.4 million in industry, 28.4 million in services, and 4 million in the construction and other private sectors).

In Table 2-1 public employment is defined as the sum of civil servants and the military, and is disaggregated into employment at the three levels of direct administration (federal, state, and municipal), education and health, judiciary and legislative, and the military sector. We will call this the sectoral share decomposition. Table 2-1 shows that the public employment share rose from 7.9 percent to 9.4 percent out of total employment from 1981 to 1990. This change is largely due to an increase in municipal employment and in the education and health sector. From 1990 on, the public employment share has stayed at about 9 percent, and the shares of all subsectors remained constant. However, employment increased in all sectors during 1992–95. For example, judicial and legislative staff increased from 0.24 million to 0.31 million, and employment in education and health increased from 2.65 million to 2.88 million.

The desegregation of employment into public employment and private employment is not exhaustive, since it does not distinguish employment

TABLE 2-1
Sectoral Shares in Employment, Selected Years, 1981–95
(percent of total)

Employment	1981	1985	1990	1992	1993	1995
Public employment	7.9	8.4	9.4	9.0	9.3	9.0
Direct administration	2.9	3.3	3.8	3.6	3.6	3.5
Federal	0.5	0.4	0.3	0.3	0.3	0.3
State	1.4	1.5	1.5	1.4	1.4	1.3
Municipal	1.0	1.4	2.0	1.9	1.9	1.9
Education and health	4.0	4.2	4.6	4.5	4.7	4.6
Judiciary and legislative	0.4	0.4	0.4	0.4	0.4	0.5
Military	0.6	0.5	0.6	0.5	0.4	0.4
Private employment[a]	92.1	91.6	90.6	91.0	90.7	91.0
Total	100.0	100.0	100.0	100.0	100.0	100.0
Total (millions)	n.a.[b]	n.a.[b]	n.a.[b]	58.8	59.9	62.5

Note: For all of Brazil.
a. Private employment includes employment in public enterprises.
b. Total employment figures before 1991 are not accurately estimated.
Source: PNAD (various years).

in public enterprises from private employment. To overcome this issue we present results below, which use the class of worker distinction. This assigns workers in public enterprises and autonomous agencies (*fundações*) to the public sector. Consequently, the share of the public sector increases to 11.5 percent during 1995. The class of worker distinction decomposes the employment at each level of government into public servants (*estatutarios*) and nonpublic servants, which subsumes employees in public enterprises and autonomous agencies. Estatutarios are civil servants who are hired officially through formal selection exams and have tenure under current law. Nonpublic servants are divided into employees with a signed work card (*com carteira assinada o CLTistas*) and workers without a signed work card (*sem carteira assinada*). Workers without and with a signed work card conform in Brazil approximately to the informal and formal private sector, respectively.[2] As can be seen in Table 2-2, almost all government employees are either public servants or have a signed work card. Only 1.4 percent of total employment consists of public sector workers without a work card.

To analyze employment patterns in the Federal District and the six most populous states (Bahia, Minas Gerais, Pernambuco, Rio de Janeiro,

TABLE 2-2
Share of Workers, by Class of Worker Distinction, 1995
(percent)

Workers	Public servants	Nonpublic servants		Total share
		With card	Without card	
Public sector workers	—	—	—	11.5
Federal	0.9	0.7	0.1	1.7
State	3.5	1.1	0.4	5.0
Municipal	1.9	1.6	0.9	4.4
Military	0.4	n.a.	n.a.	0.4
Private sector workers	—	—	—	88.5
Salaried	n.a.	28.9	21.1	50.0
Self-employed	n.a.	0.0	23.6	23.6
Employers	n.a.	0.0	4.1	4.1
Unpaid	n.a.	0.0	10.8	10.8
Total	6.7	32.3	61.0	100

— Not available.
n.a. Not applicable.
Note: For all of Brazil.
Source: PNAD (1995).

Rio Grande do Sul, and São Paulo), we calculate the relevant shares with respect to total employment in each state. We find that public employment is overrepresented in the Federal District and in Rio de Janeiro, which are among the states with the highest average wage. The share of public employment amounts to 23 percent in the Federal District and to 11 percent in Rio de Janeiro, while it is approximately 8 percent in Bahia, Pernambuco, Minas Gerais, Rio Grande do Sul, and São Paulo. Additionally, we calculate the share of public employment in each state with respect to the entire Brazilian public sector. We find that employment in the public sector is only slightly overrepresented in the poorest areas: 49 percent of public employment and 46 percent of private employment are in states with the average wage below the overall average, which does not support the argument that public employment serves as a safety net for the poorer northeastern states.

Using the class-of-workers distinction, we find that the share of government employees rises to 29 percent in the Federal District, to 14 percent in Rio de Janeiro, and to approximately 10 percent in the other states. In all six states and the Federal District the share of public servants (estatuarios) in total employment is considerably higher than the respective share of workers in public enterprises and autonomous agencies. The share of workers in public enterprises and autonomous agencies ranges from 3 percent in Pernambuco to more than 6 percent in Bahia and the Federal District. Government employees with a signed work card constitute about 1 percent of the total population, except in Bahia and the Federal District, where this share is twice as high. Much of this "informality" of government employment is at the municipal level. This is especially true for the two northeastern states (Bahia and Pernambuco). Concerning the degree of formality of private employment, we find considerable variation across states. The share of workers with a signed card in private employment is 35 to 40 percent for southern states (Rio Grande do Sul, Rio de Janeiro, and São Paulo) and the Federal District, but only 15 to 20 percent for the northeastern states. Minas Gerais, with a ratio of about 30 percent, falls in the middle.

Earnings, 1981–95

Using PNAD surveys and the commonly used *Índice Nacional de Preços ao Consumidor* (INPC) deflator, we calculate average monthly earnings of public employees between 1981 and 1995. As can be seen in Table 2-3, in 1995 average earnings were highest for judicial and legislative workers, who earned almost R$1,500 per month. Earnings were 25 percent lower for federal workers, 50 percent lower for state and military personnel, 63 percent lower for education and health workers, and 75 percent lower for

TABLE 2-3
Average Monthly Earnings, Selected Years, 1981–95
(constant September 1995 reals[a])

Public employment	1981	1985	1990	1992	1993	1995
Direct administration						
Federal	876	1,155	1,059	1,056	1,150	1,126
State	675	780	783	555	621	728
Municipal	412	386	398	330	316	361
Education and health	546	606	621	476	512	551
Judiciary and legislative	1,043	1,247	1,362	1,058	1,235	1,473
Military	669	844	687	637	622	718

Note: For all of Brazil.
a. The deflator used is INPC (Brazil).
Source: PNAD (various years).

municipal workers. In the private sector, earnings were highest in productive services, amounting to approximately R$950 per month. Compared to this, earnings in distributive services and manufacturing were about 45 percent lower, and in personal services and construction about 60 percent lower. Agricultural workers earned about 75 percent less.

Changes in average real monthly earnings by sector from 1981 to 1995 show that real monthly earnings increased about 29 percent for federal employees and 8 percent for state employees, and fell by 12 percent for municipal employees. Earnings for judicial and legislative employees rose by more than 40 percent during these years, by about 7 percent for the military, and stayed roughly constant for education and health workers in the public sector. This indicates that judicial and legislative employees enjoyed the largest increase, while municipal employees had to cope with the largest decline in real earnings. In the private sector, earnings in agriculture fell by about 10 percent and in industry by 6 percent, but rose in distributive and productive services by 6 percent, and in personal services and construction by about 16 percent.

Considerable differences in average earnings also existed across the different states. In 1995, average earnings in almost all sectors were highest in the Federal District and São Paulo, and lowest in Pernambuco and Bahia. Earnings in Minas Gerais were higher than in the two poorer northeastern states, but lower than in Rio Grande do Sul and Rio de Janeiro. Relative to earnings in the private manufacturing sector, state employees received roughly 67 to 80 percent more in Bahia and Pernambuco, and 40 to 45 percent more in the other states. In contrast, relative earnings of municipal workers were highest in Rio Grande do Sul and Rio de Janeiro, somewhat lower in Minas Gerais and Bahia, and lowest in Pernambuco and São Paulo. In absolute terms, municipal workers earned twice as much in São Paulo as in Pernambuco. In the private sector, earnings by sector relative to private manufacturing are strikingly uniform across regions. Only in Rio Grande do Sul are the earnings of agricultural workers comparatively high.

The Wage Bill, 1992–95

Using employment and average earnings for each sector, we compute the sectoral wage bill in 1995. Figure 2-1 graphs the relative importance of each of the public employment sectors. Education and health workers, who constitute about 50 percent of all government workers, absorb about 45 percent of the wage bill. Municipal employees constitute about 20 per-

FIGURE 2-1
Share of Employment and Wage Bill of Different Public
Employment Sectors

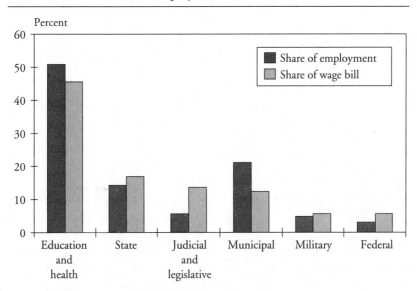

Source: PNAD (1995).

cent of total public employment, but absorb only 12.5 percent of the total
wage bill. State employees, who constitute about 15 percent of employment, absorb about 17 percent of the total wage bill. Federal and military
workers are relatively small fractions of both total employment and the
wage bill. The most dramatic difference between these two shares is for judicial and legislative workers, who constitute about 5 percent of total employment, but absorb almost 14 percent of the total wage bill. Thus, while
employment of judicial and legislative workers may be relatively small,
they are potentially critical for fiscal reasons.

To examine the trends in wage-related expenditures in the public sector, we computed the growth of the wage bill in the public and private sectors. Because of inaccurate weighting before 1991, wage bill numbers are
reliable only for the three PNAD surveys for 1992, 1993, and 1995. Figure 2-2 graphs the annual growth rate for employment, average earnings,
and the wage bill during 1992–95. In the public sector, the 20 percent annual growth of the wage bill for judicial and legislative workers dwarfs that

FIGURE 2-2
Annual Growth from 1992 to 1995 in Employment,
Average Earnings, and Wage Bill

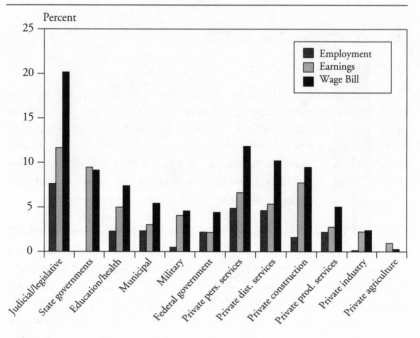

Source: PNAD surveys.

of other workers. This growth in personnel expenditures was due to both
an increase in their number (about 7.5 percent annually) and increased average earnings (about 12 percent annually). The growth of the state wage
bill exceeded 9 percent, despite a small decrease in state employment. The
wage bill for education and health workers increased by 7.5 percent annually, due to increases in both average real earnings and employment.
The federal wage bill also increased by 4.5 percent because of both new
hires and higher wages. Military employment stayed roughly constant, but
earnings increased moderately.

In the private sector average earnings grew, especially in personal and
distributive services and construction. In contrast, industry and agriculture registered modest earnings growth, and employment actually fell in
agriculture. In general, only employment growth in services exceeded the
national average of about 2 percent during this period. In the public sector, on the other hand, employment of federal, municipal, judicial and

legislative, and education and health workers rose faster than this average rate. Only state and military employment grew more slowly than the national average.

The Public-Private Wage Gap

The Uncontrolled Wage Gap

To provide evidence on the uncontrolled public-private wage gap, we start by estimating the overall wage gap between the private and public sector for the entire Brazilian labor market. We then calculate the wage gap between different segments of the public sector and the overall private sector to take into account the heterogeneity within the public sector. Finally, we analyze the impact of differences in spatial composition of the public and private labor forces on the wage gap.

DATA. The empirical analysis conducted here is based on the PNAD survey for September 1995. The PNAD is the national household survey that is undertaken annually by the Brazilian National Statistical Institute. Each dataset has more than 360,000 observations. We use two measures of labor income. The first measure is the total monthly income normally received by a worker in his or her current main job. The second measure seeks to adjust for the number of hours usually worked. It is defined as the total monthly income normally received in the main job, divided by the number of hours usually worked per week in that job and multiplied by a standard workweek of 40 hours. Since the average number of hours worked by public employees tends to be significantly smaller than the corresponding average for workers in the private sector, it does make a difference for level of the wage gap between these sectors whether or not a standardization for hours of work is conducted. To ensure that the standardized wage is a good approximation of what a worker would receive if he or she works 40 hours a week, workers working less than 20 hours per week were excluded from the analysis. We also exclude workers with zero labor income.

THE OVERALL WAGE GAP. Table 2-4 presents estimates of the overall wage gap between public and private sectors in Brazil.[3] The large positive estimates reveal that average earnings tend to be much higher in the public sector than in the private sector. The relative wage difference between the public and the private sectors amounts to 49 percent of the average

TABLE 2-4

Public Sector Wage Premium

(percent)

Measure	Public–Total private		Public–Formal private	
	Adjusted[a]	Not adjusted	Adjusted	Not adjusted
Baseline: Private				
sector wage	89	49	67	42
Average log-wage	70	45	38	18

Note: Unadjusted for sector, region, and worker attributes.

a. Adjusted refers to earnings adjusted for differences in hours worked.

Source: PNAD (1995).

wage in the private sector. It increases to 89 percent when we adjust for hours, which indicates that workers in the public sector work fewer hours per week than private sector workers.

Furthermore, Table 2-4 reports estimates of the gap between the wage of employees in the public sector and employees in the private formal sector, which may be the part of the private sector where those leaving government employment are more likely to seek employment.[4] Table 2-4 reveals that this wage gap is slightly smaller than the overall gap between the public and private sectors. More specifically, the wage gap decreases by 7 percent when we do not adjust for hours. The adjusted wage gap remains large, at 67 percent.

Estimates of the public sector wage premium measured by the average of the log-wage are also provided in Table 2-4. Log-wage differences have the advantage that they are independent of the baseline wage, and hence eliminate the need to keep track of it. Moreover, they provide estimates for the wage gap that are between the two natural (using either private sector wage or public sector wage as baseline) measures of relative differences in wages. However, a drawback is that they are not as straightforward to interpret. We include the information on average log-wages in Table 2-4 (and Table 2-5) for reasons of comparison; we provide evidence on the public-private wage differential based on regression analysis, which is stated in terms of average log-wages.

At this stage of the analysis it is difficult to meaningfully interpret these wage gaps. Three factors complicate such a comparison. First, as we have seen above, there are large differences in average earnings within the public (for example, between municipal and legislative workers) and private sectors (for example, between agricultural and service sector workers); second,

TABLE 2-5 •
Public Sector Wage Premium
(percent)

Measure	Baseline: Private wage
By sector of activity	
Federal administration	162.5
State administrations	69.9
Municipal administrations	−15.8
Judicial and legislative	231.0
Military	69.9
Education and health	18.0
By class of worker	
Federal public servants	207.0
Federal other, with signed card	166.4
Federal other, no signed card	68.2
State public servants	60.5
State other, with signed card	95.3
State other, no signed card	−1.1
Municipal public servants	−2.8
Municipal other, with signed card	−32.8
Municipal other, no signed card	−41.7
Military	71.7

Note: Unadjusted for region and worker attributes.
Source: PNAD (1995).

there are regional differences in average earnings (for example, between state employees in Pernambuco and São Paulo); and third, there are large differences across workers by individual attributes (for example, workers in the public sector tend to be better educated and older). These three factors will be addressed in the following sections. Henceforth, only wage gaps adjusted for hours worked will be discussed and reported. Interested readers can find more detailed results in Paes de Barros and others (1997).

HETEROGENEITY IN THE PUBLIC SECTOR. To analyze the degree of heterogeneity within the public sector, we use the same two decompositions for the public sector that we already proposed in the analysis of the employment shares: the sectoral share decomposition, which divides public employment into the three levels of public administration (federal, state, and municipal), public health and education, legislative and judiciary activities, and the military; and the class of worker distinction, which provides information on both the type of labor contract and the level of government. Table 2-5 presents estimates of respective wage gaps, which are calculated between the respective segment of the public sector and the overall private sector. The results indicate considerable heterogeneity within the public sector. Average wages are particularly high in federal administration, and in the legislative and judiciary sectors. The relative wage differences with respect to the overall average private wage amount to 162.5 percent and 231 percent, respectively. At the other extreme, workers in health and education and employees at the municipal level have earnings that are close to the average for the private sector, or even below it. The average wage in municipal administration is nearly 16 percent lower than the average in the private sector. In between are state administration and military personnel; wages for these two groups are close to 70 percent above the average in the private sector.

We obtain similar results when using the class of worker distinction of the public sector. Wages are particularly high among federal public servants, and federal public employees with signed work cards, which largely refers to employees in public enterprises. In both cases the wage gap is greater than 150 percent of the average wage in the private sector. For military personnel, state public servants, and employees of state enterprises, the wage gap is about 75 to 100 percent. The average wage of municipal public servants and employees of municipal enterprises is below the average for the private sector, with the wages of employees in municipal enterprises being particularly low. Overall, average wages in all segments of the public sector tend to be above those paid in the private sector. The only exceptions are the wages paid by municipal administrations and enterprises. Wages among different segments of the public sector reveal a large degree of heterogeneity in wages within the public sector, with the average wage in federal administration being more than 200 percent higher than the corresponding average paid in municipal administrations.

REGIONAL DIFFERENCES IN THE PUBLIC-PRIVATE WAGE GAP. After having analyzed public-private differentials for different segments of the public sector, we now consider the role of spatial differences in the distribution of public and private employment. The fact that public employment is overrepresented in the Federal District and in Rio de Janeiro, which are among the states with the highest average wage, implies that the wage gap would increase if public employment had the same spatial distribution as private employment. In terms of the gap in average log-wage, this means an increase from 44 percent to 46 percent; that is, public employment has a "locational disadvantage" of only 2 percent. Moreover, we find that the public-private wage gap tends to be considerably higher for metropolitan areas than for the corresponding states. This is especially true in the northeastern states of Pernambuco and Bahia, and in the State of Minas Gerais. São Paulo is the only state where the wage gap for the metropolitan area is smaller than for the corresponding gap for the entire state. The average gap between the public and private sectors is much higher in Brasília than in any state. The average wage gap tends to be high in the northeast and lower in the more developed states in the South and Southeast of Brazil, particularly in São Paulo, Paraná, and Santa Catarina. But it is also low in some poor states like Ceará and Alagoas (see Paes de Barros and others 1997).

The Controlled Wage Gap

The estimates we discuss above represent an important starting point for the wage analysis. However, they have serious limitations as a measure of the actual public-private wage differential, since they do not necessarily represent the actual difference in payment between equally productive workers in the public and private sectors. In fact, estimates of wage gaps, which do not control for worker characteristics, capture both differences in payment between equally productive workers in the two sectors and differences in the qualifications and characteristics of the labor force employed in the two sectors. Wages may be higher in the public sector simply because the labor force in the sector is older and better educated. Or they may be lower due to the possible concentration of public employment in the poorer Northeast and because women tend to be overrepresented in the public sector. Consequently, we are interested in estimating the wage gap between workers with identical observed characteristics such as gender, race, schooling, and age. Below we provide a thorough explanation of the methodology used to compare the wages of observably identical workers in the public and private sectors.

METHODOLOGY. The methodology used to compare the wages of observably identical workers in the public and private sectors consists of four steps. In the first, we regress the log-wages of workers on their characteristics and on an indicator of whether they are in the public or private sector. This means that we assume that the impact of all personal characteristics on the level of wages is the same in the public and private sectors—that is, that the difference in the wage level between the public and private sectors is the same for all types of worker. We refer to this specification as the basic model. Of course, we may think that, for example, the level of education affects wages to a different extent in the public sector than in the private sector. To address this issue, we also run regressions of log-wages on personal characteristics for the public and private sector separately and, therefore, allow personal characteristics to affect the wage level differently in the two sectors. We call this specification the general model.

In the second step, based on the estimates of the regression, we compute what would be the average wage of public employees if they were in the private sector; that is, we calculate the average log-wage that would prevail in the private sector if the labor force had the same average characteristics as the public sector workers. We refer to this type of wage gap as the controlled wage gap. Under the assumption of the basic model, which is that the wage gap between the public and private sector is the same for all types of workers, the log-wage gap between workers with identical observed characteristics is completely captured by the effect of the public-private sector indicator on wages. This is not true for the general model because this takes into account not only the effect of the public-private sector indicator on wages, but also captures the differences in the effect of individual characteristics on wages. Our estimation results reveal that no major difference exists between the two models. Consequently, we present only the results which are derived from the basic specification.

Third, we decompose the overall wage gap into the wage gap, which is due to differences in the composition of the labor force, and the controlled wage gap. To analyze differences in the composition of the labor force, we use a basic set of observed characteristics, which includes gender, race, schooling, and age. We also work with a version of this set that includes tenure at the current job. On average, workers in the public sector tend to have been in their current job for a longer period of time.[5] Since to a considerable extent this is not a result of any differential merit between employees in the public and private sectors, but one of the major advantages of jobs in the public sector, it is unclear whether we should control for this characteristic.

Fourth, we estimate the wage gap between each segment of the public sector and the overall private sector controlling for worker-specific attributes, since the wage gap between the public and private sectors is likely to differ with sector of activity and class of worker. We perform the regression analysis for the six major Brazilian metropolitan areas and Brasília. The restriction of the analysis to these seven well-defined local labor markets is useful to isolate the wage gap between the public and private sectors from possible spatial differences among local markets. However, it also has the disadvantage that the nature of public employment in large metropolitan areas is likely to be different from public employment in smaller urban areas. The contribution of federal and state employment is likely to be greater. Moreover, municipal jobs in metropolitan areas are more likely to be better paid. As a consequence, the wage gap estimated for these areas is likely to overestimate the gap for the entire urban labor market in the respective state.

Role of Differences in Worker Characteristics

The fundamental question we address here is: What fraction of the wage gap between the two sectors is due simply to differences in the characteristics of the labor force employed in the two sectors?

Table 2-6 reveals that differences in the composition of the labor force are a major explanatory factor of the log-wage gap between the public and

TABLE 2-6
Estimates of Log Wage Gap Due to Differences in Composition and Controlled Wage Gap for Metropolitan Areas

	Wage gap due to differences in composition		Controlled wage gap	
	Without tenure	With tenure	Without tenure	With tenure
Federal District	0.69	0.76	0.49	0.42
Recife (Pernambuco)	0.59	0.65	0.27	0.20
Salvador (Bahia)	0.60	0.69	0.19	0.10
Belo Horizonte (Minas Gerais)	0.63	0.71	0.14	0.07
Rio de Janeiro (Rio de Janeiro)	0.52	0.61	0.11	0.02
São Paulo (São Paulo)	0.47	0.53	−0.14	−0.20
Porto Alegre (Rio Grande do Sul)	0.56	0.65	0.13	0.04

Note: Results presented for the basic model. Wages are standardized by differences in work hours.
Source: PNAD (1995).

private sector. As can be seen in Table 2-6, the specification without tenure reveals that the gap in average log-wages due to differences in the composition of the labor force ranges from 0.47 to 0.69. Since public sector workers have longer tenure than private sector workers, and because wages increase with tenure, the public sector premium increases when we include tenure in our regression. Once we control for tenure the differences in the composition of the labor force are responsible for the average log-wage in the public sector being from 0.53 to 0.76 higher than in the private sector. Comparison of the wage gap due to composition of the labor force and the controlled wage gap reveals that, apart from the Federal District, most of the overall wage gap between the public and private sectors reflects differences in the composition of their labor forces. Therefore, we conclude that measures for the wage gap that do not control for differences in the characteristics of the labor force are almost certainly very misleading indicators of the actual wage advantage of workers in the public sector.

The wage gap, which is due to differences in the composition of the labor force, can be further decomposed in order to analyze the contribution of each observed characteristic. In the specification without tenure we find that about 80 percent of the difference in log wages, which is due to differences in the composition, is explained by the higher educational level of the labor force in the public sector. Once we control for tenure this effect decreases to about 70 percent. The remaining 30 percent is explained by the fact that public employees tend to be older and have longer tenure, with each of these two factors being responsible for 10 to 20 percent of the differential. The impact of gender and race is relatively small. The contribution of differences in race composition between the private and public sector ranges from 1 to 5 percent. The impact of gender differences ranges from 0 to −10 percent.

In sum, differences in the composition of the labor force are a major explanation for the wage gap between the public and private sector. As a consequence the controlled wage gap is much smaller than the overall gap. Still, it remains considerable for most states, even when we control for tenure:

- In the Federal District the controlled wage gap amounts to a still very large public-private wage gap of 42 percent among workers with identical observed characteristics.
- In Recife and Salvador workers in the public sector receive salaries that are 20 percent and 10 percent higher, respectively.
- The public-private wage gap is 7 percent in Belo Horizonte, 4 percent in Porto Alegre, and 2 percent in Rio de Janeiro.

- Only in São Paulo is the pattern reversed: among equally qualified workers, workers in the public sector receive salaries that are 20 percent lower than private sector salaries.

Note, however, that the nature of public employment in large metropolitan areas is likely to be different from public employment in smaller urban areas, and that as a consequence, the wage gap estimated for these areas is likely to overestimate the gap for the entire urban labor market in the respective state. This, however, is not true for São Paulo, which is the only region where the overall public-private sector wage gap is lower in the metropolitan area compared to the state. Hence, we are likely to underestimate the wage gap for the entire urban labor market of São Paulo State.

Controlled Wage Gaps by Sector and Class of Worker

In this section we estimate the wage gap between each segment of the public sector and overall private sector controlling for differences in worker-specific attributes. This is perhaps the best estimate of the "pure" premium enjoyed by public sector employees over what they would have earned had they held private sector jobs. Table 2-7 presents estimates for the controlled wage gap between each segment of the public sector and the private sector for the country as a whole. It reveals large differences among segments of the public sector. The wage advantage of government workers, measured by the controlled log-wage gap, is larger at the federal level for both public administration and enterprises. For these groups the average salaries are 23 to 46 percent higher than for comparable workers in the private sector. At the state level, the wage advantage is close to zero for public servants; for employees in public enterprises the wage advantage is between 10 and 18 percent. At the municipal level, public servants and employees in public enterprises get lower wages than workers with similar observed characteristics. Overall, the evidence corroborates the existence of a significant wage advantage in many segments of the public sector relative to similar private sector employees.

Assignment to the public sector is not random. Individuals are assumed to make rational choices about working in the private or public sector. This choice is usually based on productivity-related characteristics that also affect earnings, such as motivation, taste for public service, or preference for nonrisky employment. Furthermore, access to the public sector in Brazil is determined either by personal connections or formal selection exams, which we also cannot observe in the data. Where sorting appears on the basis of these unobserved factors, estimates are biased, which means that they give a false picture of the relative earnings position of public sec-

TABLE 2-7
Measures of the Public Sector Earnings Premium by Sector and Class,
September 1995
(percent)

Measure	Monthly[a]	Hourly[a]
By sector of activity		
Federal administration	23.1	28.9
State administrations	−7.8	−3.8
Municipal administrations	−31.9	−22.4
Judicial and legislative	43.9	55.9
Military	2.3	5.7
Education and health	−31.1	−15.6
By class of worker		
Federal public servants	40.8	46.3
Federal other, with signed card	27.0	36.3
State public servants	−15.4	−5.5
State other, with signed card	10.3	18.0
Municipal public servants	−30.5	−17.9
Municipal other, with signed card	−31.5	−20.9
All workers without signed card	−42.6	−19.7
Military	3.6	7.2

Note: Adjusted for worker characteristics: age, sex, race, tenure, and education.

a. Monthly earnings premia are not adjusted for differences in hours worked. Hourly earnings comparisons are adjusted for differences in hours worked.

Source: PNAD (1995).

tor workers. The self-selection bias may be addressed by adding a third equation to the general model that explains the individual's decision to work either in the public or private sector. Unfortunately, the information available in our data does not allow us to arrive at a well-specified selection equation. However, most of the studies on public-private wage differentials find that correcting for self-selection lowers the estimated size of the wage premium received by public sector workers.

Public-Private Differences in Pensions

Comparisons of monthly earnings of public and private workers reveal only part of the differences in the compensation between the two sectors. "Nonwage" compensation is often higher in the public sector due to more generous pension plans and other employee benefits. Most notably, the Brazilian pension system for public employees magnifies the differences between private and public sector lifetime income. As we will show, average pension relative to average wage is much higher for civil servants compared to similarly paid workers in the private sector, although contributions of civil servants are significantly lower.

Private sector workers and workers in state-owned enterprises contribute to the National Security System (*Regime Geral da Previdencia Social*—RGPS), which is administered by the federal government's *Instituto Nacional de Seguridade Social* (INSS). It is financed by payroll taxes on workers and employers.[6] Employer's payroll taxes for social security amount to 22 percent of the wage bill. The self-employed contribute roughly 20 percent of earnings. Employee contributions are based on a progressive scale and, depending on the level of wage, they range from 8 percent to 11 percent. The INSS administers a number of benefit programs for participants including the Old Age and the Length of Service Programs. Under the Old Age Program the age of retirement is 65 for men and 60 for women who work in the urban sector. Those who retired before 1991 could apply for the Old Age Program after five years of contribution to the INSS. Recent legislation has increased this minimum period of contribution such that it increases by six months per year, reaching 15 years in 2011. In 1998 the minimum period of contribution to be eligible was 8.5 years. Under the Length of Service Program pensioners receive benefits irrespective of age after meeting a certain number of years of service. (This was changed to years of contributions under the reforms in 1998–99.) The minimum period of service for having access to the benefits is 30 years for men and 25 years for women. For both programs the minimum benefit in general has to be greater than one minimum wage. The maximum benefit cannot exceed an amount that is usually close to 10 times the minimum wage (for a more detailed discussion see World Bank 2001).

Workers in Brazil's public sector participate in mandatory pension plans, which are established under the so-called *Regime Jurídico Único* (RJU). Different institutions exist to run the pension plans for federal, state, and municipal public workers. In the mid-1990s pension contributions were imposed for federal civil servants.[7] The RJU is financed from payroll taxes on workers, and to a large part from transfers from government treasuries. Until the recent introduction of employee contributions, eligibility was based on years of employment, where employment also included time of service in the private sector and leaves of absence for study and other sabbaticals. To receive the unreduced pension levels, men and women must be employed 35 and 30 years, respectively. While the RJUs have only 15 percent of Brazil's 20 million social security beneficiaries, they receive nearly 50 percent of all pension benefits paid in the country, and account for 75 percent of the consolidated pension deficits. In contrast to the private sector, public employees face no upper limit on pension amounts. Pensions of public employees are still based only on the salary of the last month, while in the INSS they were calculated on the basis of the monthly salary levels in the last three years of service, a period which is gradually being extended to cover almost all of the working life. This leads to higher pensions for public sector workers, because earnings usually increase with time of service, especially for relatively high-wage (skilled) workers.

We take into account these basic features of the Brazilian pension systems that existed until 1999 when estimating differences in pensions for public servants and those receiving social security benefits from the two main federal social security programs—the Length of Service and Old Age Programs of the INSS—and use the following techniques:

- First, using PNAD survey data from September 1995 for the seven metropolitan areas (Belo Horizonte, Federal District, Porto Alegre, Recife, Rio de Janeiro, Salvador, and São Paulo), we estimate the profile of monthly earnings for males and females, which are divided further into four worker categories (public servants, private with signed work card, private without signed work card, and private self-employed), and three education groups (0 to 8 years, 9 to 11 years, and 12 or more years of schooling). As stated above, employees in Brazil without and with a signed work card correspond, approximately, to workers in the informal and formal sectors.
- Second, using these estimated earnings profiles, and assuming that all males retire after 35 years of service and all women after 30 years of service, we estimate the average pension level for each group. For public servants we use the 36th year's salary as the estimated monthly pension. Consistent with the fact that pension levels in the INSS are calculated on the basis of the monthly salary levels in the last three years of service, we use the 34th year's salary as the estimated pension for salaried workers with a signed work card and the self-employed. For workers without a signed work card, we assume that they receive minimum pensions which equal the minimum wage. Hence, their pension levels are assumed to be equal to one minimum wage in 1995, or R$100.

- Third, we account for the fact that INSS pensions are capped at 10 minimum wages. This affects men with a signed work card who have more than 12 years of education; consequently, we restrict the pensions to be equal to R$1,000.
- Fourth, using weights obtained from nationwide PNAD data for 1995 on the shares of employees with and without a signed work card, and self-employed workers, we compute the average expected pensions for private sector men and women. We do not take into account pensions from the supplementary social security system (that is, closed or company funds).[8]
- Finally, these numbers are compared with expected monthly pensions for public servants with the same education level.

Table 2-8 reports the results of these estimations. As can be seen, public-private pension differences are greater for men than for women, and greatest for the most educated male workers. This is largely due to the pension ceiling of 10 minimum salaries. We find that the average male private sector worker with 0 to 8, 9 to 11, and 12 or more years of schooling receives,

TABLE 2-8

Estimated Monthly Pensions

(September 1995 Reals)

		Private			
Gender/education	Public	With card	Without card	Self-employed	Total[a]
Males					
0–8 years schooling	447	430	100	407	335
9–11 years schooling	772	758	100	686	558
12+ years schooling	1,747	1,793[b]	n.a.	n.a.	1,000
Females					
0–8 years schooling	264	226	100	213	190
9–11 years schooling	448	447	100	362	326
12+ years schooling	927	995	100	832	655

n.a. signifies that the sample was too small to permit reliable estimation of experience-earnings profiles.

Note: Men are assumed to retire after 35 years of service, and women after 30 years.

a. Using weights derived from nationwide PNAD employment distribution data.

b. Capped at 10 times the minimum monthly salary level, assumed to be R$100 in September 1995.

Source: PNAD (various years) and IPEA–World Bank calculations.

respectively, 75, 73, and 57 percent of the monthly pension level of his estatutario counterpart. The corresponding numbers for women are 72, 73, and 71 percent.

These large differentials in pension levels combined with the fact that pension contribution rates are 0 to 12 percent for public servants, but range between 8 and 11 percent for CLTistas, have important implications for the structure of optimal severance packages. As mentioned in the introduction, Brazil's 1988 Constitution disallows layoffs of public servants without "just cause," and considerably limits the government's ability to reduce employment in the public sector. To address this issue, between 1995 and 1997 the Brazilian government undertook a package of Constitutional reforms and introduced a number of voluntary severance programs (PDVs). Given that the federal and state governments are cash strapped and can pay only relatively low benefits to PDV takers, these large differentials in pension benefits decrease the likelihood of success of current voluntary severance programs. Actuarial calculations reveal that if raising employee contributions were the only way to bring the state system into balance, even contribution rates as high as 75 percent of salaries would be insufficient to cover current benefits in some states. This indicates that in order to solve the financial problem, the government will have to increase pension contribution rates and simultaneously reduce the pension levels for civil servants.

Voluntary Severance Programs

The PDVs were implemented both at the federal and local government levels, in public administration as well as state-owned enterprises, to encourage voluntary job separations of tenured estatutarios. PDVs imply savings in terms of a reduction in not only salary bills, but also reduce pension bills. As shown above, pensions paid to public servants are substantially higher than those paid by the INSS. Consequently, government savings in terms of the pension bill are higher when an estatutario takes a state-sponsored voluntary severance package than when a CLTista leaves public employment.

We use a simple methodology that involves the comparison of experience-earnings profiles of public and private employees to estimate the saving in salaries and pensions for groups of workers according to their sex, education, and tenure. Table 2-9 reports the results of this exercise for men and women with, respectively, 0 to 8, 9 to 11, and 12 or more years of education. In the case of men, it is assumed that the PDV taker has 17.5 years of

TABLE 2-9

Effects of Reducing Public Employment on Average Earnings,
Transfer of Obligations, and DPV[a] of Savings

(thousand reals)

Education level	State government saving			Transfer of obligations to INSS[b]	Consolidated government saving	
	Salaries	Pensions	Total		Pensions	Total
Males, with 17.5 years of service[c]						
0–8 years	51.6	23.4	75.0	17.4	6.0	57.6
9–11 years	89.7	37.9	127.5	29.1	8.8	98.4
12+ years	215.5	91.6	307.0	41.9	49.7	265.1
Females, with 15 years of service[c]						
0–8 years	27.1	21.2	48.3	14.5	6.7	33.8
9–11 years	51.4	36.0	87.4	25.1	10.9	62.3
12+ years	97.5	74.1	171.5	54.0	20.1	117.5

Note: These estimates are based on estimated earnings profiles of private and public sector workers in a nationwide sample drawn from the September 1995 PNAD survey.

a. A 6 percent discount rate was used to calculate present values.

b. These transfers do not take into account the expected contributions of these workers (and their employers in the case of salaried employees) to the INSS system.

c. Men are assumed to retire from public employment after 35 years of service and receive pensions for 20 years; women are assumed to retire after 30 years of service and receive pensions for 25 years.

Source: PNAD (1995).

service, and in the case of women, 15 years. These numbers are similar to actual tenure levels of participants in these programs (Carneiro and Gill forthcoming).

Table 2-9 provides evidence on the savings to the state government in salaries and pensions due to a voluntary quit of an estatutario. Savings in salaries are lower for men compared to women and increase with education. The same is true for savings in pensions. For estatutarios who leave under the voluntary severance program but do not qualify for early retirement, there is an uncompensated transfer of pension obligations from the state administration to the national INSS scheme. This is because these employees carry over their years of service into the private system and, after a relatively short period of contributions, become eligible for private pensions. Thus, a male PDV participant with 17.5 years of service in the public sector would be eligible for reduced INSS pensions after only 12.5 more years of work in the private sector, and for full pensions after only 17.5 years. According to our estimates, the present value of these obligations for men (and women) leaving public employment mid-career are R$17,400 (R$14,500) for low-wage workers, R$29,100 (R$25,100) for medium-wage workers, and R$41,900 (R$54,000) for high-wage workers. Thus, for example, a state PDV for 10,000 estatutarios drawn from all education-salary categories could imply a transfer of obligations of more than R$300 million in current terms from the state to the federal pension system.

Considering the transfer of obligations to the INSS, savings in pensions decrease to 6,000, 8,800, and 49,700 reals for men; and 6,700, 10,900, and 20,100 reals for women with 0 to 8, 9 to 11 and 12 or more years of education. This implies that ignoring savings due to a reduction in the pensions bill leads to an underestimation of consolidated government savings of about 12 percent, 10 percent, and 23 percent, respectively, for men with 9 to 11 and 12 or more years of education. The corresponding numbers for women are 25 percent, 21 percent, and 21 percent, respectively. Note that pension-related savings are larger for highest-wage males because private sector pensions are capped at 10 times the minimum monthly salary, and the cap is binding only for this group. Other than this group, savings are greater for women because the expected length of retirement is greater for them.

Savings due to pensions would be even higher if we account for the difference between the public pension system and the INSS. While private sector workers contribute up to 20 percent of their salaries to pensions, civil servants did not contribute anything until the 1980s (but now contribute up to 12 percent of their earnings). Consequently, the transfer of pension obligations to the INSS would to some extent be offset by payroll contributions. Under the current rules, however, the INSS system never recovers the "lost contribution" of these estatutarios—that is, what they and their employers would have contributed had they belonged to the INSS system during their years of service with the government. If one assumes that the INSS system is actuarially fair for workers who make full contributions for 30 to 35 years, this means that the INSS is "owed" employee and employer contributions (which add up to about 30 percent of earnings) for their years of tenure. The estimated present values of "lost" contributions are R$16,000, R$42,000, and R$78,000 for men with 0 to 8, 9 to 11, and 12 or more years of schooling who take PDV packages after 17.5 years of service; and R$13,000, R$25,000, and R$54,000 for the corresponding groups of women with 15 years of service. Naturally, these numbers would be smaller for PDV takers with lower tenure levels, and greater for those more senior civil servants.

Considering the generosity of public pensions, it is striking but not surprising to find that the potential benefits of PDV programs—in terms of reduced salary and pension bills—dwarfed the costs of existing programs. While our estimates in Table 2-4 indicate that the potential saving for these groups ranges between R$34,000 (for least-educated women) and R$265,000 (for educated men), the average benefits that were paid ranged from R$5,000 to R$25,000. One of the main reasons is that state governments are cash strapped and could not afford to pay more. As a consequence, though, take-up rates were low, and a promising source for reducing the long-term fiscal burden on state and federal governments remained largely untapped.

Conclusion

Our analyses in this chapter corroborate the view that there are significant earnings gaps in many segments of the Brazilian public sector relative to similar private sector employees, but it is far from clear that public sector workers are systematically over- or undercompensated. In sharp contrast, differentials in pension levels were large and systematically higher for government employees compared with similar private sector retirees. The estimates in the mid-1990s indicated that compared to their private sector counterparts, pension levels of civil servants are 25 to 50 percent higher, depending on their salary level, gender, and occupation. Recent pension reforms for private sector workers may have widened these differentials.

Based on this analysis, we recommend steps for reducing public sector payroll expenditures that differ across the various branches and levels of government. Table 2-10 presents the set of measures that we consider appropriate. Several points should be kept in mind in using this table. First, for efficiency and equity reasons the analysis is based on the principle that compensation should be the same for equally qualified workers in the public and private sectors. Second, the analysis presents strategies for reducing payroll expenses at all levels of government. Clearly, federal, state, and municipal priorities will dictate whether in fact downsizing efforts should be broad, or instead targeted to some workers (for example, lower-level administrative staff) while sparing others (for example, education and health workers). Finally, this analysis should be viewed as general guidance. Specific steps should be determined after more detailed analysis of public-private earnings differences at each level of government.

TABLE 2-10
Measures to Reduce Public Payroll Expenses While Maintaining or
Improving Labor Market Efficiency

	Reduce salary/benefits	Reduce pensions	Reduce employment
Judicial and legislative	✓	✓	√
Federal administration	✓	√	
State administration		√	✓
Municipal administration			✓
Education and health		√	√
Military			
Federal enterprises	✓	√	?
State enterprises	√	√	?
Municipal enterprises			?

✓ signifies that this is a priority countrywide measure, though the measure may not be appropriate for some states, municipalities, or occupations.
√ signifies that this is a recommended countrywide measure.
? indicates that our analysis does not allow generalizations.

The measures suggested by the analysis are:

- Judicial and legislative payroll expenses should be controlled by lowering salary and pensions and by reducing employment levels.
- Reducing personnel expenses in federal administration and federal and state enterprises mainly requires lowering salary and pension levels, though employment reduction in selected occupations and enterprises may also be necessary.
- Reducing personnel expenses in state administrations is best done by employment reduction preceded by tenure revocation and reforms to make state pension programs less generous.
- Reduction of personnel expenses for education and health workers and municipal administrations and enterprises should be done mainly by reducing employment, preferably after revoking tenure for civil servants.

Additionally, administrative reforms for public employment may include reduction in tenure rights, enforcement of working hours, introduction of stricter performance monitoring, and the requirement for civil servants to make contributions for pensions at the same rate as for INSS benefits. This would reduce public-private differentials in earnings and pensions, and thus improve labor market efficiency. Moreover, reduction in public employment would become easier and cheaper to achieve.

Concerning the pension levels, social security reform has become a priority concern in Brazil's effort to carry out a lasting fiscal adjustment. In 1998, the overall pension deficit was 4.8 percent of GDP. In the same year the Brazilian government responded to this challenge by introducing a set of reforms that put the social security system (RGPS) on a better actuarial base. Concerning access to pensions for civil servants, the government has changed the requirements for eligibility. It furthermore attempted to increase pension contributions by civil servants. This may be a first step in reducing the differences in compensation between public and private sector workers and in building a sustainable and just social security system that better fits the country's budgetary constraints.

Notes

1. Efficiency in this context means that the public employer minimizes the cost for a given output, and hence does not pay higher wages than necessary to attract sufficiently capable workers.

2. CLTistas are governed by the labor code for the private sector. This expression derives from the *Consolidação das Leis do Trabalho* (CLT) of 1943 that forms the main body of Brazilian labor legislation. Among other things it determines that all workers must have a booklet where all individual labor contracts and changes to them over time are registered by the employers. By definition, a formal worker has a booklet signed by his employer. For more information on Brazilian labor legislation, see Chapter 3.

3. For more information on the estimation of the overall wage gap, see Technical Annex A.

4. Employees in the private formal sector are all employees in the private sector who have a formal labor contract.

5. For Brazil, using the PNAD September 1995, we find that tenure at the current job, even when adjusting for characteristics such as age, education, and gender, is longer for public sector workers in all states except São Paulo.

6. The INSS system comprises four major subsystems: time of service, disability, old age, and special programs.

7. Rio Grande do Sul introduced a 2 percent contribution rate in 1996. Federal employees have had to contribute to their pensions since 1992, when contribution rates were set as a progressive scale. In 1997 this scale was replaced with a flat contribution rate of 11 percent.

8. The supplementary social security fund is privately managed, intended to supplement the RGPS benefits, and dominated mostly by pension funds of pub-

lic enterprises. The number of contributors is about 3 million (compared to 60 million in the RGPS).

References

Carneiro, Francisco G., and Indermit S. Gill. Forthcoming. "Effectiveness and Financial Costs of Voluntary Separation Programs in Brazil: 1995–1997." *Revista Perspectiva Económica.*

Paes de Barros, Ricardo, Indermit S. Gill, Miguel Foguel, and Rosane Silva Pinto de Mendonca. 1997. "Labor Market Prospects of Public Employees in Brazil: An Empirical Evaluation." Economic Note No. 24. Country Department I, Latin America and the Caribbean Region, World Bank, Washington, D.C.

PNAD (Pesquisa Nacional por Amostra de Domicílios). Various years. Brazil.

Rama, Martin. 1997. "Downsizing and Severance Pay in Developing Countries." World Bank, Washington, D.C.

World Bank. 2001. *Brazil. Critical Issues in Social Security.* A World Bank Country Study. Washington D.C.

3 Assessing the Impact of Regulations on Informal Workers in Brazil

Edward J. Amadeo, Indermit S. Gill, and Marcelo C. Neri

As one of the alleged contributors to *custo Brasil*—the abnormally high costs of doing business in Brazil—labor legislation that both raises labor costs and makes them more uncertain has been a topic of some discussion for the last decade. The introduction in 1994 of the *real*, the new anchored currency, and the resultant decline in inflation, removed an instrument for keeping real wages flexible. Increased openness resulted in steadily rising unemployment rates (especially for more experienced industrial sector workers in areas such as São Paulo). These factors resulted in a steady buildup of pressure for labor market reforms. A sharp rise in open unemployment rates in 1998 precipitated by the Asian crisis of October 1997 brought labor market reforms to the forefront.

As Brazil prepares to take on the difficult task of amending labor-related clauses in the Constitution and the labor code, a debate rages over whether inappropriate or outdated labor legislation is at all binding in developing countries. The argument is that if, for example, minimum wages are set at above-market-clearing levels, these laws will simply be ignored rather than restricting employment. Similarly, if the workweek is specified at unrealistically low levels, employers and workers will agree on higher weekly hours, in effect annulling the mandate. If payroll tax rates are set at high levels and if the programs they fund are poorly designed, workers and employers will conspire to avoid paying them altogether. One of the results of unsuitable mandates and inadequate enforcement capacity would be the emergence of an illegal, unregulated, or "informal" labor market, so that even if labor legislation changes were made, the effects on aggregate labor market outcomes would be insignificant. On the other hand, some proponents of labor reform argue that the excessively high taxes and labor market restrictions contribute to the increase in the informal sector, because they provide incentives for evading formality. Using empirical evidence, they hint at a positive correlation between the level of payroll taxes or high firing restrictions and the level of informality, and hence recommend a reduction in taxes and labor market restrictions.

This chapter shows that it is difficult to make sweeping generalizations on the question of whether labor laws matter and how they affect the size of and conditions in the informal sector. The more interesting and tractable question for policy purposes is, which laws matter, where, and why? This chapter suggests that the economic and political history of a country may be a critical determinant of the relative importance of legislation on wages and employment. A few examples of how the economic and political history of Brazil (and the manner in which labor laws are enforced) has affected outcomes in both regulated and unregulated labor markets are:

- Newcomers to Brazil are initially perplexed by the use of multiples of the legal minimum salary in individual and collective contract negotiations, in determining floor and ceiling pension benefits, and in official statistics on employment and earnings. The roots lie in a period of high inflation and widespread illiteracy of the workforce. Changes in the legally specified minimum salary—based on changes in the cost of living due to inflation—seem to have provided a widely accepted and frequent signal to workers and employers to adjust nominal wages accordingly. We provide evidence that a significant number of workers are paid exactly the legal minimum wage, and adjustments in this wage are matched by salary adjustments even in Brazil's unregulated sector and, perhaps because of habit persistence, even in today's low-inflation environment.
- Brazil's labor laws specify that workers must be paid within the first week of the month. We discuss evidence that this law—which was critical in periods of high inflation—appears to be obeyed by employers in both the formal and informal sectors, even in today's low-inflation environment.

- Persistent high income inequality and a prolonged period of socialist policies has led to labor laws with a prolabor bias, and to labor courts acquiring a similar bias in their verdicts on disputes. Under Brazilian law, labor courts have policy-setting powers, in the sense that labor courts in judging a particular case are entitled to formulate policies in areas where the labor code and the Constitution are ambiguous in the opinion of the court. Increased ambiguity of labor laws combined with a prolabor bias of dispute resolution has resulted in workers who are dismissed from either formal or informal employment being able to extract generous severance benefits from their former employers.

These examples indicate that the subset of binding laws does not depend only on the design of labor legislation, but is also country specific.[1] Labor markets must be studied and understood country by country, not by compiling and analyzing cross-country data designed to help arrive at a summary verdict. In contrast to the general notion, we will show that labor legislation in Brazil not only affects the formal, but also the informal, sector. Changes in labor legislation should take this into consideration.[2]

In this chapter, we first present some stylized facts about the Brazilian labor market and examine the evolution of labor market indicators, such as employment structure, job creation and unemployment, and labor income and earnings ratios in recent years. We briefly describe the evolution of labor legislation in Brazil from 1943 until 1998, explaining in detail the main labor laws, and discuss the main issues and objectives of the labor market reforms implemented and proposed in 1997–98. We examine the adherence to labor laws in the formal and informal sectors by looking for "pressure points" or evidence of clustering of labor market outcomes, such as wages and hours worked, exactly at the limits set by the law; and by discussing whether changes in the labor legislation led to changes in these labor market outcomes.

Relevant Labor Market Indicators

The opening of the economy since the late 1980s and the sharp reduction of inflation since 1994 have changed the macroeconomic environment in Brazil.[3] The analysis of relevant labor market indicators concentrates on the 1990s, with special emphasis given to the last four years after the launching of the Real Plan. In the case of variables that have more "structural" determinants, such as unemployment and the level of informality of the labor market, the analysis goes back to the 1980s.

Job Creation and Unemployment

Despite the low rate of growth in the 1980s, neither job creation nor un-employment was a major problem during this decade. The level of employment grew continually as more than 15 million new jobs were created. The labor force participation rate increased almost continuously from 1979 to 1987, then fell slightly toward the early 1990s. The rate of open unemployment fluctuated during the 1980s, increasing during the recession years of 1981–83, but never surpassed 5 percent. Despite the adjustments associated with the opening of the economy, the early 1990s were not very different from the 1980s. In the recession of 1990–92, employment decreased but then recovered, growing almost 10 percent between 1991 and 1996. Compared to the 1980s there has been a slight increase in the rate of unemployment. However, it has remained low and stable, oscillating between 4 and 6 percent. Only in 1997 and 1998 did unemployment rise to above 6 percent, prompting concerns about joblessness.

The Structure of Employment

According to data of the Pesquisa Nacional por Amostra de Domicílios (PNAD—the annual nationwide household survey), the structure of employment by type of working relation remained relatively stable during the 1980s. The share of formal workers remained around 32 percent, the share of informal workers around 22 percent, and the share of self-employed around 26 percent. Public servants accounted for approximately 12 percent, and nonpaid workers for around 7 percent.

Data of the *Pesquisa Mensual do Emprego* (PME—monthly household surveys in the six main metropolitan regions)[4] show a persistent increase of the share of self-employed since 1986. Between 1986 and 1996 the share of self-employed went from 16.5 percent of the metropolitan labor force to 23 percent. The share of informal wage earners fell between early 1984 and 1989 and then started increasing, to reach almost 25 percent of the labor force in 1996. As a consequence, the share of the remaining wage earners (formal, public, and nonpaid workers) fell from an average of 58 percent during 1985–90 to less than 47 percent in 1996. Hence, around 10 percent of the labor force moved from legal wage earner status to either informal or self-employed status since the late 1980s.

As for the sectoral structure of employment nationwide, PNAD data for the 1980s show a stable share of industry and manufacturing employment, and a reduction in agricultural employment compensated by an increase in service. Both PNAD and PME data for the 1990s show a marked decrease in manufacturing employment and an increase in service sector employment. There is a clear movement in favor of job creation in the nontradable sector and against the tradable sector during the 1980s and the 1990s.

Labor Turnover and Job Quality

Looking at a selected set of countries in the early 1990s, the share of workers in the manufacturing sector with less than one year in service is 10 percent in Japan, 12 percent in Germany, 15 percent in France, 28 percent in the United States, and 33 percent in Brazil. For manufacturing workers with less than five years of service, the share in the labor force is 37 percent in Japan, 41 percent in Germany, 42 percent in France, 62 percent in the United States, and 71 percent in Brazil. Hence job tenure is greater in Japan, Germany, and France than in the United States and Brazil. Even when considering all sectors, workers change jobs frequently in Brazil and the United States and very infrequently in Germany and other European countries. In contrast, the duration of unemployment, while increasing, remains short in Brazil and the United States, and considerably higher in Germany and European countries. In Japan the frequency and duration of unemployment spells are both relatively low.

Table 3-1 presents available data on labor turnover in the Brazilian formal sector. The data should be read as follows. In 1985, on average, 2.8 percent of workers in all Brazilian legally registered firms with more than five employees changed their job every month. In 1989, 40 percent of the workers changed their jobs over the year. Thus, during 1989–93, 28 percent or more of workers in legally registered firms changed their jobs in the period of one year. Turnover is lower in the manufacturing and service sectors than in the trade sector where, in turn, turnover is lower than in the construction sector.[5]

The labor turnover statistics presented in Table 3-1 are based on the *Relação Annual de Informações Sociais* (RAIS) and the *Cadastro Geral de Empregados e Desempregados* (CAGED) data, which are based on legally required self-reporting by firms. This sample comprises legally registered firms with more than five employees. Consequently, they do not cover the informal segment of labor markets. It is possible to build turnover measures based on the longitudinal aspect of PME data for the six main Brazilian metropolitan regions. The turnover rate in the informal sector is three to four times greater than the already high turnover rate found for the for-

TABLE 3-1
Labor Turnover Rates, Brazilian Formal Labor Market,
1985–93

Year	Monthly average	Annual
1985	2.80	n.a.
1986	3.67	n.a.
1987	3.72	n.a.
1988	3.80	n.a.
1989	3.49	39.66
1990	3.26	38.20
1991	2.69	35.75
1992	2.26	28.05
1993[a]	2.73	32.81

n.a. Not applicable.
a. January–October 1993. RAIS and CAGED data.
Source: Ministry of Labor, Law 4923. Calculations, Amadeo and others (1994).

mal segment of the labor market. The high level of labor turnover is sometimes viewed as evidence of the flexibility of the labor market, especially if one takes into account illegal employees. However, high levels of turnover may also be associated with low levels of investment in firm-specific human capital (see Amadeo and others 1993). Furthermore, as we will discuss below, the design of the Brazilian severance fund Fundo de Garantia por Tempo de Serviço (FGTS) may artificially raise the level of turnover in the formal sector by providing strong incentives for workers to induce their dismissal in order to access their FGTS balances.

Labor Income

From 1980 to 1990, gross domestic product (GDP) increased by 17 percent while the labor force increased 40 percent, implying a decrease of 17 percent in average productivity. In a "competitive" labor market, wages would have fallen to accommodate the reduction in productivity. In fact, the average labor income per worker did fall 22 percent between 1980 and 1990.[6] The path of the average labor income followed the oscillations of output, falling during the 1981–83 recession, increasing in the 1986 boom (the Cruzado Plan), then declining at the end of the decade. In the 1990s, real labor income also oscillated according to the output cycle in

1991–92, falling by 17 percent between 1991 and 1992, then recovering by 35 percent between 1992 and 1996.

Sectoral Earnings Ratios

In the 1980s relative earnings moved strongly in favor of manufacturing wages and against nontradable sectors. This movement resulted from the increase in labor absorption in the service sector without a corresponding increase in output, on one hand, and the protectionist tariff and exchange rate policies which favored the manufacturing sector, on the other hand. The 1990s were marked by a symmetric movement with the opening of the economy and the pronounced appreciation of the exchange rate reducing the competitiveness of the tradable sectors, with negative effects on employment and relative earnings in manufacturing. Relative earnings between manufacturing and service sector workers fell from 1.6 during 1992–93 to 1.3 in 1996. Between manufacturing and trade workers it fell from 1.5 in 1992 to 1.27 in 1996.

The Brazilian Labor Code

We now turn to the main characteristics and elements of the Brazilian labor code and the main changes to it since it was created in the 1940s.[7]

The Consolidated Labor Code

The main body of Brazilian labor legislation was introduced in the 1940s, and was consolidated into the Consolidação das Leis do Trabalho (CLT) in 1943. The CLT is a large, often overlapping set of rules that determines individual and collective rights and duties of workers, unions, and firms. The law mandates that all workers have a booklet in which all individual labor contracts and changes to them are registered by the employer. Consequently, a worker with a booklet signed by his employer (*com carteira assinada*) is considered a formal worker. Signing the booklet implies an obligation on the part of employer and employee to contribute to social security.[8]

Besides the obligation to sign the booklet, the law stipulates a set of minimum conditions an employment relationship must meet. The most important rules address maximum hours of work per week, maximum overtime working hours, minimum payment for overtime work, minimum wage, prepaid annual vacations. The rules include special protection clauses for women and children that forbid the dismissal of pregnant women and provide for paid vacation before and after childbirth for the mother, special work conditions for night shifts, one-month prenotification of firing, and protection against unjustified dismissals. Between 1962 and 1988 the main changes were:

- In 1962, introduction of a mandatory end-of-year bonus of one monthly wage (called the "thirteenth salary").
- In 1963, introduction of a mandatory family allowance.
- In 1965, introduction of a wage-adjustment law which determined the minimum rate of wage adjustments of all workers in the economy.
- In 1966, creation of an individualized severance fund (FGTS) in place of a clause forbidding dismissal of workers with more than 10 years of tenure.
- In 1986, creation of an unemployment insurance program which today covers about 25 percent of the country's labor force.

Reform of Brazilian labor regulations requires either changes in labor legislation or constitutional reform. In addition, reforms can be implemented immediately by the executive branch through executive decrees. Amendments to the Constitution require a two-thirds majority vote in both the upper and lower houses of Congress, twice. Changes in clauses of the CLT require a single vote in the upper and lower house and can be approved by simple majority. Examples of reforms that do not require votes in the two houses are the elimination of incompatibilities between the labor code and the introduction of occupation-specific contracts. They further may refer to minor changes, such as allowing shorter hours per week, or improvement of the inspection of occupational safety regulation. Extending the duration of unemployment benefits or allowing temporary layoffs without any severance payment can be approved by simple majority. Changing rules of union finance and membership, minimum wage-setting procedures, or reforms of the unemployment insurance system require a Constitutional change.

The Reforms of 1988

In 1988 a new federal Constitution was approved and new labor clauses introduced. The main changes in labor legislation concerning individual rights introduced in the Constitution of 1988 were:

- Reduction of the maximum number of hours a worker worked per week before receiving overtime wages from 48 hours to 44 hours, and an increase in the minimum payment for overtime hours from 120 percent to 150 percent of the worker's regular wages.

- Reduction of the maximum daily working time for continuous work shifts from eight hours to six hours.
- Creation of a mandatory vacation bonus of one-third of the worker's wages.
- Increase in the paid maternity leave for mothers to 120 days, and introduction of five days' paid childbirth leave for the father.
- Increase in the firing costs for unjustified dismissals (which includes reductions in workforce due to economic reasons) from 10 percent of the FGTS balance to 40 percent.

This is the list of the minimum individual rights for private sector and state enterprise workers. In general, therefore, the new Constitution clearly mandated higher nonwage benefits and made dismissals costlier for employers. Working conditions can be improved further through negotiations between the individual worker and the firm, or through collective bargaining. In 2001, the government introduced legislation that would allow collectively bargained contracts that provide nonwage benefits less than those stipulated in the CLT.

Severance Rules and Unemployment Compensation

Until 1965, to fire a worker without proper justification the employer had to pay one month's salary for each year of work in the firm. The compensation was calculated on the basis of the highest wage received during the work contract. It was a duty of the employer to prove the dismissal was justified, and the conditions for justified dismissals were clearly defined in the law. In 1966, this system changed and a severance fund was created, called the FGTS. The FGTS provides an individualized fund for each worker. Every month the employer contributes the equivalent of 8 percent of the employee's current wage to the fund. This implies that the worker's FGTS increases with tenure and that the amount accumulated in the Fund per year corresponds approximately to one monthly wage. In general, the FGTS can be accessed only by the worker upon dismissal without just cause or upon retirement.[9] When workers are dismissed without just cause (*sem justa causa*) they also have the additional right to receive a penalty in proportion to their FGTS. Thus, until 1988, the dismissed worker received access to his or her accumulated balance in the FGTS, and additional compensation of 10 percent of the FGTS balance at the time of dismissal if this dismissal was considered to be without just cause. In 1988 this fine for unjust dismissal was increased to 40 percent of the FGTS.

Besides this fine, the employer must notify the worker one month before he or she is fired. This is the *aviso prévio* law, or a mandate for the employer to provide "advance notification" of firing. During the month the worker receives the advance notification of firing, he or she is allowed, according to the law, to take two hours a day to look for a new job. This implies a minimum cost of 25 percent of the worker's monthly wage. In fact, the cost is usually higher since firms end up paying the notification fee to workers and dismissing them immediately.

The total cost of dismissal is thus 25 to 100 percent of the monthly wage plus 40 percent of the FGTS. The FGTS depends on the number of months the worker has worked for the firm. Table 3-2 shows the costs for the firm as a multiple of monthly wages, according to the number of years of the worker's contract, under the assumption that the firm dismisses the worker upon notification. For example, if the worker stayed with the firm one year, the cost of dismissal is, at most, 1.41 monthly wages. The cost to dismiss a worker who has been with the firm for five years is, at most, 3.19 monthly wages, and so on.

According to PMEs in the six largest metropolitan regions during 1982–98, 72 percent of workers who reported separations from their jobs were in fact fired, 85 percent of whom received the FGTS. There are two points to note here. First, the share of dismissals among those exiting employment rose from 67 percent to 76 percent after the Constitution raised firing fines from 10 percent to 40 percent. This result indicates that higher firing fines do not reduce dismissals but, on the contrary, may even increase them. Second, about 65 percent of the workers that reported voluntary separation during 1982–98 also reported that they had access to the FGTS. This hints at illicit agreements between firms and workers regarding access to FGTS funds. The fact that being fired is the main mechanism which allows access to the FGTS may be a significant incentive to

TABLE 3-2
Total Cost of Firing a Worker
(multiple of monthly wages)

Tenure	1 yr.	2 yrs.	3 yrs.	4 yrs.	5 yrs.	10 yrs.	15 yrs.	20 yrs.
FGTS fine	0.41	0.84	1.27	1.72	2.19	4.72	7.66	11.07
Aviso previo	1.00	1.00	1.00	1.00	1.00	1.00	1.00	1.00
Total	1.41	1.84	2.27	2.72	3.19	5.72	8.66	12.07

induce dismissal. This may be exacerbated by credit constraints and by the fact that the fund is administrated by the government, which, because of poor management, typically generates real returns below market returns.

Since 1986, besides advance notice, access to the FGTS, and the 40 percent fine for unfair dismissal, the worker also has the right to unemployment compensation benefits under the *Seguro de Desemprego* program. The unemployment compensation program offers partial coverage for up to four months of unemployment (extended to five months after 1996). To become eligible for the benefit, the worker must (a) have been dismissed without just cause, (b) have had a formal labor contract during the last six months or have been legally self-employed for at least 15 months, (c) be unemployed for at least seven days, (d) not receive any other pension, and (e) not have any other type of income sufficient to guarantee his own subsistence and that of his family. The value of the benefit cannot be lower than the value of the minimum wage, is adjusted monthly for inflation, and is related to the average wage received by the worker in the last three months in his or her previous job.

Wage Laws

An important change in the CLT was the introduction of the Wage Adjustment Law in 1965. Before this date, wage adjustments were fixed through collective bargaining between workers and employer unions, and through individual negotiations between the individual worker and his or her employer. Only the minimum wage was determined directly by the president of the republic, although most of the time it automatically incorporated the prescriptions given by indexation clauses imbedded in the law.

The Wage Adjustment Law gave the government the right to determine the minimum rate of adjustment of all wages in the formal sector of the economy. The first wage law stipulated that nominal wages should be adjusted once a year, at a date which was specified for each occupation, following a formula which took the past and expected future rate of inflation and the growth rate in GDP per capita as the base for the adjustments. The specific formula and the adjustment period changed many times over the years as the rate of inflation increased.

In mid-1995, one year after the introduction of the Real Plan, the Wage Adjustment Law was abolished. Today, upward adjustment of wages is negotiated between employers and employees, but for all practical purposes downward adjustment of wages is prohibited by the Constitution. Attempts to do so open employers to lawsuits, which are generally re-

TABLE 3-3
Stylized Facts of Wage Indexation Regimes, 1980–2000

Starting Date	Dec. 1979	March 1986	June 1987	Jan. 1989	May 1989	March 1990	Sept. 1991	Dec. 1992	July 1995
Duration (months)	63	15	20	4	10	18	15	9	84
Stabilization plan	—	Cruzado	Bresser	Summer	—	Collor	—	—	Real
Transition phase[a]	Instant	Instant	Gradual	Instant	Instant	Instant	Gradual	Gradual	—
Rule type[b]	Time	State	Time	Time	Time	—	Time, R	Time, R	—
Trigger point	6 m	20%	1 m	—	1 m	—	4.2 m	4.2 m	—
Average lag[c]	8 m	—[d]	4 m	—	1 m	—	4 m	4 m	—

a. This attribute indicates whether the transition to the new wage indexation regime was done in an instantaneous or a gradual manner.

b. For time-dependent rules the trigger point is specified in terms of months between adjustments. For the state-dependent rule the trigger point was specified in terms of accumulated price index variation between adjustments. R means regressive adjustments, that is, lower wages get higher adjustments.

c. Refers to the average lag between price rises and their incorporation into wages.

d. In the state-dependent case the lag is endogenous.

solved in favor of the worker. This was irrelevant during a time of high inflation, but now quite possibly adds to the rigidity of the labor market.

Payroll Taxes and Mandatory Contributions

The CLT and the 1988 Constitution stipulate a comprehensive set of minimum standards any individual contract must follow. The rules do not provide much space for negotiation between employers and workers. The result is a rigid set of minimum rules, which reduces the flexibility of the labor contract in the face of changes in the economic environment. In addition to the costs imposed by this inflexibility, there are more direct and obvious nonwage costs due to payroll taxes and mandatory benefits required by the law.

Table 3-4 shows the composition of the labor cost in Brazil. The cost of labor can be decomposed into four parts:

- The basic contractual wage (60 percent of total cost = 100/165.4).
- Mandatory benefits, which include the annual one-month bonus (*décimo terceiro salário*), the contribution to the severance fund FGTS, vacations, and other benefits (23 percent of total cost = 37.6/165.4).

TABLE 3-4
Wage and Nonwage Labor Costs
(monthly)

Component	Percent	Total
Basic Wage		100.0
Annual bonus	8.3	108.3
Vacations	11.3	119.6
Severance fund contribution (FGTS)	8.0	127.6
Other mandatory benefits[a]	10.0	137.6
Total pay (*basic wage + mandatory benefits*)		137.6
SESI, SENAI, SEBRAE (*employer associations*)	3.1	140.7
INSS[b] + accident insurance + education +		
INCRA	24.7	165.4

Note: Normal number of hours = 44 weeks.

a. These are benefits that cannot be calculated for all workers since they depend on gender, kind of work done, economic sector, and so forth. These include family allowances, pregnancy leaves, and transport subsidies.

b. Workers contribute 8, 9, or 10 percent of their wages to social security, depending on the wage.

- Contributions to the official training system (*Serviço Nacional de Aprendizagem Industrial*—SENAI, and *Serviço Nacional de Aprendizagem Comercial*—SENAC), to finance an institution which assists small enterprises (*Serviço de Apoioàs Pequenas Empresas*—SEBRAE), and a contribution paid by firms to finance a workers' assistance service (*Serviço Social de Industria*—SESI, or *Serviço Social do Comércio*—SESC) (2 percent of total cost = 3.1/165.4).
- Contribution to the federal social security system (INSS) and to fund educational services (*salário educação*) and an on-the-job accident insurance fee mandatory for all firms and proportional to the payroll (14.8 percent of total cost = 24.5/165.4).

In addition to these contributions based on payroll costs, employers are also charged levies on revenues to pay for additional INSS-related obligations (*cofins*), which in 1999 were raised from 1 to 2 percent. Additionally, employers have to pay contributions to the Fundo de Aparelho de Trabalhador (FAT), which funds unemployment compensation, job search assistance, and active labor programs such as training and microenterprise support schemes (PIS/PASEP). These labor-related levies can add up to between 2 and 3 percent of employer revenues.[10]

Reforms Proposed and Implemented in the 1990s

Brazil faces formidable challenges in the area of labor legislation. As pointed out, the set of laws that constitute the labor code have their basis in rules formulated in the 1940s, with additional—sometimes overlapping or inconsistent—legislation added over the years in response to both genuine labor market concerns and for shortsighted political reasons. Today, the regulation of the labor market is a daunting task for the Ministry of Labor for the following reasons:

- The plethora of laws has led to uncertainty about which regulations apply and under what circumstances, which results in frequent disputes between employers and employees.[11]
- These disputes are resolved by labor courts, which have earned the reputation of having a strong prolabor bias. Under Brazilian law, labor courts have policy-setting powers, in that labor courts—in judging a particular case—are entitled to formulate policies in areas where the law is ambiguous in the opinion of the court.[12]
- No employment contract is strictly legal unless approved by the Ministry of Labor, which leads to the Ministry having to devise and validate special contracts for specific working conditions, without which employers are left vulnerable to expensive lawsuits.

- Collective bargaining between workers and employers can be an instrument for formulating more definite contracts, but collective bargaining rules in Brazil and the practices they have engendered are often insensitive to work-specific conditions.
- The high rates of payroll contributions and the low benefits of programs they fund encourage evasion and informality.

Consequently the five fundamental aims of the government's reform agenda are to:

- Reduce the uncertainty of labor costs for employers.
- Create the conditions for more durable employee-employer relationships, so that both employers and employees voluntarily choose to stay together because the contract can be changed without friction in response to changing work and market conditions.
- Create the environment for more representative collective bargaining.
- Reform implementing institutions to ensure better enforcement of contracts.
- Reduce the incentives to become informal.

Addressing these issues, the government implemented some labor reforms in 1997. They allowed the introduction of temporary contracts of employment with lower payroll taxes and considerably lower dismissal costs. In general, reforms that have been debated over the past few years include the following:

- *Eliminating contradictions between labor legislation and the constitution.* The Ministry has submitted a bill for consideration by Congress that seeks to eliminate contradictions between labor legislation and worker rights guaranteed under the dismissals to reduce the perverse incentives for workers to induce dismissal.
- *Severance laws.* While reform of the FGTS has not been formally attempted, there have been proposals suggesting delinking the access to the fund from dismissals in order to reduce the perverse incentives for workers to induce dismissal. A 1998 Ministry of Labor proposal to reduce the rate of employer contributions to fund the FGTS from 8 percent to 2 percent of payroll met with opposition within and outside the government, and was dropped. If seriously considered, this could be accompanied by reform of the unemployment compensation system to function more like an unemployment insurance plan (that is, actuarially based). In 1998, the government proposed the allowance of temporary layoffs, which are funded by credits of the FAT. The employer has to repay these funds if he does not rehire the worker at the end of the layoff.

- *Maximum hours worked.* The government is considering a reduction in weekly work hours (*jornada de trabalho*) from 44 to 40.[13] One of the proposals of the current administration is to reduce the hours of work that qualify a person for a full-time contract (which entitles the person to greater benefits than part-time work). The objective of this measure is to make the workweek more flexible by permitting daily work to range from 5 to 8 hours, and weekly hours from 26 to 40 hours.

- *Temporary contracts.* In 1997, the government introduced legislation that would allow employers to hire new workers on temporary contracts, during which non-INSS-related payroll taxes would be waived and dismissals would be less costly. These measures were expected to lead to increased employment because the nonwage costs of labor would be reduced.

- *Union representation.* For a single sector or occupation, Brazilian labor laws do not allow for more than one union per municipality—the *unicidade sindical* provision. For all practical purposes, this legislation outlaws plant-level collective bargaining. The Ministry of Labor has proposed that this law be altered to facilitate collective bargaining to reflect firm-level conditions. The Ministry has also proposed changes in the mechanisms by which unions are financed, making union fees voluntary rather than mandatory. In 2001, the government initiated efforts to allow union-negotiated contracts to set conditions "below" the floor set by the CLT.

- *Policymaking powers of labor courts.* Brazilian labor laws give labor courts policy-setting powers (*poder normativo*) in that these courts can establish policy on issues which are left unclear by the CLT and the Constitution. As a result, labor court rulings have influence far beyond the case being arbitrated, in effect serving a policymaking role that should be the responsibility of the Ministry of Labor. Reforms being contemplated to curb this policymaking role of labor courts while also reducing ambiguities in the labor law are thus likely to reduce the uncertainty regarding the full cost of labor, and hence result, in increased labor demand.

- *Minimum wage.* Brazil has a nationwide minimum wage that is, at the same time, the minimum legal wage in the private sector and the minimum payment for pensions of the social security system. Appropriate reforms would attempt to (a) regionalize the minimum wage, (b) delink social security pensions from the minimum wage, and (c) delink public employee salaries from the minimum wage.

The Effects of Labor Legislation on Informal and Formal Workers

The informal sector is defined as the set of economic units that do not comply with taxes and regulations imposed by the government (Hernando de Soto 1989). Following accepted practice, throughout this chapter we distinguish formal from informal employment by determining whether or not the contract has been ratified by the Ministry of Labor; that is, whether the worker has a signed work card (com carteira assinada) or not (sem carteira assinada).[14] For reasons of comparison between the formal and informal sector, our analysis concentrates on wage earners. We thus ignore the (informal) self-employed. In this section we analyze and contrast the effect of various labor regulation schemes on the formal and informal segments of the labor market. We focus on labor regulations concerning minimum wages and maximum working hours.

We provide evidence that informal jobs in Brazil are not necessarily unregulated. In other words, we argue that institutions and the legal apparatus affect both formal and informal workers. The distinction between legal and illegal employment appears rather to be associated with the incentives and costs for both the employer and the employee of maintaining a legal contract and, to a much lower degree, with the quality of jobs in terms of working conditions and wages. In this respect, the high proportion of informality of labor contracts on the one hand may be seen as emanating from poor design of the programs—the social security system, the severance fund, the fund for providing unemployment compensation and more active labor programs, and various other schemes that are funded by high levels of mandatory contributions. On the other hand, it supports the view that, as Maloney (1998) puts it, the informal sector may be seen as a way to avoid inefficiency arising from labor market regulation, rather than the regulations themselves. Given that signing the work card requires paying rather high contributions to the social security system, and that links between INSS benefits and contributions are low, some workers may have an incentive to evade labor legislation and seek informal employment.

Brazil offers unique conditions for testing the effects of regulation on formal and informal labor market outcomes for the following reasons:

- A substantial share of employees work in the illegal sector.
- Labor market surveys in Brazil have traditionally explicitly asked whether or not employees possess working permits (carteira de trabalho), allowing us to distinguish formal from informal employees.

- Large household surveys allow us to follow the same individuals through short periods of time. This longitudinal aspect allows us to analyze changes in several labor market outcomes at an individual level.
- Perhaps most important, a regulated labor market exists and these regulations change from time to time, offering "natural experiments" to study the effects of regulation.

The final point merits elaboration. Institutional effervescence in Brazil is due in part to adoption of the new Brazilian Constitution in 1988, and in part by the transition from hyperinflation before 1994 to almost zero inflation in 1998. The former offers the possibility of estimating the impact of various labor code provisions (for example, changes in maximum hours allowed, payroll taxes, and firing fines) on informal and formal wage employees by exploring the variation in labor market outcomes before and after the new Constitution.

To assess to what extent labor legislation affects the formal and informal sector, we start by looking at the percentage of workers in the formal and informal sector that comply with the limits set by the legislation. We then ask whether minimum wage and maximum hour legislation actually distort the wage and hour distribution in the informal and formal sector workers and answer this question by first assessing the size of the clustering exactly at the limits set by the law.

- *Wages.* In the case of wages we assess how many individuals earn exactly one minimum wage. The idea here is that in the absence of regulation the wage distribution would be continuous, which means that each point of the distribution would have a zero mass. If the minimum wage law forces a change in the distribution, then we will observe a mass point at the minimum wage level.
- *Hours worked.* Similarly, in the case of hours worked we assess the proportion of individuals who work the maximum number of hours allowed without requiring the payment of overtime.

Second, we study the effects of changes in labor legislation on the distribution of wages and hours worked. This dynamic approach provides a check against habit formation in labor markets. As pointed out, history does matter, and the wage and hour level that we observe may be reminiscences from the past. For example, people in the informal sector may frequently work 44 or 48 hours a week because it is a long-established tradition that also happens to be present in the labor code. To tackle this issue, we test whether the relevant labor regulations are binding before *and* after the change is introduced.

- *Wages.* We choose dates of minimum wage changes and assess the share of employees who adjust their earnings at the official minimum wage adjustment rates. We have already mentioned that changes in legally specified minimum salary had an important signaling effect during periods of high inflation. Now we show that wage adjustments are matched by salary adjustments in Brazil's unregulated sector, even in today's low-inflation environment.
- *Hours worked.* Similarly, we assess the proportion of individuals who work the maximum number of hours that are allowed for formal workers without requiring the payment of overtime.

Minimum Wage Regulation

Analysis of Distribution of Wage Levels

Our empirical strategy to gauge the effects of wage regulation is the direct analysis of earnings distribution. The idea is to assess the relative concentration of the mass of the distribution of labor market variables at the minimum wage level observed. If there is a point with positive mass at the minimum wage, the size of the spike of the frequency distribution at the minimum wage level constitutes a key statistic to quantify the effectiveness of the wage floor imposed.

We start this analysis by providing evidence on the percentage of wage earners paid above the minimum wage (see Table 3-5). As can be

TABLE 3-5
Wage Earners Paid above the Minimum Wage
(percent)

	All	*Legal*	*Illegal*
Recife	90	100	83
Salvador	91	100	83
Belo Horizonte	96	100	93
Rio de Janeiro	98	100	96
São Paulo	98	100	97
Porto Alegre	97	100	94

Note: By metropolitan region.
Source: PME, September 1998.

seen, minimum wages are binding in the formal sector, but in the informal sector the percentage of wage earners paid below the minimum wage level is strikingly low, ranging from 17 percent in Recife to 3 percent in São Paulo.

The fact that we do not observe formal wage earners below the minimum wage does not necessarily mean that the minimum wage law affects formal sector wages. It may be just too low. If this is the case, then the distribution of formal sector wages should in principle be continuous at each point in the distribution. If a minimum wage regulation is introduced and is binding, then all the workers that initially earn below or equal to the minimum wage should earn exactly the minimum wage after the introduction. Given that the minimum wage law is binding, the frequency distribution at the minimum wage level indicates the share of people who would have earned the minimum wage or less without the legislative constraint. This is not the correct interpretation for informal sector workers, as we still observe some workers earning less than the legal minimum. However, if we observe a point with positive mass at the minimum wage in this sector, then this indicates that some employers in the informal sector respect minimum wage laws, and that consequently minimum wage laws affect the earnings distribution of informal sector workers.

Table 3-6 presents the relative concentration of wage levels for February 1998 at exactly one minimum wage in the six main metropolitan regions according to PME. Ten percent of all employees earned exactly one minimum wage. The point to be noted here is that the share of illegal employees (14 percent) earning one minimum wage is double the share observed for legal employees (7 percent). As can be seen in Table 3-6, this

TABLE 3-6
Wages Exactly Equal to One Minimum Salary
(percent)

	All	Legal	Illegal
Recife	18	15	23
Salvador	24	20	29
Belo Horizonte	10	8	14
Rio de Janeiro	8	4	12
São Paulo	2	1	5
Porto Alegre	6	4	7
Total	10	7	14

Note: By metropolitan region.
Source: PME, September 1998.

TABLE 3-7
Wages Exactly Equal to One Minimum Salary
(percent)

	Legal	Illegal	Public
North	9	21	11
Northeast	14	20	14
Southeast	6	15	6
South	6	15	4
All Brazil	8	18	9

Note: For all of Brazil.
Source: Pesquisa Nacional por Amostra de Domicílios (1996).

greater share of illegal employees earning exactly one minimum wage is observed in all six metropolitan regions.

Table 3-7 presents the share of total legal and illegal employees earning exactly one minimum wage in September 1996 for the whole country, according to the nationwide PNAD. Again, the share of minimum wage earners is highest in the illegal sector, compared to the formal and the public sector. In Tables 3-6 and 3-7 the share of employees earning exactly one minimum wage is larger in the illegal sector. This reflects the fact that the wage distribution of informal employees lies to the left of the distribution of the formal sector, which to some extent may be due to differences in worker characteristics such as age and education.

Results of Maloney and Nuñez (2001) strongly support our findings. Using a sample from the PNAD,[15] the authors show, as can be seen in Figure 3-1, that the minimum wage law strongly alters the wage curve in the informal sector.

Analysis of Distribution of Wage Adjustments

We have shown that minimum wage laws do affect the wage distribution of formal and informal sector workers. We now address the issue of whether this is a vestige of the past, or whether wages really move with changes in labor legislation. The indirect effect through which the minimum wage policy affects illegal employee earnings has been called the "lighthouse effect" (*efeito-farol*) of regulations. It is claimed that official wage rules would act as a "voluntary" reference price to illegal employees. However, as Maloney and Nuñez (2001) point out, the fact that inflation was moderate in 1998 indicates that the minimum wage is not only a signal in a high-inflation country, but appears to be an important benchmark

FIGURE 3-1
Wage Distribution of Formal and Informal Male Workers, Brazil 1998

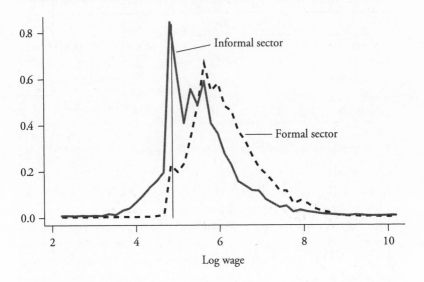

Source: PNAD (1998).

for "fair" remuneration. A complementary, country-specific channel in Brazil is that illegal employees may get the benefits of labor market regulation by suing their employers for evading the minimum wage law. If a court decision is favorable to employees, firms have to pay all benefits denied to illegal employees.

To shed light on the connection between illegal employee wage and wage law description, we take advantage of the longitudinal aspect of earnings information present in PME data. Our approach consists of determining the share of employees with earnings adjustment rates exactly equal to the official minimum wage adjustment rates at the respective adjustment dates. This allows us to describe how earnings adjustment rates evolve through time and identify their focal points. The idea is that employers in the informal sector may frequently pay minimum wages to some informal sector workers because it serves as a kind of reference point. But if we observe that changes in the legally specified minimum wages result in changes in actual wages paid, then we can conclude that the minimum wage law is binding.

Figure 3-2 presents the shares of legal and illegal employees that received earnings adjustments rates exactly equal to the ones of the mini-

FIGURE 3-2
Proportion of Wage Adjustments Exactly Equal to
Minimum Wage Adjustments, Legal and Illegal Employees

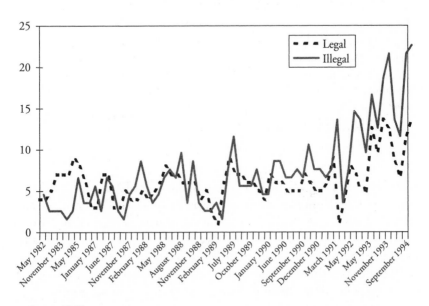

Source: PME.

mum wage at minimum wage adjustment dates that occurred during
1982–95.

Table 3-8 summarizes the information presented in Figure 3-2 as averages of selected periods. The data show that (a) the two adjustment dates
after the launching of the Real Plan (September 1994 and May 1995) presented a sharp rise in the influence of the minimum wage on salary levels
in all three universes analyzed; (b) if we abstract from the post–Real Plan
period there is not a clear trend in the degree of minimum wage influence
in the legal employee universe analyzed; and (c) there is a sharp rise in the
influence of minimum wages on the informal employee segment. All
things remaining the same, in the first half of the 1980s less than 3 percent
of illegal employees adjusted at the minimum wage adjustment rate, while
this ratio rose to more than 10 percent in the first half of the 1990s.

To compare the short-term movements of earnings at a monthly level
between the two sectors, we proceed as follows. First, we calculate the ratio
of a month's nominal earnings with respect to the earnings of the previous

TABLE 3-8

Proportion of Wage Adjustments Exactly Equal to Minimum Wage
Adjustments at Dates When the Minimum Salaries Were Changed

(percent)

Period	All	Legal	Illegal
May 1980 to February 1986	6.00	6.38	2.75
March 1986 to February 1990	5.27	5.47	4.82
March 1990 to January 1994	7.04	6.86	10.29
September 1994 to May 1995	14.00	12.00	21.50
Average	6.25	6.21	7.03

Note: Average across selected periods.
Source: PME.

month (that is, one plus the monthly nominal earnings rate of change).
For each month we plot the distribution of this ratio. We find that the
main focal point corresponds to a nominal earnings ratio of one, which
means that nominal incomes had been rigid between two consecutive
months. It is interesting to note that in all graphs the illegal segment presents a greater share of people with constant earnings.

At the same time, illegal employees present, in general, a greater am-
plitude of the rates of change of nominal earnings measured by the spread
between the 3rd and the 97th percentile of the distribution. The main
characteristics of the distribution of illegal employees' monthly adjustments distributions is the existence of plateaus or focal points equal
to 1.5 and 2. Legal employees present these focal points during November and December, which are probably connected to the payment of the
mandatory annual bonus (décimo terceiro salário) in one or two receipts.
Concerning illegal employees' distributions, however, these focal points
are relatively more important and more spread out through the year.

Regulations on Hours Worked

Working hours are an important determinant of job quality. Consistent
with our analysis of minimum wages, we start by providing evidence on
the percentage of workers who work hours below the maximum hours
limit. Before the Constitution of 1988, the maximum number hours
worked without the obligation of the payment of overtime was 48. In
1998 this limit changed to 44. As can be seen in Table 3-9, between 60
and 80 percent of formal sector workers work 44 hours or less. Compared
to minimum wages, a rather large fraction works below the maximum

TABLE 3-9

Proportion of Workers with Hours Worked Below
or Equal to Maximum Hours Limit

(percent)

Metropolitan region	All	Legal	Illegal
Recife	60	60	59
Salvador	61	66	56
Belo Horizonte	63	65	61
Rio de Janeiro	66	67	66
São Paulo	67	71	64
Porto Alegre	73	80	66

Note: The legal limit is 44 hours.
Source: PME (September 1998).

legal limit. This may be due to the effect of overtime hours, which are not
forbidden, but have to be remunerated differently. Since 1988, overtime
has been paid at 1.5 times the worker's wage rate. Unfortunately, in the
PME no information is available on whether or not overtime is paid.
However, Table 3-9 shows that differences in the percentage of workers
who work above the legal limit are strikingly small for Recife and Rio de
Janeiro, but large for Porto Alegre and São Paulo.

Using distributions of hours worked of legal and illegal employees on a
yearly basis from 1982 to 1996, we find that the distributions of illegal
employees are in most cases above those of legal employees. Except for the
years 1985, 1989–91, and 1993, in terms of first-order stochastic domi-
nance, illegal employees work more than legal employees. That is, the
number of hours in any given percentile of the distribution of illegal
employees is greater than the corresponding percentile in legal employees hours distribution. The distribution of illegal employees hours also
second-order stochastically dominates the corresponding distribution of
legal employees in all years except 1982, 1988, and 1994.

To analyze whether the maximum hours legislation distorts the hours
distribution in the formal and informal sector, we evaluate the relative
concentration of the mass of the distribution of hours effectively worked
at the level of the parameters set by the law. Table 3-10 reveals that the
main focal points found for legal employees hours distribution are also
found for illegal employees distribution. There are clear plateaus at 40, 44,
and 48 hours. The 40 hours focal point is not related to a legal limit, but
rather corresponds to the weekly working week (*jornada*) of 40 hours. In

TABLE 3-10

Effective Workweek before and after New Constitution

Hours per week	Legal employees		Illegal employees	
	1987	1990	1987	1990
0–30	9	11	9	9
30	5	5	4	6
30–40	5	7	4	5
40	30	31	21	22
40–44	1	1	1	1
44	3	**20**	3	**8**
44–48	6	4	4	4
48	**32**	15	**25**	19
48–60	6	4	14	15
60 and more	3	2	15	11
All	100	100	100	100

Note: All Brazil. The legal maximum was lowered from 48 to 44 hours in 1988. Figures in bold are of particular interest.

Source: PME (1987, 1990).

1987, the percentage of employees who worked 48 hours amounted to 32 percent in the formal sector, and only 7 percent less in the informal sector. Consequently, the largest mass point is found at the legal maximum hours limit in both sectors, which hints at the fact that the hours legislation distorts the hours distribution in the legal and the illegal sector.

To understand whether changes in labor legislation affect the distribution of hours worked in either sector, we exploit the change in the maximum hours limit introduced by the Constitution in 1988. The reduction of the jornada de trabalho from 48 hours to 44 hours in the Constitution of 1988 is reflected in a decrease in the share of workers working 48 hours by 17 percent in the formal sector and 6 percent in the informal sector. Similarly, the share of workers working 44 hours increased from 1987 and 1990. This clearly reveals that changes in the legislation concerning the weekly working week did affect illegal employees, but to a lower extent than formal sector workers.

Conclusion

In this chapter, we studied the effect of minimum wage and maximum working hours labor legislation on the wage and hours distribution of formal and informal wage earners. We found that labor legislation concerning minimum wages and maximum hours distorts the wage and hours distribution not only in the formal labor market, but also in the informal labor market. This provides evidence that evading the costs for both the employer and employee of maintaining a legal contract, such as payroll taxes, social security contributions, and firing fines, does not necessarily imply that other labor legislation does not affect illegal employment. Table 3-11 summarizes our main results.

That labor legislation affects the illegal labor market may be explained by the following reasons: First, concerning minimum wage, the argument of the "lighthouse effect" (efeito-farol) of regulations has been put forward, which claims that the official wage rules act as a "voluntary" reference price to illegal employees. Second, the fact that inflation was moderate in 1998 indicates that the minimum wage is not only a signal in a high-inflation country, but appears to be an important benchmark for "fair" remuneration. A similar argument may apply to the number of work hours. Moreover, the high costs of social security for employees; the low

TABLE 3-11
Brazil: Some Measures of Conformity with Labor
and Social Security Laws

| | Sector of employment | |
	Formal: with signed card	Informal: without signed card
Indicator		
Payroll taxes (% of workers whose firms...)		
Paid INSS contributions	94.5	4.5
Paid FGTS contributions	95.0	5.0
Wage regulations (% of workers with...)		
Paid exactly one minimum wage	7.0	14.0
Wage change = minimum wage increase		
March 1990 to January 1994	6.9	10.3
September 1994 to May 1995	12.0	21.5
Hours restrictions (% of workers)		
Workweek equal to jornada		
1987 (before Constitution)	32.0	25.0
1990 (after Constitution)	20.0	8.0

Note: Following convention, formal employment implies having a carteira de trabalho assinada (working card or booklet signed by the employer), which signifies ratification of the contract by the Ministry of Labor.

link between contributions and benefits; and the low quality of many social security benefits combined with the ambiguity in the design of labor legislation and the slanted nature of its enforcement by labor courts may increase the incentive to evade payment of social security contributions.

Finally, Brazilian employees can take their employers to court—which has sweeping powers under current Brazilian law—to force them to pay for their legal working rights, whether or not their contract had been ratified by the Ministry of Labor. Given the high probability of the cases being resolved in favor of workers, employers accord these workers all the rights under the labor law even when they do not have legal contracts. The nature of enforcement of labor laws therefore endows informal sector workers "ex post legality," even though they are "ex ante illegal." Thus, all things being equal, the incentives to stay informal are higher for workers who are assured of protection under labor legislation regardless of the nature of their contract; labor legislation only alters their financial relationship with the government.

Notes

1. A corollary of this, which is far more obvious, is that the current political economy of a country affects the possibility of successful labor reforms.

2. Recent research in Latin America (see, for example, Maloney 1998) has challenged the notion of the traditional dualistic view of the labor market, which considers the informal sector as a disadvantaged part of the labor market, which is segmented due to high labor costs in the formal sector. Some authors emphasize that given the high labor costs in the formal sector, some workers actually may choose to become informal.

3. This section draws on Amadeo and others (1993).

4. Note that the PNAD covers total labor population, while the PME is restricted to the six main metropolitan areas.

5. Turnover is relatively low in the formal service sector mainly because this sector includes workers employed in large public utilities and other state enterprises.

6. Real labor income measures the income of all employed workers, including illegal (informal) wage earners and the self-employed.

7. This section draws upon Amadeo and others (1993) and *Ministerio do Trabalho* (1998).

8. Employee contributions for social security are based on a progressive scale and vary between 8 and 11 percent.

9. Withdrawals are possible for large health expenses or acquisition of a home.

10. PIS/PASEP rates are 0.65 percent of personnel costs of private sector firms and 1 percent of the wage bill of nonprofit establishments, but are 1 percent of the revenues of state enterprises.

11. For example, under one part of the law a worker who worked for less than the full hours per week for a year is entitled to a *proportional* amount of paid vacation and the mandatory Christmas bonus of a worker who worked full time all year, but is entitled to *full* benefits under another part of the law.

12. Using administrative data from the CAGED, one researcher reports that in the early 1990s more than 1.5 million labor cases were disputed every year. Based on a sample for Minas Gerais, 96 percent of the disputes were for workers with one to five minimum monthly wages. Seventy percent of those disputes had less than two minimum wages.

13. That is, the maximum number of hours of work per week without the payment of overtime wages.

14. A similar system exists in Peru. Note that this definition of informal sector worker is more precise than the conventional definition of informality initiated by the WTO, which classifies informal workers as nonprofessional self-employed workers in firms with less than five employees or domestic workers.

15. The sample they use consists of workers between 16 to 65 years of age who work between 30 and 50 hours a week. Informal salaried workers as defined as those working for firms with five employees or less, and formal salaried workers as those working for firms with more than five employees.

References

Amadeo, Edward, Ricardo Paes de Barros, José Márcio Camargo, and Rosane Silva Pinto de Mendonça. 1993. "Institutions, the Labor Market and the Informal Sector in Brazil." Inter-American Development Bank, Washington, D.C.

———. 1994. "Institutions, the Labor Market and the Informal Sector in Brazil." Institute of Applied Economic Research and Department of Economics, Catholic Pontifical University-Rio. Processed.

Amadeo, Edward, Ricardo Paes de Barros, José Márcio Camargo, Rosane Silva Pinto de Mendonça, Valéria Pero, and André Urani. 1993. "Human Resources in the Adjustment Process." Discussion Paper, No. 317. Rio de Janeiro: Institute of Applied Economic Research.

De Soto, Hernando. 1989. *The Other Path.* New York: Harper and Row.

Maloney, William F. 1998. "Does Informality Imply Segmentation in Urban Labor Markets? Evidence from Sectoral Transitions in Mexico." *World Bank Economic Review* 13: 275–302.

Maloney, William F., and Jairo Nuñez. 2001. "Measuring the Impact of Minimum Wages: Evidence from Latin America." Policy Research Working Paper No. 2597. World Bank, Washington D.C.

Ministerio do Trabalho. 1998. *Relatorio da forca-tarefa sobre politicas de emprego: diagnostico e recomendacoes.* Governo Federal, Brasilia, August.

PME (Pesquisa Mensual do Emprego). 1998. September. Brazil.

PNAD (Pesquisa Nacional por Amostra de Domicílios). 1996. Brazil.

PART

II

Labor Supply
and Labor Demand
in Argentina

CHAPTERS 4 AND 5 ANALYZE the determinants of labor demand and supply in Argentina using a quantitative approach.

Chapter 4 takes up the question of variations in labor supply over the economic cycle. The approach employed in the chapter can be summarized as follows. First, the authors examine the basic patterns—trend (long-term) and cyclical (short-term)—in labor force participation of men and women. Then they determine the underlying cause of year-to-year fluctuations in labor force participation, distinguishing between the added worker and the discouraged worker effect. The added worker effect refers to an increase in labor force participation, when a demand-induced fall in employment arises, while the discouraged worker effect has the opposite implication. The likely explanations for these patterns are provided, contrasting Argentina's experience with other countries. Next, the trends and structure of unemployment are analyzed to determine the extent to which increased labor force participation can account for the increased unemployment in recent years, and the extent to which reduced employment growth is responsible. Finally, the chapter discusses the policy implications of these findings, both in terms of what Argentina can expect over the longer term as benefits to labor reform, and the likely consequences of current labor supply patterns—for the sustainability of labor policies—if the proposed reforms are not implemented.

Based on this analysis, Chapter 4 concludes that reforms to encourage efficient employment and wage-setting practices—while directly promoting sustainable growth of labor demand—are also likely to favorably influence short-term labor supply patterns. In Argentina, high real wages tend to be maintained during recessions, even though unemployment rates increase. An increase in unemployment rates leads to a drop in income for many households, which induces secondary workers, such as women, to enter the labor force. This results in a strong added worker effect, which may put even more pressure on unemployment. Hence, labor force participation of secondary workers in Argentina tends to be anticyclical, leading to exaggerated fluctuations in measured unemployment rates. Labor reforms that encourage wage flexibility will result in reduced cyclical volatility of unemployment rates, not just because employment fluctuations will be moderated by wage adjustments, but also because labor supply fluctuations will be less exaggerated. The discouraged worker effect will be strengthened, countering the significant added worker effect that leads to increased labor supply when the economy is weak. This would in turn allow the government to concentrate on the task of instituting policies for raising long-term employment growth, instead of being distracted by temporary but sharp increases in unemployment, which are politically difficult to ignore.

Chapter 5 provides quantitative estimates of the likely payoff—in terms of greater employment—to initiatives that improve labor market functioning. The analysis allows for a comparison between strategies that rely only on economic growth to reduce unemployment and those that combine these strategies with labor policy reform. Numerical estimates of employment growth that would occur due solely to economic expansion, that is, without labor reforms which raise or lower labor costs, are approximated by the output elasticity of aggregate employment, holding wages or unit labor costs constant. Similarly, the wage elasticity of employment can be used to quantify the effects of labor policy reforms on employment growth. Since the estimations require assumptions on issues such as the degree of substitutability between labor and capital in the production process, the chapter reports these results under a variety of assumptions.

The estimated wage elasticity can reasonably be regarded as about -0.5, implying that a 10 percent fall in labor costs—other things remaining unchanged—will raise employment by 5 percent. Estimated output elasticities range between 0.1 and 0.4. The average estimate is about 0.25, implying that a 10 percent increase in output will result in a 2.5 percent increase in employment. With the output elasticity estimate being roughly half the absolute magnitude of the wage elasticity, the main implication is that Argentina cannot rely solely on economic growth to lower the high unemployment rates it has experienced since 1995, but must undertake labor reforms.

Argentina's monetary and exchange rate policies have resulted in low inflation rates, but they also limit the policy instruments the government has at its disposal. Fiscal discipline and labor market deregulation are perhaps the two most important policy priorities. While comprehensive labor reform is politically difficult to implement since it involves confronting powerful labor unions, Argentina did lower labor taxes in the mid-1990s and introduced legislation allowing for special labor contracts (modalidades promovidas). These contracts allowed the hiring of certain categories of workers without paying labor taxes or severance payments, and under longer probationary periods. When these laws were simplified, employers were quick to take advantage of the new law, and by 1998 more than 12 percent of formal employees had been hired under these more flexible terms. Employment growth accelerated to more than 3.5 percent annually between 1995 and 1998, and unemployment fell from 20 percent to about 12.5 percent. But in mid-1998, under political pressure during the run-up to elections in 1999, the government essentially revoked the special contracts law, reduced probationary periods, and made the centralized collective bargaining laws even more centralized. By 1999, unemployment rates had begun to climb again, and were around 15 percent in 2000. Under pressure to tighten fiscal discipline, the Argentine government increased some labor taxes in 2001. After essentially reversing by the end of the decade the progress made in the mid-1990s, Argentina made a discouraging start with respect to labor policy reform in the new millennium.

Three years of economic stagnation have resulted in unemployment rates rising to about 20 percent again. In late 2001, Argentina defaulted on its public debt, triggering a political crisis.

4 Understanding Labor Supply Dynamics in Argentina

Carola Pessino, Indermit S. Gill,
and José Luis Guasch

The evolution of a labor force is influenced either by changes in the population size or changes in labor force participation (LFP). Changes in population size are determined by the rates of natural increase and net migration. These patterns—especially the rate of natural increase—are relatively slow to change. LFP may exhibit either long-term of short-term changes. Long-term tendencies in the change of LFP, such as increased participation of women, are due to sociological and other factors, which are also slow to change. Speaking of "trend" labor force growth based on growth of the population base and these long-term changes in LFP is not unreasonable. But the size of the labor force also responds to shorter-term (or cyclical) changes, which operate largely through rapid—though often predictable—changes in the LFP rate. These changes have received considerable attention in recent labor policy debates in Argentina, and are the main concern of this chapter.

In Argentina, unemployment rates have risen sharply since 1990, reaching about 18 percent in 1995. Since then they have remained at about 15 percent. Recent labor policy discussions about the origins of the high unemployment in Argentina have involved decomposition of changes in unemployment into a component related to labor demand (or an unexpected slowdown of employment growth) and another related to labor supply (or unexpected increases in LFP, especially of women). In joining this debate, we contend that the definition of "unexpected" fluctuations in labor supply employed so far ignores a fundamental attribute of the Argentine labor market, that is, that LFP is positively correlated with the unemployment rate over the business cycle. The main contribution of this paper is to explain shorter-term LFP patterns in Argentina using established theory and econometric techniques, to re-examine the decomposition of unemployment using these results, and to draw policy implications from these exercises.

In Argentina, the change in female LFP explains most of the change in total LFP from 1974 to 1995. Female participation rates rose by 45 percent from 1974 to 1995, while male participation rates were the same in 1995 as in 1974. In this chapter, we examine variations in female LFP using data up to October 1995. We distinguish trend from cyclical behavior and illustrate, through econometric techniques, the correlation between LFP and unemployment rates. Based on this analysis we determine the extent to which higher LFP—or increased labor supply—can legitimately be blamed for the rapid increase in unemployment since 1990.

The approach employed in this chapter can be summarized as follows: First, we examine the basic patterns—trend (long term) and cyclical (short term)—in LFP of men and women. Second, we determine the underlying cause of year-to-year fluctuations in LFP, decomposing the effects of demand-induced reduction of employment on labor supply in "added worker" and "discouraged worker" effects: The added worker effect implies that LFP of secondary workers increases as unemployment rises, while the discouraged worker effect leads to the opposite conclusion. We provide likely explanations for these patterns, contrasting Argentina's experience with that of other countries. Third, we examine the trends and structure of unemployment. This enables us to determine the extent to which increased LFP can account for the increased unemployment in recent years, and the extent to which reduced employment growth is responsible. Finally, we discuss the policy implications of these findings.

Trends in Participation and Unemployment

Population, Labor Force, and Employment

Before turning to the discussion about changes in LFP, we provide some evidence on the evolution of total population and employment. As can be seen in Table 4-1, total population in all 25 urban conglomerates in Argentina increased from 23 million in 1980 to 30.7 million in 1995. Following the increase in total population, the economically active popula-

TABLE 4-1

Argentina: Labor Force, Employment, and Unemployment, 1980–95

Year	Total population	Economically active pop.	Employed	Unemployed	Unemployment rate (%)
1980	23.00	8.73	8.48	0.25	2.81
1981	23.50	8.89	8.45	0.44	4.95
1982	24.00	9.10	8.59	0.51	5.60
1983	24.45	9.12	8.64	0.47	5.21
1984	24.90	9.32	8.84	0.47	5.10
1985	25.45	9.57	8.95	0.63	6.53
1986	26.95	9.89	9.29	0.60	6.12
1987	26.40	10.19	9.56	0.63	6.19
1988	26.90	10.41	9.73	0.68	6.54
1989	27.50	10.68	9.83	0.85	7.96
1990	28.00	10.72	9.92	0.79	7.42
1991	28.60	11.10	10.35	0.75	6.76
1992	29.10	11.44	10.63	0.82	7.12
1993	29.75	11.88	10.77	1.11	9.35
1994	30.35	12.08	10.73	1.34	11.14
1995	30.70	12.64	10.43	2.21	17.48

Note: All urban areas. Numbers are averages of April/May and October; estimates for 1995 are for May only.

Source: "Secretaria de Programacion Economica," printed in *Informe Económico,* First Quarter, 1995.

tion increased from 8.73 million in 1980 to 12.64 million in 1995. Employment increased steadily from 1980 until 1993, ranging from 8.48 million to 10.77 million, and declined to 10.43 million in 1995. However, employment rates decreased from 97.14 percent in 1980 to 82.52 percent in 1995. Unemployment increased steadily from 250,000 in 1980 to 850,000 in 1989, followed by a decrease until 1991. In 1995, the recession induced by the so-called Tequila Crisis reached its peak, which is reflected in a drastic increase in the number of unemployed. From 1993 to 1995, it nearly doubled, climbing to 2.21 million in 1995, which corresponds to an unemployment rate of 17.48 percent.

Between 1980 and 1991 Argentina's population grew at an annual rate of 1.4 percent. This growth in population—which is high compared to Europe (0.3 percent) and North America (1 percent)—is mostly due to the rate of natural increase. While the stock of migrants is important, changes in the number of migrants are not large enough to significantly affect overall labor supply as well as employment, unemployment, or wages. Moreover, the number of legal immigrants from neighboring countries has increased in absolute numbers, but not as a proportion of the population.[1]

Employment growth in Argentina has fluctuated considerably since 1974. According to Ministry of Economy household data for Greater Buenos Aires, employment grew at an annual rate of 1.1 percent between May 1974 and October 1995. Compared to other countries, GBA fared moderately well in terms of employment growth. Employment growth has been strongest in North America (1.7 percent annually since 1974) and weakest in the European Community (EC) (0.2 percent annually) and the European Free Trade Association (EFTA) (0.2 percent), with Argentina (1.1 percent), Oceania (1.2 percent), and Japan (1.1 percent) falling in the middle. (For a more detailed discussion see Pessino 1997.) However, when population growth is taken into account, Argentina fares the worst, with an annualized rate of growth in population of 1.3 percent (in GBA). Employment growth minus population growth averages a 0.16 percent decrease per year. In this respect, Argentina is much closer to the EC and EFTA. Using this index, North America and Japan fared the best, generating the highest employment growth relative to population growth. Furthermore, in Argentina there was an increase in the overall LFP rate, implying that LFP growth was higher than population growth. The labor force grew at a 1.95 percent annualized rate during the period, which compares to an annual population growth of 1.3 percent. We will show that this growth was largely due to the increase in female LFP.

Labor Force Participation

LFP rates—the number of people working or seeking work as a share of population aged 15 to 64—in Greater Buenos Aires rose by more than 10 percentage points (from 58.1 to 68.5 percent) between 1974 and 1995, as can be seen in Table 4-2.[2] This increase was accounted for entirely by increased female LFP rates: female participation rates rose by 45 percent over 1974 levels (more than 16 percentage points), while male participation rates were about the same in 1995 as they were in 1974. Furthermore, while male LFP rates fluctuated only slightly around the 84 percent level during the two decades preceding 1995, changes in female LFP rates were much more pronounced. Female participation rates increased very rapidly from October 1991, peaked in May 1993 at 51 percent, then decreased by

TABLE 4-2
Labor Force Participation, by Gender
(percent)

Year	All	Female	Male
1974	58.1	36.6	85.3
1975	58.4	36.3	85.9
1976	58.3	35.7	86.2
1977	57.9	35.8	85.1
1978	57.8	37.8	83.8
1979	58.1	37.3	84.3
1980	60.6	38.1	84.8
1981	60.1	38.5	83.6
1982	60.0	38.5	84.5
1983	58.6	36.6	83.0
1984	59.8	38.3	83.5
1985	60.6	39.6	83.6
1986	62.0	42.8	84.4
1987	62.6	43.4	84.3
1988	62.8	43.8	83.8
1989	64.0	45.5	84.3
1990	63.8	45.0	84.1
1991	63.2	44.4	83.2
1992	64.4	45.9	84.5
1993	66.5	49.7	84.8
1994	65.9	48.8	84.2
1995	68.5	53.0	85.1

Note: For Greater Buenos Aires, people 15 to 64 years of age.

two percentage points, peaked again in May 1995 at 53 percent, and declined again in October 1995. Participation rose relatively steadily between 1983 and 1989 (by between 1 and 2 percentage points per year), but has exhibited sharper fluctuations since 1990. From 1992 to 1993, and again from 1994 to 1995, female LFP rates rose by about 4 percentage points within a single year. As a consequence, understanding the trend and changes in LFP rates in Argentina requires understanding the trend and changes in female LFP.

Not only aggregate and female LFP rates exhibited an upward trend from 1974 to 1995. Pessino (1997) shows that participation rates of teenagers and older people increased from 1987 to 1995, as well. Using microeconomic household data on male wage earners and the self-employed aged 25 to 54 for Greater Buenos Aires, Pessino furthermore finds that aggregate real monthly earnings dropped drastically from 1986 to 1990. Real wages behaved similarly. They increased substantially between 1991 and 1993, before starting to decrease again. Hence, from 1991 to 1993 aggregate participation rates and participation rates for women, teenagers, and older people increased.

The change in labor supply due to change in the price of labor can be decomposed into two effects: the substitution effect and the income effect. Classical theory predicts that the substitution effect is positive, which means that the family member that receives higher wages will work more hours. The sign of the cross-substitution effect (for example, the effect of wages of husbands on the labor supply of their wives) is not determined by theory. The same holds for the income effect. If wages of a member of the household decrease, family income decreases. It is often assumed that a fall in family income induces members to work more. Given that the income effect is positive and dominates the cross-substitution effect,[3] a decrease in a husband's wages will increase the labor supply of his wife.

With the exception of 1990 and 1991, female LFP increased during a time of rising unemployment rates. According to Lundberg (1985), the response of LFP rates to a demand-induced fall in employment consists of two components—the added worker effect and the discouraged worker effect. The added worker effect usually refers to a temporary increase in the labor supply of married women whose husbands have become unemployed or face restriction in their work hours. The discouraged worker effect refers to workers who drop out of the labor force or refrain from entering it, because they anticipate that wages will be lower or job search costs higher. The finding that female LFP increases with unemployment rates suggests that in Argentina the added worker effect dominates the discouraged worker effect.

Compared to OECD countries, female LFP rates are quite low in Argentina. In OECD countries, female LFP rates averaged 48 percent in 1973, and 60 percent in 1990.[4] Hence, female LFP in Argentina during this period was smaller than in OECD countries.[5] The increase in female LFP in Argentina is very similar to that of North America and Oceania, despite much higher population growth in Argentina. Other countries have an even higher growth trend in female LFP. In some sense, therefore, Argentina is lucky to have slower growth in LFP, since it would have generated a much higher rate of unemployment, if one assumes that LFP is inelastic with respect to wages and income and that relative wages do not adjust to the increased labor supply of women. The difference between employment and labor force growth is negative in all OECD countries, leading to growing unemployment rates. The countries that fare best (in terms of low unemployment growth) are the United States and Japan. Argentina faced a 0.8 percent shortfall per year in employment relative to labor force growth. High population growth combined with relatively low LFP growth compared to other countries hints at the fact that there exists a considerable reserve of potential workers in Argentina. This may be quite responsive to economic stimuli (for example, increasing wages and declining household wealth that accompany business cycles). The considerable year-to-year fluctuations exhibited by female LFP rates since 1990 are consistent with this observation.

Summarizing, there are three noteworthy observations regarding female LFP rates. First, they remained largely unchanged from 1974 to 1983. The 45 percent rise in LFP rates between 1974 and 1995 is thus a phenomenon of the subsequent decade. Second, female LFP rates exhibit considerable fluctuations. Third, compared with OECD countries, Argentina faces low female LFP rates and low LFP growth relative to population growth.

Unemployment

In Greater Buenos Aires (for which the most reliable and detailed data are available) the unemployment rate quadrupled from 5.1 percent in October 1987 to 20.2 percent in May 1995, as can be seen in Table 4-3. The rapid increase in the unemployment rate from October 1987 until May 1995 was similar for men and women. Table 4-3 illustrates that male and female unemployment rates increased by approximately 290 percent. Looking at worker groups by age, it can be seen that workers who were aged 35 to 49 faced a somewhat greater increase in unemployment rates than younger workers. This is in line with the fact that growth in the unemployment rate was lower for single workers compared to married workers.

White-collar workers faced a higher growth in unemployment rates compared to blue-collar worker. Note, however, that all the groups that faced low unemployment growth had a relatively low level of unemployment rate in October 1987. Differences among sectors and education in unemployment growth during this period are very small. Comparing increases in unemployment rates for two subperiods—October 1987 to October 1994, and October 1994 to May 1995—and for the period as a whole—October 1987 to May 1995—it can be seen that the rise in unemployment rates was even more uniform than during 1987–95 as a whole. Thus, while there were differences in the rate of increase of unemployment

TABLE 4-3
Unemployment Rates, Inflows, and Duration,
October 1987 and May 1995

	Rate[a]		Inflows[b]		Duration[c]	
	Oct. 1987	May 1995	Oct. 1987	May 1995	Oct. 1987	May 1995
All	5.1	20.2	1.5	4.2	5.6	8.6
By Gender:						
Male	4.4	17.1	1.3	4.2	5.2	7.2
Female	6.3	24.8	1.8	4.1	5.8	10.0
By Age:						
Male 20–34 years	4.2	15.3	1.1	3.9	5.0	7.2
Male 35–49 years	2.9	11.9	1.0	3.4	4.8	6.2
Female 20–34 years	7.3	25.2	1.8	4.1	6.2	10.0
Female 35–49 years	4.2	19.0	1.5	2.9	4.4	11.0
By Sector:						
Manufacturing	5.5	19.0	2.1	3.5	4.0	9.6
Services	4.5	16.7	1.3	3.4	6.0	8.4
Construction	11.0	36.2	4.0	12.7	4.4	4.4
By Occupation:						
White collar	3.8	16.8	1.3	4.0	5.2	7.8
Blue collar	7.1	24.3	2.2	5.1	5.2	8.6
By Education:						
Primary incomplete	7.6	23.4	2.3	6.4	5.6	6.8
Tertiary complete	2.2	6.7	0.6	1.2	6.2	11.6
By Marital Status:						
Male single	8.6	28.6	2.2	5.9	5.4	8.2
Male married	2.8	11.6	0.9	3.3	5.2	6.4
Female single	8.4	30.0	2.0	5.0	6.2	10.0
Female married	5.3	22.6	1.8	3.8	5.4	10.2

Note: For Greater Buenos Aires. The groups in each category are not always exhaustive, and are chosen for illustrative purposes.

a. Unemployment rates are percentage of labor force.

b. Inflows are percent per month.

c. Unemployment duration is in months, computed by multiplying the duration of incomplete spells by two.

across age, sector, occupation, education, and marital status, these numbers are more striking for their similarity than their differences. Thus, while these groups have quite different unemployment rates—for example, female, younger, less-educated, blue-collar workers have higher unemployment rates—this structure remained relatively unchanged before and after the reforms.

Unemployment rates are the product of inflows into unemployment (that is, the fraction of workers that become unemployed in any month) and the duration of unemployment spells. Thus, for example, in 1995 construction workers had high inflow rates (about 12.7 percent compared with 3.5 for services and manufacturing), but relatively short duration of unemployment (about 4.5 months, and about 9 months for manufacturing and services). These numbers translate into an unemployment rate of 36 percent for construction, roughly twice the rate for manufacturing and services.

The average inflow into unemployment in Greater Buenos Aires increased from 1.5 percent per month to 2.8 percent between 1987 and October 1994, and rose to 4.2 percent in May 1995. This implies an overall increase of about 180 percent. There was more variation in inflow rates than in unemployment rates across categories of workers. For example, the percent change in inflows from October 1987 to May 1995 with respect to 1987 was 1.8 times higher for men than for women. Similarly, the percent change in the inflow rates of construction workers was more than 3 times higher compared to manufacturing, while the percent change of white-collar workers was 1.5 higher compared to blue collar workers.

The average duration of unemployment spells increased less dramatically—from 5.6 months in October 1987 to 8.6 months in October 1994—which corresponds to an increase of 54 percent. It then remained unchanged. With the exception of older women and manufacturing workers, the increase in unemployment rates in 1995 was driven largely by increased inflows into unemployment, and not by longer unemployment spells. Since relative unemployment rates (for different worker groups) remained quite stable between 1987 and 1995, but relative inflows changed considerably, it stands to reason that unemployment duration of different workers would also have changed significantly as well. In fact, unemployment rates of workers with different attributes tend to move together over the reference period.

Another question that concerns policymakers is whether the unemployment increase that took place between October 1994 and May 1995 was an aberration, perhaps due to an unfortunate combination of an external shock (the Tequila Effect) and increased LFP, which was encouraged by the economy's strong performance between 1992 and 1994. Table 4-4 provides evidence of the composition of the unemployed according to their labor force status, age, and gender in May 1995. Of the 1 million unemployed in May 1995, 21 percent were reentrants, 14 percent were new entrants, and 65 percent were previously employed individuals. Among the latter group, 61 percent were men, while women dominated the groups of unemployed who entered or reentered the labor market (70 percent). Furthermore, unemployed new entrants, as expected, were mostly young. In contrast, males between 20 and 49 years of age formed the bulk of the unemployed with previous employment. While these findings are not conclusive evidence that increased LFP of women is not responsible for increased unemployment, they do provide reason to be skeptical of such claims.

Using standard econometric techniques (probit analysis) to determine the characteristics that are associated with unemployment rates, we find mainly that being male, having more education, not being a new entrant into the labor force, working in larger firms, and working in nontradeable (service) sectors other than construction significantly lowers the probability of being unemployed. But being educated is no guarantee against unemployment: older, educated workers are more likely to be unemployed than older, less-educated workers. There also exists some evidence that having other sources of income allows workers to stay unemployed longer. Comparing probit analysis results for May of each year between 1992 and 1995, we find considerable stability of these relationships.[6]

Determinants of Labor Force Participation

Methodology

Unemployment can increase either because fewer jobs are available or because more workers decide to look for jobs. Whether the rise in unemployment is largely demand induced or is the result of increased LFP has very different welfare implications for workers. This implies that understanding the relation between the dramatic changes in female LFP in Argentina and the high level of unemployment has important policy implications. As explained, the response of LFP rates to a demand-induced fall in employment can be decomposed into an added worker effect and a discouraged worker effect. Added workers are, for example, women or school-aged children who increase their labor supply as the family head becomes unemployed or faces restriction on his or her work hours. Discour-

TABLE 4-4
Distribution and Duration of Unemployment, by Age, Gender, and Previous Labor Market Status, May 1995

	Reentrants to labor force	New entrants	Previously employed	All
Distribution of the unemployed (percent)				
Males				
15–19 years	17.0	77.1	19.4	—
20–34 years	33.8	22.9	33.9	—
35–49 years	24.7	0.0	26.3	—
50–64 years	24.5	0.0	20.4	—
Females				
15–19 years	9.9	54.2	15.5	—
20–34 years	43.9	33.8	41.8	—
35–49 years	30.4	9.0	30.3	—
50–64 years	15.8	3.0	12.4	—
All				
15–19 years	12.0	61.4	17.9	—
20–34 years	40.9	30.4	37.0	—
35–49 years	28.6	6.2	27.8	—
50–64 years	18.5	2.1	17.3	—
Males	30.1	31.1	61.0	—
Females	69.9	68.9	39.0	—
Duration of unemployment (months)				
Males				
15–19 years	5.4	7.3	4.2	5.2
20–34 years	5.0	10.9	3.9	4.5
35–49 years	5.0	—	4.0	4.1
50–64 years	3.2	—	8.8	7.9
All	4.6	8.1	5.0	5.2
Females				
15–19 years	3.6	6.5	4.7	5.4
20–34 years	5.1	9.8	6.1	6.4
35–49 years	8.3	8.2	7.7	7.9
50–64 years	8.9	12.4	7.3	8.2
All	6.5	7.9	6.5	6.8
All	6.0	8.0	5.6	6.0

— Not available.
Source: INDEC-EPH.

aged workers may be women who refrain from entering the labor force be-cause their cost of looking for acceptable employment rises to such a de-gree, during a recession, that it no longer pays for them to make the effort.

To address the question of how LFP rates respond to changes in un-employment rates, we assume that participation rates are functions of the cycle and a time trend. The time trend is included to reflect the impact of slowly changing social factors and other gradually moving variables omit-ted from the equation. The cycle may affect each demographic group in a different way. As a cycle measure we use the unemployment rate of prime-aged male workers, which is expected to influence the level of participa-tion since the costs of search are affected by the availability of jobs.[7] Using male unemployment rates also allows us to test whether in Argentina the added worker effect or the discouraged worker effect applied during the recent years. We also analyze the determinants of female LFP decisions.

Following the methodology used by Pencavel (1986), Killingsworth and Heckman (1986), Clark and Summers (1981), and Pessino and Gi-acchino (1994), we estimate variants of the following regression of LFP on trend (t) and cycle (U^P) for Greater Buenos Aires during 1974–95 for eight gender-age groups.

$$L_{it} = \alpha_i + \beta_i \, U^P_t + \gamma_t \, t + \varepsilon_{it} \tag{1}$$

L_{it} is the LFP of group i in year t, expressed as a percentage of total pop-ulation in group i, U^P_t is the unemployment rate of males aged 35 to 49 in year t. The superscript "P" on U designates this as the prime-aged ref-erence group. The responsiveness of the participation rate to the business cycle is measured by β, while γ is the coefficient for the linear time trend. Note that β may vary across groups. The equation error is represented by ε_t and the index i runs over eight gender-age groups. We assume that the errors follow an (AR1) process and present the results of estimating those equations by maximum likelihood techniques in Table 4-5.[8]

Of course, the equations that we are estimating do not provide a de-tailed explanation of LFP of each of the groups. Rather, our purpose is to estimate a model that captures the relation between LFP and cyclical fluc-tuations in the unemployment rate. A positive coefficient on U^P tells us that LFP of the respective group moves in the same direction as U^P, and hence is evidence of the predominance of the added worker effect. If we find that a higher rate of unemployment of male workers is associated with lower LFP of this group, that is, that the coefficient on U^P is nega-tive, we have evidence of a discouraged worker effect.

TABLE 4-5
Labor Force Participation: Cyclical and Trend Factors Specification (1),
Females and Males

	α Constant	β Cycle	γ Trend	δ Autocorrelation
Females				
15–19 years	34.445[a]	1.257[a]	–0.407[a]	0.372[a]
	(0.995)	(0.272)	(0.061)	(0.145)
20–34 years	46.947[a]	1.067[a]	0.117[a]	0.365[a]
	(0.950)	(0.262)	(0.058)	(0.145)
35–49 years	33.548[a]	0.745[a]	0.441[a]	0.517[a]
	(1.146)	(0.251)	(0.064)	(0.134)
50–64 years	18.050[a]	0.544[b]	0.341[a]	0.430[a]
	(1.165)	(0.294)	(0.069)	(0.141)
All females	33.892[a]	0.821[a]	0.226[a]	0.615[a]
	(0.943)	(0.170)	(0.049)	(0.123)
Males				
15–19 years	49.343[a]	0.453	–0.220[a]	0.508[a]
	(1.452)	(0.324)	(0.081)	(0.135)
20–34 years	95.580[a]	0.310[a]	–0.064[a]	0.044
	(0.289)	(0.109)	(0.021)	(0.156)
35–49 years	97.097[a]	0.154[a]	–0.028	0.460[a]
	(0.314)	(0.076)	(0.018)	(0.139)
50–64 years	75.857[a]	0.407	0.039	0.441[a]
	(1.176)	(0.292)	(0.069)	(0.140)
All males	85.001[a]	0.274[a]	–0.068[a]	0.290[b]
	(0.365)	(0.110)	(0.023)	(0.149)

Note: Biannual data from 1974/1–95/1. April 1986 is missing. Data are usually measured in April/May and September/October. The number of observations is 42. The estimation method is the maximum likelihood method correcting for autocorrelation. Standard errors are in parentheses.

a. Significant at 5 percent level.

b. Significant at 10 percent level.

Source: INDEC-EPH.

To check the robustness of our results, we run three further regressions, which are variants of the standard specification described in equation (1). The other three regressions use the following specifications:

- Trend, U^P and industrial production index (IPI).

$$L_{it} = \alpha_i + \beta_i U^P_t + \gamma t + \delta \log(IPI)_t + \varepsilon_{it} \qquad (2)$$

- Trend, U^P, period dummy for 1991–95 and period dummy interacted with cycle measure.

$$L_{it} = \alpha_i + \beta_i U^P_t + \gamma t + D*Dummy91 + \theta U^P_t *Dummy91 + \varepsilon_{it} \qquad (3)$$

- Trend only.

$$L_{it} = \alpha_i + \gamma_t t + \varepsilon_{it} \qquad (4)$$

IPI refers to the index of industrial production and is introduced as a direct measure of the cycle. δ is the coefficient on IPI. Dummy91 is a dummy which assumes value 1 if the period is 1991 or after, and equals 0 otherwise. D and θ are the coefficients on Dummy91 and the U^P interacted with Dummy91, respectively. We will refer to the period following 1991 as the postreform period. Specification (3) allows us to test whether the added worker effect is, rather, a phenomenon of the period following 1991. The estimation results of specifications (1), (2), and (3) are presented in Tables 4-5, 4-6, and 4-7. Specification (4) is used in the analysis of the predictive power of the models, which we will present below.

Trend and Cyclical Effects

As can be seen in Table 4-5, the coefficient on trend is negative for all males, which indicates that over the past two decades the participation rate of males decreased. This decline occurred mainly because of the decrease of the LFP rate of teenage males of about 0.44 percentage points per year, and a decline in the participation rate for males aged 20 to 34 by 0.13 percentage points. For males, the estimates of the cycle coefficient β show positive values for all age groups; however, only the positive values for the groups aged 20 to 34 and 35 to 49 are statistically significant at the 5 percent level. The value of β equal to 0.31 for men aged 20 to 34 indicates that a 1 percentage point decrease in the unemployment rate of prime-aged men increases the participation rate of men aged 20 to 34 by 0.31 percentage point. The response of males aged 35 to 49 is lower, but positive. Hence, we can conclude that the higher the unem-

TABLE 4-6

Labor Force Participation: Cyclical and Trend Factors
Specification (2), Females

Age	α Constant	β Prime-aged unemployment	γ Trend	δ Industrial production	ρ Autoregressive correction
15–19	88.328[a]		−0.117	−12.180[a]	0.701[a]
	(16.750)		(0.085)	(3.687)	(0.111)
	45.702[a]	1.185[a]	−0.385[a]	−2.510	0.429[a]
	(17.100)	(0.299)	(0.072)	(3.802)	(0.141)
20–34	61.562[a]		0.313[a]	−3.345	0.510[a]
	(17.730)		(0.058)	(3.924)	(0.134)
	23.903	1.171[a]	0.085	5.108	0.250[b]
	(15.820)	(0.267)	(0.059)	(3.517)	(0.151)
35–49	28.417[b]		0.569[a]	1.040	0.486[a]
	(15.710)		(0.049)	(3.479)	(0.136)
	7.235	0.932[a]	0.389[a]	5.859[b]	0.482[a]
	(15.130)	(0.268)	(0.067)	(3.366)	(0.137)
50–64	−2.705		0.420[a]	4.543	0.478[a]
	(17.080)		(0.052)	(3.781)	(0.137)
	−23.425	0.841[a]	0.258[a]	9.241[a]	0.348[a]
	(17.060)	(0.293)	(0.068)	(3.794)	(0.146)
All Females	42.896[a]		0.389[a]	−2.112	0.705[a]
	(11.330)		(0.058)	(2.494)	(0.111)
	14.443	0.986[a]	0.183[a]	4.328[b]	0.551[a]
	(10.220)	(0.184)	(0.049)	(2.272)	(0.130)

Note: Biannual data from 1974/1–95/1. April 1986 is missing. Data are usually measured in April/May and September/October. The number of observations is 42. The estimation method is maximum likelihood method correcting for autocorrelation. Standard errors are in parentheses.

a. Significant at 5 percent level.
b. Significant at 10 percent level.
Source: INDEC-EPH.

ployment rate for prime-aged males, the higher the participation rate for these groups.

As we have seen, changes in female LFP dominate changes in aggregate LFP. Consequently, we gain more insight into the participation behavior by looking at female participation rates. Contrary to men, the trend in fe-

TABLE 4-7

Labor Force Participation:

Cyclical and Trend Factors Specification (3), Females

Age	α	β	γ	θ^a	D^b	ρ
5–19	35.331^c	0.724^c	–0.405^c	0.534^c	0.158	
	(0.821)	(0.329)	(0.534)	(0.220)	(0.154)	
	35.312^c	0.611	–0.388^c	0.701	–1.043	0.154
	(0.828)	(0.445)	(0.069)	(0.497)	(2.812)	(0.154)
20–34	47.572^c	0.761^c	0.110^d	0.357	0.388^c	
	(1.065)	(0.342)	(0.059)	(0.258)	(0.144)	
	47.442^c	0.370	0.175^c	0.965^d	–4.122	0.382^c
	(1.045)	(0.437)	(0.074)	(0.502)	(2.922)	(0.144)
35–49	33.861^c	0.583^d	0.436^c	0.197	0.491^c	
	(1.194)	(0.333)	(0.063)	(0.268)	(0.136)	
	33.862^c	0.586	0.436^c	0.192	0.0350	0.491^c
	(1.212)	(0.428)	(0.078)	(0.501)	(2.964)	(0.136)
50–64	18.929^c	0.125	0.326^c	0.516^d	0.395^c	
	(1.177)	(0.375)	(0.065)	(0.284)	(0.143)	
	18.747^c	–0.456	0.424^c	1.390^c	–6.043^d	0.467^c
	(1.273)	(0.467)	(0.084)	(0.544)	(3.212)	(0.138)
All Females	34.357^c	0.610^c	0.215^c	0.283	0.579^c	
	(0.924)	(0.221)	(0.046)	(0.189)	(0.127)	
	34.295^c	0.305	0.270^c	0.800^c	–4.010^c	0.663^c
	(1.059)	(0.258)	(0.058)	(0.314)	(1.906)	(0.117)

Note: Biannual data from 1974–95. April 1986 is missing. Data are usually measured in April/May and September/October. The number of observations is 42. The estimation method is maximum likelihood method correcting for autocorrelation. Standard errors are in parentheses.

a. θ is the interaction of Dummy91 and prime-aged unemployment.

b. D is the coefficient of Dummy91. Dummy91 equals 1 if the period is 1991 or after, and equals zero between 1974 and 1990.

c. Significant at 5 percent level.

d. Significant at 10 percent level.

Source: INDEC-EPH.

male LFP was positive from 1974 to 1995. Except for teenagers, all age categories show a strong positive trend during this period. Prime-aged women (aged 35 to 49) increase their LFP by 0.9 percent a year, followed by older women (0.7 percent a year), and those aged 20 to 34 (0.2 percent a year).

Female teenage LFP decreases by 0.8 percent per year. Table 4-5 further suggests that the aggregate response of female LFP to changes in U^P amounts to 0.82, and that female participation rates are strongly countercyclical, at least if one measures the cycle by the unemployment rate of prime-aged males. Notice that the younger the group, the higher the response to the cycle. For female teenagers an increase by 1 percentage point in U^P raises their participation by about 1.26 percentage points. These results show that young individuals and females exhibit substantial cycle sensitivity.

According to these estimates, over the past two decades, there has been a declining trend in the participation rate for all males, and an increasing trend in the participation rate for all females. With respect to males, the trend decline occurred mainly because of the decrease in male teenage participation of about 0.4 percentage points per year, and a decline in the participation rate for males aged 20 to 34 by 0.15 percentage points. The estimates of β (the cycle coefficient) for males show positive values for all age groups; however, only the positive values for the groups aged 20 to 34 and 35 to 49 are statistically significant at the 5 percent level. This means that the behavior of these groups is countercyclical: the higher the unemployment rate for prime-aged males, the higher the participation rate for these groups.[9]

The estimation results of specification (2), which introduces the IPI as a direct measure of the business cycle, are presented in Table 4-6. When U^P is excluded from the regression, the coefficient on log(IPI) becomes negative when it is significant. That is, using another measure of the cycle does not change our conclusion about the countercyclical behavior. Evidence becomes less clear when we include both U^P and log(IPI). Teenagers respond countercyclically to both. Prime-aged, older females, and the entire sample of females continue to respond countercyclically to U^P, but procyclically to log(IPI).

The years of 1991–95 is the period of structural reform. It was characterized by a boom in terms of GDP and industrial production growth, while at the same time unemployment increased. Consequently, we expect differences in the structural parameters of the regressions. Regressing female LFP on unemployment of prime-aged male workers (U^P), a time trend, Dummy91 and the interaction of Dummy91 with U^P, we find that, except for women aged 35 to 49, there is a significant effect of this interaction. As can be seen in Table 4-7 the added worker effect grew stronger since 1991 for the less stable part of the female labor force. Table 4-5 shows that for teenagers, for example, a 1 percent increase in U^P increases their LFP rate by 1.2 percentage points. Now we can show that until

1990, a 1 percent increase in U^P augments their participation by only 0.7 percentage points. The remaining 0.5 percentage point was added after 1991.[10]

Contrasting these results with similar estimations for the United States (see, for example, Pencavel 1986; and Killingsworth and Heckman 1986), we find that our results differ mainly in that, while we find countercyclical LFP for both men and women, U.S. data indicate no cyclical effects for men, but procyclical LFP for some of the female cohorts. That is, it appears that in the United Kingdom and the United States in the analyzed period there is a prevalence of discouraged female workers during a recession, while in Argentina the phenomenon of added female workers prevails.

We should not be surprised by the difference in cyclical patterns in LFP (especially of females) between Argentina and more developed countries, such as the United Kingdom and the United States. First, females, on average, have lower LFP rates in Argentina than in those countries, so there is a larger pool that can enter the labor market when facing higher unemployment rates for males. Second, Argentina does not yet have a widely available capital market to which families can turn to maintain consumption during a recession. Hence, it is not surprising that they turn to secondary earners in the household—women and non-prime-aged men—to support the family if the primary earner becomes unemployed.[11] Since the economic reforms of the Convertibility Plan in 1991,[12] smooth wage adjustments have been hampered by individual and collective bargaining laws and practices that evolved during a period of high inflation. Strong unions and centralized collective bargaining agreements hindered wage reductions. Attempts to reduce dismissal costs for all existing jobs have faced strong opposition. It is estimated that around 95 percent of the labor force are covered by these centralized collective bargaining agreements (Pessino 2001). Any reduction in wages is considered to be a layoff of the worker, and hence makes him or her eligible for severance payments. New collective bargaining agreements cannot reduce benefits granted to workers in previous agreements, except if a firm declares a crisis, and if the new type of agreement is approved by the Ministry of Labor.

Consequently, employment bears the brunt of the adjustment during a downturn. Furthermore, in Argentina the fixed costs of labor contracts are substantial due to high mandatory severance payment and high payroll taxes. Thus, wages—for those who still have jobs—remain high, prompting a queuing for jobs, which is reflected in both higher LFP and unemployment. This last factor may be quite important in explaining the increase in observed LFP between October 1994 and May 1995 and, if confirmed, has important policy implications.

Predictive Power of the Model

Concerning the fit of our models, we find that specification (1) predicts LFP rates in May 1995 reasonably well, but does not capture well the peaks of 1989 and 1993.[13] The predictions improve considerably when we add the industrial production index, log(IPI). For example, the below-trend LFP during 1980–86, which corresponds to years of stagnation in GDP and IPI, is better captured because of the procyclical nature of LFP with respect to the IPI measure of the cycle. Including the male unemployment rate interacted with the dummy for the reform-convertibility period increases the predictive power of the model even further. Estimations by age group may be more meaningful since different age groups behave quite differently to changes in the economy.

A handy test of the predictive power of the regressions was available, since at the time of estimation we had the results of the October 1995 wave of the INDEC-EPH. Using the four alternative models, we predicted LFP for October 1995. The results are presented in Table 4-8. For females, specifications (1) and (2) are best, while for males, models (1), (2), and (4) do equally well. The average predictive power of the models appears to be good, indicating that the theoretical foundations and econometric formulation are consistent with the data.

Using these estimates, we can examine the extent to which "abnormally" large increases in LFP are responsible for the observed increase in unemployment levels in 1995. Interpreting departures from a linear trend as "abnormal," actual participation levels for both females and males in May 1995 appear to be about 5 and 2 percentage points above their normal trend levels. For females, this means an actual participation rate of 55 percent compared with the trend LFP of about 50 percent. Similarly for males, an actual LFP rate of 86 percent compares to a trend rate of 84 percent. But well-established theory suggests, and our empirical analysis for Argentina shows, that cyclical factors are important, as well. When cyclical factors are incorporated, the "surprise" component of the increase in labor supply in May 1995 diminishes significantly. May 1995 participation rates are still abnormally high, but by much smaller margins: less than 1 percentage point for both males and females.

Determinants of Female Labor Force Participation

The facts about female LFP presented so far do not necessarily say much about the causal relation between male unemployment rates and female LFP. To address this issue we provide further evidence using cross-section

TABLE 4-8
The Predictive Power of Alternative Models of Labor Force Participation

Group	Actual LFP (percent)	Predicted LFP of model:				
		1	2	3	4	Average
Females						
15–19 years	27.1	29.8	29.4	30.8	25.6	28.9
20–34 years	63.1	62.9	63.5	64.2	59.3	62.5
35–49 years	58.7	60.1	61.0	60.6	57.7	59.9
50–64 years	39.7	38.2	39.7	39.9	36.6	38.6
All	51.7	52.0	52.7	52.7	49.7	51.8
Males						
15–19 years	44.3	44.5	46.0	46.7	43.2	45.1
20–34 years	92.8	94.0	94.2	93.8	92.9	93.7
35–49 years	97.3	97.5	97.6	97.5	97.0	97.4
50–64 years	82.1	81.7	83.4	82.9	80.4	82.1
All	84.1	84.9	85.4	85.3	84.0	84.9

Note: The four models are: (1) trend and cycle represented by unemployment of prime-aged males, U^P; (2) trend, U^P, and IPI; (3) trend, U^P and period dummy for 1991–95 interacted with cycle measure; and (4) trend only. Actual LFP calculated using October 1995 INDEC-EPH.

data. Our approach is two-fold. We first estimate a linear probability model, which describes the determinants of the female LFP decision. Second, we compare the probability of a wife being employed conditional on having an unemployed husband—Prob(wife is employed|husband is unemployed)—with the probability of a wife being employed conditional on her husband being employed—Prob(wife is employed|husband is employed).

The linear probability model confirms that women do respond to the wages and employment prospects of their husbands by changing their labor supply. On the basis of 1,697 observations of married women aged 15 and 64, preliminary results for May 1995 show that:

$$LFP = -0.500 + 0.024 \text{ Education}$$
$$\quad\;\; (-3.3) \quad\; (7.9)$$

$$+ 0.049 \text{ AGE} - 0.00065 \text{ AGE}^2 - 0.04 \text{ KIDS}$$
$$\quad (6.5) \qquad\quad (-7.4) \qquad\qquad\; (-3.7)$$

$$- 0.00006 \text{ WAGE\_H}$$
$$\quad (-4.7)$$

where KIDS is the number of children under 14 years of age, and WAGE_H is the log wage of the husband. The t-statistics are reported in parentheses. This indicates that LFP of working-age women increases when the wage of the husband decreases. With respect to husbands' employment status and education level we find that women whose husbands are employed are less likely to participate in the labor force.

$$LFP = -0.40 + 0.028 \text{ Education}$$
$$(-2.6) \quad (7.3)$$

$$+ 0.048 \text{ AGE} - 0.00065 \text{ AGE}^2 - 0.04 \text{ KIDS}$$
$$(6.5) \qquad (-7.3) \qquad\qquad (-4.2)$$

$$- 0.061184 \text{ EMPL\_H} - 0.0109 \text{ EDUC\_H}$$
$$(-1.9) \qquad\qquad (-2.9)$$

EMPL_H equals one if husband is employed, and zero otherwise, and EDUC_H is education of husband.

In a next step, we compare the probability of a wife being employed conditional on having an unemployed husband with the probability of a wife being employed conditional on her husband being employed. If the added worker effect dominates, we expect that, on average, wives of unemployed husbands are more likely to be employed than wives of employed husbands. Hence, the difference between the two probabilities should be positive. As can be seen in Table 4-9, a wife whose husband is unemployed has a higher probability of participating in the labor force (both employment and unemployment) than a wife whose husband is employed. We see that in most years the difference between columns (3) and (6) is positive, with the exception of 1986 and 1987, which were years of relatively low male unemployment. Differences in LFP increase between 1988 and 1991, drop in 92, and then increase from 1993 to 1994. Except in 1991, when we expected to have small differences, these data show signs of a strong added worker effect for married women in the peak unemployment years.[14] As a consequence, if there is an exogenous increase in overall unemployment (caused, for example, by sectoral variability in the demand for labor), the effect will be magnified by the accompanying rising unemployment of females that "added" to the labor force to help overcome this fluctuation in family income.

During the period studied, Argentina had cycles of high inflation that tended to be followed by stabilization plans that opened the economy to both international capital movements and trade in goods. This resulted not only in lower inflation rates, but also in lower real exchange rates. The

TABLE 4-9
Female Labor Force Status, by Husband's Employment Status

| | Husband | | | | | |
| | Unemployed | | | Employed | | |
Wife	Employed (1)	Unemployed (2)	In LF (3)	Employed (4)	Unemployed (5)	In LF (6)
Oct. 1985	37.6	6.4	44.0	32.6	0.9	42.5
Oct. 1986	34.2	1.2	35.4	34.3	1.3	35.6
Oct. 1987	31.7	2.3	34.0	33.2	1.8	35.0
Oct. 1988	38.1	6.0	44.1	36.2	2.3	38.5
Oct. 1989	40.7	5.2	45.9	36.2	1.7	37.9
Oct. 1990	51.1	1.5	52.6	37.8	1.1	38.9
Oct. 1991	54.1	0.0	54.1	36.8	1.3	38.1
Oct. 1992	41.8	3.8	45.6	38.0	1.9	39.9
Oct. 1993	45.5	5.4	50.9	39.1	4.1	43.2
Oct. 1994	42.4	9.8	52.2	37.6	5.5	43.1
May 1995	37.7	15.6	53.3	37.4	10.2	47.6

change in real exchange rates introduced sectoral reallocations of resources and people. In particular, low real exchange rates correspond to a relative rise in wages in the service sector, which is the sector in which women are relatively highly represented. Furthermore, a change in the real exchange may increase unemployment.[15] Consequently, periods of stabilization that are combined with an opening of the economy or, put differently, a competitive shock through lower real exchange rates, may lead to an increase in male unemployment. Given that the added worker effect dominates, the increase in male unemployment will be accompanied by an increase in female LFP. If simultaneously the change in the real exchange rate implies an increase of the relative wage in the sector in which women are more likely to work, female LFP will be intensified, exerting additional pressure on unemployment rates.

Summary and Policy Implications

Main Findings

First, LFP in Greater Buenos Aires rose by 18 percent from 1974 to 1985, fuelled entirely by increases in female participation rates, which increased substantially since 1990. Female participation rates rose by 45 percent from 1974 on, while male participation rates remained unchanged. Participation rates of teenagers and older people also increased (or did not decrease) from 1987 to 1995, and increased sharply during 1994–95.

Second, the increase in unemployment from 6 percent in 1987 to 20 percent in May 1995 cannot be explained by changes in female LFP. Despite seemingly rapid growth of the female labor supply compared to 1974 levels, increased female LFP can at best account for less than 6 percentage points of the change in the unemployment rate. This is largely due to the low initial rates of female participation (relative to countries with similar income and education levels), so that *absolute* increases in female workers are not sufficiently large to confirm conjectures that increased supply, and not slowing demand, is responsible for the rapid rise in unemployment.

Third, the aggregate response of female LFP to changes in prime-aged male unemployment indicates that female participation rates are strongly countercyclical. The response to the cycle is negatively related to age. Furthermore, a wife whose husband is unemployed has a higher probability of being in the labor force than a wife whose husband is employed. The difference between these two probabilities is higher in periods when unemployment peaked. These findings indicate that in Argentina the phenomenon of added female workers prevails.

Fourth, additional evidence indicates that reentrants (including retirees) and new entrants to the labor force account for only about one-third of the total unemployed in GBA in October 1995: almost two-thirds of the unemployed were previously employed, and while about two-thirds of reentrants and new entrants were female, almost two-thirds of the unemployed who were previously employed were male. While these findings do not prove that unexpected increases in LFP are not mainly responsible for the high levels of unemployment since 1987, they do provide another reason to be cautious in making such claims.

Finally, we find that analyses of current labor market trends that attribute recent unemployment increases largely to unexpected or abnormally large labor supply increases inadvertently understate the importance of policy reform in stabilizing and increasing labor demand.[16] Interpreting departures from a linear trend as abnormal, actual participation levels for both females and males in May appear to be about 5 and 2 percentage points above their normal trend levels. But established theory suggests, and empirical analysis shows, that using only trend values as expected LFP ignores an important feature of the Argentine labor market. In Argentina LFP is systematically influenced by cyclical factors. Once we account for cyclical factors, the surprise component of the recent increase in labor supply diminishes significantly. May 1995 participation rates are still abnormally high, but by a margin of less than 1 percentage point for both males and females.

Policy Implications

The pattern of unemployment indicates that it is a widespread phenomenon and is not restricted to a few clearly identified worker groups. The relatively uniform increase in unemployment rates across worker categories points to falling labor demand as the main cause of growing unemployment. In this chapter we show that LFP rates are positively correlated with unemployment rates in Argentina. This should be taken into account when drawing inference from changes in LFP on unemployment, and hints at the fact that the government should aim at increasing employment growth. Figure 4-1 summarizes a simple exercise conducted to illustrate the importance of measures to raise the trend rate of employment growth. Data on employment and labor force growth clearly show that employment is growing more slowly than the labor force by a widening

FIGURE 4-1
Employment and Labor Force

Source: Ministry of Labor and Social Security, based on data from INDEC-EPH and *Secretaría de Programación Económica* (Department of Economic Policy).

margin; the result, naturally, is higher unemployment. In the preceding chapter we showed that relying on output growth is not enough to increase employment. Labor market reforms are necessary. Hence, the government would be advised to concentrate on policies that increase labor demand and employment, such as making wage- and employment-setting practices more flexible, reducing payroll taxes, and minimizing interventions that encourage workers to hold out for higher wages.

Reforms that encourage efficient employment and wage-setting practices—while promoting sustainable growth of labor demand—are likely to favorably influence short-term labor supply patterns as well. As we have explained, in Argentina wage adjustments are hindered by individual and collective bargaining laws and practices, which evolved during a period of high inflation. Consequently, employment bears the brunt of the adjustment during a downturn. Empirical studies indicate that in countries with relatively flexible labor markets, such as the United States, LFP is procyclical. In Argentina, higher unemployment rates, which result in lower expected household income, induce additional workers to join the labor force. Consequently, the LFP of secondary workers tends to be anticyclical because of the added worker effect, leading to exaggerated fluctuations in measured unemployment rates. Labor reforms that encourage wage flexibility will result in reduced cyclical volatility of unemployment rates, not just because employment fluctuations will be moderated by wage adjustments, but also because labor supply fluctuations will be less exaggerated. This in turn will allow the government to concentrate on the task of instituting policies for raising long-term employment growth, instead of being distracted by temporary but sharp increases in unemployment, which are politically difficult to ignore.

Notes

1. It is believed that there are between 800,000 to 1 million foreigners working illegally in Argentina, mostly as maids and construction and agricultural workers (*Migrant News* 1996). Between 1980 and 1991, the population born in foreign countries decreased by 14 percent for the country as a whole, and by 16 percent in Greater Buenos Aires.

2. Since data are not readily available for the rest of the country, we use data for Greater Buenos Aires for all estimations, unless stated otherwise. Greater Buenos Aires accounts for more than 50 percent of the GDP and nearly 40 percent of the population.

3. Of course, the income effect must not be larger than the cross-substitution effect, if the latter is positive.

4. In North America female LFP rates averaged 69 percent in the 1990s.

5. In fact, one of the major consequences of development during this century has been the incorporation of women in high numbers into the labor force. Since Argentina has lagged in development with respect to OECD countries, it is not surprising to find that female LFP rates are lower in Argentina than in OECD countries, and have been growing at a slower pace.

6. Estimates of probit results for October 1991 and October 1994 can be found in Pessino (1997, pp. 196–7).

7. Alternatively, we may use a demographically adjusted unemployment rate as a measure for the cyclical conditions; however, because the quality of available jobs may vary over the cycle, we refrain from using this variable so as not to introduce simultaneity bias.

8. We control for autocorrelation since the Durbin-Watson statistic reveals serially correlated errors. Higher-order serial correlation was rejected by the data. Since the data are usually measured in April/May and September/October, we also introduced a seasonality dummy, since May and October are presumably different in terms of LFP. Only the participation rate for teenage females showed lower entrance into the labor force during October, without significantly altering the other coefficients.

9. Note that for men aged 35 to 49 we can have spurious correlation between LFP and U^P and, given the correlation between U^P and unemployment for males aged 20 to 34, results should be interpreted carefully.

10. Excluding the observations from 1993 onward, the estimates of α lose significance but do not switch signs. This evidently shows that the 1993 period is influencing the results, and that it was a period of strong countercyclicity in female LFP.

11. In fact, using employment transition probabilities from household data, Lundberg (1985) found that there is a small but significant added worker effect for the United States, and attributes this finding mainly to the existence of credit constraints for some households.

12. The Convertibility Plan was an exchange rate–based stabilization program introduced in October 1991 after the end of the hyperinflation in 1990. The plan eliminated tariffs on imported capital goods, which substantially reduced the relative price of capital. Further economic reforms included trade liberalization and extensive privatization of state-owned companies.

13. In October 1983, the sample size of the INDEC-EPH became much smaller, and the actual values of LFP are less precise. Note the large increase in LFP that is not captured by the estimates.

14. We have a large drop in the absolute number of husbands unemployed— from 68,800 to 42,700—and the relatively lower number of unemployed may have strong reasons to be unemployed, such as general disadvantages or sickness that make the wife the sole provider.

15. A lower real exchange rate means that imported goods are cheaper. Among other things, Argentina imports capital goods. A lower price of capital goods with

respect to the higher price of labor implies a strong substitution effect toward capital and against labor if production processes allow such adjustments. See Chapter 5 for moderate elasticities of substitution between labor and capital.

16. In Chapter 5, Pessino, Gill, and Guasch address labor demand issues, measuring the output and wage elasticities of labor demand during the same period as this paper, and imputing the benefits to labor reform in contrast to a policy of simply relying on economic growth to increase employment and reduce unemployment rates.

References

Clark, K. B., and L. H. Summers. 1981. "Demographic Differences in Cyclical Employment Variation." *Journal of Human Resources* 16: 61–79.

Killingsworth, Mark R., and James J. Heckman. 1986. "Female Labor Supply: a Survey." In O. Ashenfelter and R. Layard, (eds.), *Handbook of Labor Economics*, Volume I. Elsevier Science Publishers, pp. 103–204.

Lundberg, Shelly. 1985. "The Added Worker Effect." *Journal of Labor Economics* 3 (1): 11–37.

Migrant News. March 1996.

Pencavel, John. 1986. "Labor Supply of Men: A Survey." In O. Ashenfelter and R. Layard, (eds.), *Handbook of Labor Economics*, Volume I. Elsevier Science Publishers, pp. 103–204.

Pessino, Carola. 1997. "Argentina: The Labor Market during the Economic Transition." Chapter 6 in Sebastian Edwards and Nora Lustig, (eds.), *Labor Markets in Latin America: Combining Social Protection with Market Flexibility*. Washington, D.C.: The Brookings Institution.

_____. 2001. "Convertibility and the Labor Market." Paper prepared for the Conference *The Currency Board's First Decade: Argentina and the Convertibility Law*. BCRA, April 5 and 6.

Pessino, Carola, and Leonardo Giacchino. 1994. "Rising Unemployment in Argentina: 1974–1993." Paper prepared for the 13th Latin American Meeting of the Econometric Society, Caracas, República Bolivariana de Venezuela.

5 Increasing Labor Demand in Argentina

CAROLA PESSINO, INDERMIT S. GILL,
AND JOSÉ LUIS GUASCH

IN THE YEARS FOLLOWING the initiation of economic reforms in the late 1980s, Argentina's employment growth has increasingly lagged behind output growth. Between 1990 and 1993, employment grew by about 2 percent annually, compared to a much higher economic growth rate of approximately 8 percent. The result was an increase in average labor productivity by approximately 5.5 percent per year between 1990 and 1993 (Pessino 1997). In 1991, the Convertibility Plan—an exchange-rate-based stabilization program—was introduced, which also eliminated tariffs on imported capital goods. As a consequence, the relative price of capital declined. Evidence on the combined effects of the Convertibility Plan, introduction of subsidies for domestic capital, and falling interest rates indicate that the price of capital relative to labor fell between 26 to 40 percent between 1990 and 1994 (Bour 1995). Thus, the "output effect" on employment triggered by the reforms was counteracted by a "substitution effect," leading to an increase in the price of labor relative to capital. The effect of trade liberalization, combined with the appreciation of the peso, particularly hurt employment of unskilled labor, but led to an increase in dollar-dominated wages. This implied that average real wages began to rise until 1994.

From 1974 to 1995, total employment grew at an annual rate of 1 percent, and the population grew at approximately 3 percent. This implied that net employment growth—that is, employment growth minus population growth—decreased by 0.29 percent per year. Growth of labor force participation exceeded population growth by 0.5 percent, resulting in a difference between employment growth and labor force growth of 0.79 percent. The government introduced programs to encourage private employment. Public programs to help displaced workers and new entrants to a labor market in transition were also initiated. Furthermore, the government responded with measures to lower labor costs and smooth adjustments by reforming wage-setting and employment regulations. But employment growth remained sluggish. In 1994, in spite of GDP growth of about 6 percent, employment stagnated or even declined. In 1995, during the recession induced by the so-called Tequila Crisis, GDP growth and employment fell, and unemployment soared to about 20 percent.

A likely explanation for the relatively slow employment growth in the early years despite healthy GDP growth is that the costs of labor remained high. Although productivity increased, it was not enough to compensate for the increase in average real wages. At the same time, Argentine labor legislation mandated that employer contributions to payroll taxes amounted to approximately 33 percent between 1990 and 1995. There is also the cost of a mandated 13th monthly salary, mandatory compensation for work-related injuries, and severance payments. In the case of layoffs "without just cause," severance payments are mandatory and advance notice of one or two months must be given to the worker. The Employment Law passed in 1991 determined that severance compensation be equal to one month's salary per year of service, with a minimum payment of two months' wages and a maximum yearly payment of three times the average wage of the collective bargaining agreements that apply to the worker.

To provide alternatives to the predominant form of contracting in Argentina, which is by law of indefinite duration, the government introduced new forms of group-specific, fixed-term contracts. These contracts featured lower payroll taxes and severance payments.[1] However, the law required union approval of these contracts. But unions largely resisted them. Hence, it is not surprising that, as Hopenhayn (2001) shows, this reform seems not to have had a great impact. In 1995 a further reform introduced a trial period for all contracts and special employment promotion contracts. These contracts did not require the previous approval of trade unions. They induced increased hiring, but also reduced longer-term employment. In 1999 the reform was reversed.

GDP, productivity, and unemployment grew steadily between 1990 (the end of hyperinflation) and 1994. This contradicted the widespread belief that economic growth induced by macroeconomic stabilization would be a major contribution to job creation. The unemployment rate rose steadily from about 5 percent in October 1990 to about 10 percent in October 1993, and to 11 percent in May 1994. With the falloff in GDP growth in 1995, and a continued rise in the relative price of labor, employment growth fell. The unemployment rate rose sharply to almost 20 percent in May 1995, triggering a heightened interest in labor market issues. The fact that the relative price of labor did not adjust downward after the drop in GDP growth may be blamed on the slow progress of the labor reforms. The effects of the labor market rigidities had become worse in the more competitive, low inflation environment of the postreform period. While substantial reforms had taken place in monetary affairs and goods and services markets, no far-reaching labor market reform took place in the 1990s. Some claim that this asymmetry may have contributed to the high unemployment rates (Mondino and Montoya 2000).

Changes in unemployment and wages depend on changes in both labor demand and supply. Issues related to labor supply and unemployment were discussed in the previous chapter. Here we examine the determinants of labor demand from a policy perspective. Classical theory predicts that—given the long-run neutrality of money—the main determinants of labor demand can be identified as output (GDP), since the demand of labor is derived from the demand of commodities and services, and the relative price of labor with respect to other input factors such as capital. The relative price of labor determines the costs of using labor in production. We use different assumptions for the technology of production to compute the own-wage and output elasticities of labor demand. Simply put, the own-wage elasticity of labor demand provides a numerical guide to the "payoff" of labor market reforms that lower the cost of labor in terms of an increase in employment. Estimates of the output elasticity of labor demand, holding wages and other labor costs constant, provide quantitative estimates of the effect of renewed output growth on increases in employment, given that labor market functioning is left unaltered. Our results can then be combined with estimates of the influence of different policy measures on labor costs, which are provided in World Bank (1996), to impute the employment effects of these policy reforms.[2] We hope that quantitative estimates of the responsiveness of employment to, alternatively, higher growth and labor policy reform, will enrich the policy debate in Argentina and in other Latin American countries.

Methodology, Technology, Data, and Issues

In Argentina, beset by high inflation and concerns of macroeconomic stability until the late 1980s, labor market issues were a secondary concern. Since the economic reforms in the early 1990s, however, employment, unemployment, and wage policies have assumed importance. The paucity of labor-related data will increasingly hamper informed decisionmaking on critical issues. The construction of appropriate labor series is difficult, and application of econometric techniques to available labor-related data in Argentina is troublesome. Still, this chapter illustrates both the benefits of such exercises and the value of reliable data in facilitating informed decisionmaking. In what follows we briefly describe the methodology and data used. We then discuss the relevant issues.

Methodology

Assuming two factors of production labor (L) and capital (K), a constant returns to scale (CRS) production function and profit maximization, the own-wage elasticity of labor demand, holding output, and price of capital r constant, is given by

$$\varepsilon_{LL} = -[1-s]\sigma < 0 \tag{1}$$

where s = wL/pY is the share of labor in total revenue of the firm (w is the price of labor, p is the price of output Y) and where σ is the elasticity of substitution between labor and capital.[3]

A dual approach is based on cost minimization, which assumes that the cost of an input factor is determined by the product of the profit-maximizing input demand and the factor price. Adding up all factor costs yields the total cost. Since the profit-maximizing input demands are functions of input prices, the level of output, and the technology, total cost can be written as

$$C = C(w, r, Y); \quad C_i > 0, C_{ij} > 0, \quad i, j = w, r \tag{2}$$

Using Shephard's lemma (see Varian 1992), we then write conditional labor demand as a function of the prices of labor and capital, output, and technology:

$$dC/dw = L^* = L^d (w, r, Y) \tag{3}$$

where dC/dw is the marginal effect of wages on total costs and L* is the profit-maximizing demand for labor. Capital demand is derived similarly. The own-wage elasticity of labor demand ε_{LL} equals equation (1). The only difference is that now s = wL/C, which is the share of labor in total costs.

Representations of Technology

The form of technology in an economy is generally not known. For this reason, we provide estimates of the elasticities of interest based on different production functions that represent a broad range of technologies. These technologies include Cobb-Douglas, constant elasticity of substitutions (CES), generalized Leontief, and transcendental logarithmic technology.

(a) Cobb-Douglas Technology

$$C = C(w, r, Y) = Zw^{1-\beta}.r^{\beta}.Y \tag{4}$$

where β is the share of capital and Z is a constant. Using Shephard's lemma, we get

$$L^d = A.w^{(-\beta)}.r^{\beta}.Y \tag{5}$$

$$\ln L = \ln A + (-\beta)\ln w + \beta \ln r + \ln Y \tag{6}$$

A is a constant. The output elasticity and σ, the elasticity of substitution between L and K, are restricted to equal 1. The own-wage elasticity of labor demand ε_{LL} is given by $(-\beta)$.

(b) Constant Elasticity of Substitution Technology

$$C = Y[\alpha^{\sigma}.w^{1-\sigma} + (1-\alpha)^{\sigma}.r^{1-\sigma}]^{1/(1-\sigma)} \tag{7}$$

Using Shephard's lemma, the labor demand equation is:

$$L^d = \alpha^{\sigma}w^{-\sigma}Y$$

$$\ln L = \sigma\ln\sigma - \sigma\ln w + \varepsilon_{Ly} \ln Y \tag{8}$$

α is labor's share of revenue if the factors are paid their marginal product. σ is the elasticity of substitution and is a constant, but does not necessarily equal 1. The own-wage elasticity of labor demand ε_{LL} now is given $(-\sigma)$. The output elasticity ε_{Ly} is restricted to equal 1.

(c) Generalized Leontief Technology

$$C = Y[a_{11}w + 2a_{12}w^{0.5}r^{0.5} + a_{22}r] \tag{9}$$

Using Shephard's lemma, the labor demand equation becomes:

$$L^d = a_{11}Y + a_{12}Y(w/r)^{-0.5} \tag{10}$$

Neither elasticity of substitution, output elasticity, nor own-wage elasticity of labor demand is restricted to be a constant; they vary with the ratio of input prices.

(d) Transcendental Logarithmic Technology (Translog)

$$\ln C = \ln a_0 + a_1 \ln w + 0.5 a_2 [\ln w]^2 + a_3 \ln w.\ln r + 0.5 b_1.[\ln r]^3$$
$$+ b_2 \ln r + b_3 \ln Y + b_4 \ln Y.\ln r + a_4 \ln Y.\ln w \qquad (11)$$

Using Shephard's lemma, we arrive at the following labor demand function:

$$wL/C = a_1 + a_2 \ln w + a_3 \ln r + a_4 \ln Y \qquad (12)$$

Again the elasticities are not constants, but depend on the parameters and both factor prices.

These technologies vary not only in their assumption with respect to the different elasticities, but also in the data required to estimate the respective parameters of interest. Given the data problems we face, using different functional forms provides an important device for checking the robustness of our results.

Data Sources and Concepts

To estimate labor demand elasticities, we use all the data available for 1974–95. The main sources of information are publications of the *Ministerio de Economía* (Ministry of Economy), the INDEC-EPH household surveys, and national accounts published first by the Central Bank, and then by the Ministry of Economy. The lack of reliable industry- and enterprise-level surveys is a serious shortcoming for our purposes. Worse, in Argentina no complete national accounts on the quantity of factors and their remuneration have been published since 1975. Consequently, homogeneous and consistent aggregate data are not available, and the data we use in this study come from different private and public sources. Most of it had to be reconstructed, combining data from different sources, in order to cover the whole period analyzed.

LABOR DEMAND. Employment data differ in coverage and sources. Concerning coverage, we have series for Greater Buenos Aires, for manufacturing workers, and for wage workers, or combinations thereof. Generally speaking, when coverage is taken into account, all series show very similar patterns. The two main sources are the INDEC-EPH surveys and the *Informe Economico del Ministerio de Economía* (Economic Report of the Ministry of Informe 1995). The different series for Greater Buenos Aires show very similar patterns. The main difference between Ministry of Economy and INDEC numbers arises in 1994 and 1995, when INDEC-EPH numbers show a greater decrease in employment than do Ministry of Economy numbers. We therefore use both series in our estimations to make sure that our results are not sensitive to the choice of series. Most of the results we present refer to the manufacturing sector. While total employment reveals an upward trend, this is not necessarily for the manufacturing sector, especially in the period following the Convertibility Plan. This may be due to the fact that in Greater Buenos Aires, the import-competing sectors in manufacturing, such as textiles and clothing, and metallic products, faced a concentration in the employment decrease, while the share of the service sector in total employment increased since 1991 at the expense of that of manufacturing.[4]

OUTPUT. GDP series are from the Ministry of Economy. Indexes of industrial production are from the Central Bank (1974–80) and the *Fundacion de Investigaciones Económicas Latinoamericanas*—FIEL (Latin American Economic Research Foundation) (1980–95). Based on these data, we construct three series: real per capita GDP, real GDP, and industrial production. They display very similar patterns over the sample period.

PRICE OF LABOR. Nominal wage data for 1970–79 are from FIEL, and data for 1980–95 are from the Ministry of Economy, FIEL, or INDEC-EPH. FIEL data are restricted to the manufacturing sector, while from 1980 on all sectors are included. Using these different sources makes the nominal wage series less than satisfactory, which implies that the real wage series (that is, nominal wages deflated by the consumer price index) are rather unreliable. Until the mid-1980s the two series are similar, but in 1987 they began to diverge. From 1990 on even the slopes differed. We define real labor costs as wages adjusted for payroll taxes and deflated by the wholesale price index. The different series for real labor costs track one another closely.

PRICE OF CAPITAL. Constructing a reliable series on the price of capital is a different task. Given the data constraints we had, we opted for the following solutions. We use the implicit price of gross domestic investment from the national accounts, and deflate it either by the wholesale price index (WPI) or implicit prices in GDP. Alternatively, we use the price of domestic and imported machinery deflated by the WPI.

RELATIVE PRICE OF LABOR. More reassuringly, there is considerable consensus in the series for the price of labor relative to capital, which is most relevant for our estimation of labor demand. The exception is for 1995: three series show a decline, while two show a moderate increase. The divergence is again caused by the difference between labor costs that include an adjustment for compliance rate changes for payroll taxes and those that do not, and different deflators in the wage and capital series.

Issues

The objective of this chapter is to estimate the output elasticity of labor demand, holding wages and other labor costs constant, and the own-wage elasticity of labor demand. As shown in the methodological section, these are derived from the production or cost functions of the firms, which suggests the use of firm-level data. These data were not available for the estimation of long-term elasticities and, consequently, we have to rely on aggregated data. As noted in the literature (for example, Hamermesh 1993), there are several methodological concerns that arise when using aggregate data instead of establishment-level data. These imply that parameter estimates do not usually correspond to elasticities at the firm level. This has to be kept in mind when interpreting our results.

For example, one series of our employment data refers to manufacturing employment in Greater Buenos Aires. Hence, because we do not estimate elasticities at the firm level, we cannot answer the question of how a firm would change its employment in response to a shock to its own wages. What we do estimate is a change in employment net of all shifts of employment that occur among firms in the manufacturing sector in Greater Buenos Aires, including those that are induced by changes in relative costs across firms with different factor intensity. Ignoring biases that may result from other issues, such as measurement error and endogeneity, Hamermesh (1993) points out that estimates derived from studies using highly aggregated data will understate the true firm-level value. Furthermore, using aggregate employment[5] data introduces the standard problem of linear aggregation of nonlinear relationships. And it means that we simply add up the number of workers. This is a common procedure, but embodies the rather strong assumptions that workers are equally productive and separable from other inputs.[6] Using employment as a proxy for the quantity of labor may also lead to biases if worker hours are correlated with factor prices and outputs. Because we use time-series data and are interested in estimating long-term elasticities, we may ignore this problem due the fact that in the long term, variations in employment and worker-hours are generally highly correlated.

A further data issue arises from the fact that the frequency of the data is annual, covering 1974–95. This gives us only 22 data points. There are some biannual data available for the same period, but only for some variables. Since not all the variables could be included in the estimations, and there were other measurement and time aggregation problems, estimators tended to be less efficient using the biannual data, even after correcting for first-order autoregressive (AR1) and second-order autoregressive (AR2) specifications, including seasonal dummies and deseasonalizing the time series. However, the variable of the annual data set shows a high variance, which improves the efficiency of the estimation of the parameters of interest. Moreover, in our data, aggregate employment and output series display strong serial correlation. The solutions adopted in this chapter are to choose output and employment series that are less aggregative—for example, industrial output, manufacturing sector employment, and wage employment—and to apply econometric procedures that adjust for autocorrelation in the data.

Another important concern is whether to take quantities or prices as exogenous for the econometric implementation. Ideally, both the price and quantity of labor should be treated as endogenous. Therefore, one must be able to argue that supply of labor is either completely inelastic or completely elastic in response to exogenous changes in demand. So, the choice usually boils down to whether price or quantity is viewed as exogenous. Input prices are likely to be endogenous variables because a change in wages, for example, affects demand of labor, but also its supply. For each point in time for which we have an observation, we observe a certain combination of employment and wages. Comparing these outcomes, we can see changes in employment and changes in wages, but ex ante we do not know whether these changes are due to a change in demand or a change in supply of workers. One way to solve this issue is to use so-called instrumental variables, which in our case are variables that are correlated with input prices, but not with labor demand. Or to be more precise, we seek variables affecting the supply of labor, but not its demand. Consequently, we present results using instruments. The instruments we use are the logs of the real exchange rate (TRC2), real GDP per capita (Y1), real GDP index (Y2), urban population in Greater Buenos Aires (PBLURB), and annual percent change in CPI (INFL). Unfortunately, in this context, good instruments are hard to find. With aggregate data, if the supply of labor is relatively inelastic in the long term, demand parameters are best estimated using specifications that treat the quantity of labor as exogenous. This recommends the use of a production function, such as the generalized Leontief and the translog production functions, which include factor quantities as regressors.

Econometric Specification and Results

As shown in the Methodology section, the own-wage and output elasticity of employment can be estimated either by relying on the production function directly, or by using the cost function approach and estimating factor demand functions. In what follows, we provide evidence of the estimates of these elasticticities for the technologies presented above. Furthermore, we will discuss the single factor estimation and its results. We use different time series for employment and output to check the robustness of our results and to control for autocorrelation. We address the issue of endogeneity of input prices by using instruments.

Cobb-Douglas Technology

We start with the analysis by estimating the own-wage elasticity of labor demand and the output elasticity of labor demand based on a Cobb-Douglas technology. For this technology the share of labor in total revenue of the firm ($s = wL/pY$) corresponds to the share of labor, which equals $1-\beta$. As σ, the elasticity of substitution between labor and capital equals 1. It is easy to see from equation (1), that the own-wage elasticity of labor demand ε_{LL} equals minus the share of capital ($-\beta$). Table 5-1 reports estimates of ε_{LL}, which are obtained from estimating equation (6), using different output (Y) and employment (L) series.

Diagnostic tests reveal the presence of autocorrelation. Taking into account that there exists first order autocorrelation, these estimates imply that for employment in Greater Buenos Aires (EM1 and EM2), the own-wage elasticity of labor demand ε_{LL} is about –0.65. This means that holding output constant, a 1 percent increase in wages reduces employment net of all shifts of employment that occur among firms in Greater Buenos Aires by 0.65 percent. The elasticities for manufacturing employment (EM4) and wage employment in the manufacturing sector (EM6) are –0.74 and –0.71, respectively. Table 5-1 reveals ε_{LL} ranges from –0.50 to

TABLE 5-1
Cobb-Douglas Technology
(Estimates of ε_{LL})

L Used	Y Used	Specification	ε_{LL}	T-statistic
EM1	Y2	AR1	−0.635	−3.19
EM2	Y2	AR1	−0.674	−2.84
EM4	Y2	OLS	−0.628	−8.21
EM4	Y3	OLS	−0.472	−6.04
EM4	Y2	AR1	−0.742	−6.95
EM4	Y3	AR1	−0.493	−4.52
EM5	Y2	AR1	−0.497	−2.31
EM6	Y2	OLS	−0.640	−8.83
EM6	Y2	AR1	−0.713	−7.25

EM1   Employment in GBA (15 to 64 years), from INDEC-EPH.
EM2   Employment in GBA (all ages), from *Ministério de Economía Informe Económico*.
EM4   Manufacturing employment, from INDEC-EPH and Ministério de Economía.
EM5   Total wage employment, from INDEC-EPH and Ministério de Economía.
EM6   Wage employment in manufacturing, from INDEC-EPH and Ministério de Economía.
Y2   Real GDP Index, from Ministério de Economía (1980–95) and the Central Bank (1974–80).
Y3   Industrial Production Index, from FIEL and Central Bank. See technical annex B for details.

−0.75, which is consistent with estimates of the National Accounts in the 1970s (not updated since), and with a simple estimation of the share of labor. The share of labor can be estimated multiplying average wages (900 pesos) by aggregate employment (12 million employees) and dividing this product by GDP (300 billion pesos). This yields an estimate of the share of labor of 0.35, which corresponds to a share of capital β of 0.65. Our finding of the share of labor $1-\beta$ is consistent with the results of other authors. Delfino (1984) finds a share of labor in manufacturing of approximately 0.40 in 1973. Using data from the National Accounts of the Central Bank of Argentina, Elías (1988) reports a series on the share of capital income in GDP, whose average during 1950–80 is close to 0.6.

Constant Elasticity of Substitution Technology

The CES technology continues to assume that the elasticity of substitution σ is a constant, but loosens the restriction imposed in the Cobb-

TABLE 5-2
CES Technology: Cost Function Approach
(Estimates of σ, ε_{LL}, and ε_{LY})

L Used	Y Used	Specification	σ	ε_{LL}	ε_{LY}
EM4	Y3	OLS W3	0.16	−0.10	1.08
			(2.19)	(−2.20)	(0.36)
EM4	Y3	IV* AR1 W3	0.35	−0.21	0.34
			(3.28)	(−3.24)	(1.49)
EM4	Y2	IV* AR1 W3	0.51	−0.31	0.52
			(1.77)	(−1.76)	(0.86)
EM6	Y3	OLS W3	0.19	−0.11	0.13
			(2.38)	(−2.32)	(0.52)
EM6	Y3	IV* AR1 W3	0.41	−0.25	0.45
			(3.70)	(−3.65)	(1.91)
EM6	Y2	IV* AR1 W3	0.62	−0.37	0.72
			(2.03)	(−2.00)	(1.11)

EM4   Manufacturing employment, from INDEC-EPH and Ministério de Economía.
EM6   Wage employment in manufacturing, from INDEC-EPH and Ministério de Economía.
Y2   Real GDP Index, from Ministério de Economía (1980–95) and the Central Bank (1974–80).
Y3   Industrial Production Index, from FIEL and the Central Bank.
Note: To calculate ε_{LL} it was assumed that $s_L = 0.6$. Instruments used were LTRC2, LY2, or LY3, LPBLURB, and INFL.

Douglas technology that σ equals 1. Table 5-2 shows estimates of σ, the own-wage elasticity of labor demand ε_{LL} and the output elasticity of labor demand ε_{LY}. The employment data used is manufacturing employment (EM4) and wage employment in the manufacturing sector (EM6). Specifications using the more aggregate categories of labor for all sectors in Greater Buenos Aires (EM1, EM2, and EM3) did not produce tight estimates of the parameters of interest. The reason may be that the trend captures most of the movements in these series and that using data for manufacturing and services sectors masks the true elasticities in each sector of the economy. To finesse this problem, most subsequent estimates rely on employment in the manufacturing sector.

The effect of wages on manufacturing employment, as measured by the wage elasticity of labor demand, is stronger when using wage employment in manufacturing, which excludes self-employed and owners, compared to employment in manufacturing. As Table 5-2 shows, the elasticities are

–0.37 and –0.31, respectively. Because input prices are likely to be endogenous, we choose instrumental variable estimations. In this context, we need instruments that are correlated with input prices and henceforth labor supply, but not with labor demand. The instruments we use here are the logs of the real exchange rate (TRC2), real GDP per capita (Y1), real GDP index (Y2), urban population in Greater Buenos Aires (PBLURB), and annual percent change in CPI (INFL). Using instrumental variables substantially increases the estimated elasticity of substitution, which implies that the absolute value of the own-wage elasticity of labor demand ε_{LL} increases. Instrumental variable estimates of the output elasticity, ε_{LY} lie between 0.34 and 0.72. The estimates are sensitive to the use of GDP or industrial production. They tend to be higher but of lower statistical significance for the real GDP index (Y2), relative to estimates based on the industrial production index (Y3). Note that CES technology restricts ε_{LY} to be equal to 1. Our estimates indicate, however, that the output elasticity is statistically different from 1. This does not necessarily tell us that firm technology is not CES, but may be due rather to the level of aggregation in our data.

Under the assumption that firms make zero profits and operate in competitive markets, an alternative way of estimating the elasticity of substitution σ based on CES technology can be derived, which allows us to check the robustness of our results. We proceed as follows. From the production function we take the first derivatives with respect to labor and capital and obtain:

$$\partial Y/\partial L = \alpha \, (Y/L)^{1-\rho} \tag{13}$$

$$\partial Y/\partial K = [1-\alpha](Y/K)^{1-\rho} \tag{14}$$

Note that $\rho = 1-1/\sigma$. When equating (13) to w/p and (14) to r/p and adding an error term, we obtain the estimable equations:

$$\ln(Y/L) = \alpha_1 + \sigma_1 \ln (w/p) + u_1 \tag{15}$$

and

$$\ln(Y/K) = \alpha_2 + \sigma_2 \ln (r/p) + u_2 \tag{16}$$

where σ_1 and σ_2 are alternative estimates of σ (see Berndt [1991] for a discussion on these alternative estimates of σ). Under the assumption of cost minimization the ratio of equations (15) and (16) is equal to the factor price. Taking logs and differentiating with respect to $\ln(w/r)$ yields:

$$-\partial \ln(K/L)/\partial \ln(w/r) = \sigma \tag{17}$$

Hence an estimable form of this equation is:

$$\ln(K/L) = \alpha_3 + \sigma_3 \ln(w/r) + u_3 \tag{18}$$

As can be seen, estimation of equations (16) and (18) require a measure of capital input, and the price of its service r. Both are likely to be measured with error, and hence estimations based on this approach should be less reliable than the results obtained from (15). Table 5-3 shows that σ_1, which is derived from (15), ranges from 0.5 to 0.7. Under the assumption that $s_L = 0.6$, the own-wage labor demand elasticity of ε_{LL} lies between -0.3 and -0.5, which correspond to the above findings. Again, elasticities of substitutions are higher when using Y2 instead of Y3. And given the same output measure, σ_1 is higher when wage employment in manufacturing, instead of manufacturing employment, is the employment measure. Difficulties in inferring ε_{LL} when including an imperfectly measured price of capital can be overcome in a labor-demand equation by specifying w and r separately. We now turn to estimates based on the so-called factor-demand equations.

TABLE 5-3
CES Technology: Production Function Approach
(Different estimates of σ)

Variables Used for Output and Employment	σ_1	σ_2	σ_3
Real GDP index (Y2)	0.67	0.32	1.15
Manufacturing employment (EM4)	(5.73)	(2.08)	(7.55)
Industrial production (Y3)	0.48	0.28	—
Manufacturing employment (EM4)	(3.90)	(0.93)	—
Real GDP index (Y2)	0.70	—	1.21
Manufacturing wage employment (EM6)	(5.95)	—	(7.75)
Industrial production (Y3)	0.51	—	—
Manufacturing wage employment (EM6)	(4.29)	—	—

Note: Instruments used were log of the real exchange rate (TRC2), log of real GDP or industrial production (Y2 or Y3), urban population in GBA (PBLURB), December-to-December percent change in the CPI (INFL). See technical annex B for details. All estimates are AR1 corrected instrumental variable estimates, with t-statistics in parentheses.

Estimation of Single Factor Demand Equations

To estimate Shephard's condition, equation (3) can be written in logarithmic form as a log-linear equation.

$$\ln L = \alpha' + \varepsilon_{LL} \ln w + \varepsilon_{LK} \ln r + \varepsilon_{LY} \ln y + u \tag{19}$$

where α is a parameter and u represents an error term. ε_{LK} is the cross-elasticity of demand for labor in response to a change in the price of capital services. This specification allows us to obtain direct estimates of constant-output elasticity of demand for labor ε_{LL}, ε_{LK}, and the employment-output elasticity ε_{LY}.[7] Table 5-4 presents the results of this estimation.

Again we find that ε_{LL} ranges from -0.4 to -0.5, which is consistent with the estimates of σ and the labor share estimated above. However, the

TABLE 5-4
Single Factor Demand Equations
(Estimates of ε_{LL}, ε_{LK}, and ε_{LY})

Variables used for employment, wages, and output	ε_{LL}	ε_{LK}	ε_{LY}
Manufacturing employment (EM4)	−0.396	0.580	0.080
Nominal wages (W3), industrial production (Y3)	(−4.03)	(2.42)	(0.35)
Unrestricted			
Manufacturing wage employment (EM6)	−0.472	0.718	0.127
Nominal wages (W3), industrial production (Y3)	(−4.88)	(3.05)	(0.57)
Unrestricted			
Manufacturing employment (EM4)	−0.412	0.412	0.189
Nominal wages (W3), industrial production (Y3)	(−4.30)	(4.30)	(1.05)
Restricted			
Manufacturing wage employment (EM6)	−0.493	0.493	0.272
Nominal wages (W3), industrial production (Y3)	(−5.19)	(5.19)	(1.57)
Restricted			

Note: Instruments used were log of the real exchange rate (TRC2), log of real GDP or industrial production (Y3), urban population in GBA (PBLURB), December-to-December percent change in the CPI (INFL). See technical annex B for details. All estimates are AR1 corrected instrumental variable estimates. t-statistics in parentheses.

estimates of the cross-elasticity of demand for labor ε_{LK} and the output elasticity ε_{Ly} appear to be inconsistent with the previous estimates. Given a constant returns to scale production function, profit maximizing behavior and competitive market, the cross-elasticity of demand for labor in response to a change in the price of capital equals the negative of the own-wage elasticity, which means that $\varepsilon_{LL} + \varepsilon_{LK} = 0$. An F-test of the estimates cannot reject the null hypothesis that ε_{LK} equals $- \varepsilon_{LL.}$ Consequently, we impose this restriction in the following estimations and find that the estimate of ε_{LK} decreases, while that of ε_{LY} increases in size and significance.

Generalized Leontief Technology

To estimate the generalized Leontief technology, we impose constant returns to scale and estimate equations (20) and (21) jointly, using a seemingly unrelated regression estimator (SURE) with the imposed cross-equation restriction. We apply three-stage least squares estimation to correct for the simultaneous equation bias. This procedure provides the following results for the labor demand equation (10) and the capital demand equation, using manufacturing employment (EM4) and real GDP index (Y2):

$$L/Y = -0.0029 + 0.0098 \, (w/r)^{-0.5} \tag{20}$$
$$(-1.26) \quad (4.12)$$

$$K/Y = 0.0063 + 0.0098 \, (w/r)^{-0.5} \tag{21}$$
$$(2.47) \quad (4.12)$$

Using these estimates, the elasticity of substitution σ, the own-wage elasticity of labor demand ε_{LL}, and the constant-output capital demand elasticity, ε_{KK} can be calculated (see Berndt 1991). These elasticities are no longer constant, but vary over the sample interval. As can be seen in Table 5-5, elasticities are much higher than the above-presented estimates. However, the absolute value of ε_{LL} does not exceed 0.8, thus remaining below 1. The estimates appear to be sensitive to the way total costs are computed and the measure of the actual capital stock used. This is a drawback, because measurement errors in capital stock are usually high. The implied labor share in these estimates is around 0.30, which is consistent with our previous results.

Transcendental Logarithmic Technology

In the two-factor case, the transcendental logarithmic (translog) technology has the advantage over the CES technology that the elasticities are not re-

TABLE 5-5
Generalized Leontief Technology
(Estimates of σ, ε_{LL}, and ε_{KK})

Year	σ	ε_{LL}	ε_{KK}
1974	1.01	−0.71	−0.30
1975	0.99	−0.69	−0.29
1976	0.92	−0.65	−0.27
1977	0.93	−0.66	−0.28
1978	0.96	−0.67	−0.29
1979	0.99	−0.69	−0.30
1980	1.08	−0.76	−0.32
1981	1.08	−0.76	−0.32
1982	1.02	−0.72	−0.31
1983	1.07	−0.75	−0.32
1984	1.13	−0.80	−0.33
1985	1.04	−0.73	−0.31
1986	1.06	−0.74	−0.32
1987	1.04	−0.73	−0.31
1988	1.02	−0.72	−0.31
1989	1.04	−0.73	−0.31
1990	1.03	−0.72	−0.31
1991	1.05	−0.73	−0.31
1992	1.10	−0.77	−0.32
1993	1.11	−0.78	−0.33
1994	1.10	−0.78	−0.33
1995	1.08	−0.76	−0.32
Mean	1.04	−0.73	−0.31

stricted to be constant, but are allowed to vary with the values of the factor inputs or prices. Elasticities based on translog technology are usually estimated in a system of factor demands, known as KLEM (capital, labor, energy, and materials). Again, we are constrained by the data at hand because information on energy and other materials is not available. This may introduce biases in the estimates we present in Table 5-6. We estimate the cost (11) and share (12) equations jointly using iterated three-stage least squares.[8]

Table 5-6 presents the estimates of the translog technology imposing different restrictions on the production function. The number of restrictions increases as we move from left to right. The first column corresponds to the nonhomothetic case, the second to the homothetic, the third to the homogeneous, the fourth to the linear homogeneous, and the fifth to the

TABLE 5-6
Transcendental Logarithmic Technology

	Nonhomothetic	Homothetic	Homogeneous	Linear homog	Cobb-Douglas
$\ln a_0$	−55.824	−72.021	−1.376	−4.462	−4.462
	(2.01)	(2.49)	(2.30)	(164.77)	(271.54)
a_1	1.324	0.300	0.297	0.304	0.302
	(2.05)	(27.53)	(27.40)	(27.77)	(33.54)
a_2	0.133	0.051	0.099	−0.029	
	(2.27)	(1.02)	(2.34)	(0.56)	
b_3	23.346	30.421	0.330		
	(1.96)	(2.46)	(2.55)		
a_4	−0.223				
	(1.59)				
b_5	−4.855	−6.404			
	(1.91)	(2.43)			
Restrictions	0	1	2	3	4
Mean of ε_{LL}	−0.256	−0.528	−0.368	−0.793	−0.698
Mean of ε_{KK}	−0.114	−0.232	−0.163	−0.343	−0.302
Mean of σ	0.369	0.760	0.531	1.136	1
Mean of ee	0.131	0.172	0.670	0	0

Note: Three-stage least squares estimates. Absolute value of ratio of estimated parameter to standard error in parentheses.

Cobb-Douglas restriction. Using the likelihood ratio test, the hypothesis of homotheticity cannot be rejected at the 5 percent level.[9] We reject the hypothesis of homogeneity, linear homogeneity, and Cobb-Douglas technology. Under the preferred—homothetic—specification, the estimated average elasticity of labor demand with respect to wages is −0.528, and the elasticity of substitution σ is 0.760. The elasticity of total costs with respect to output ε_{CY} is 0.828. $1- \varepsilon_{CY}$ can be used as a measure of returns to scale ee, which takes a positive value if returns to scale exist, and a negative value otherwise.[10] Under the assumption of homotheticity, $\varepsilon_{CY} = \varepsilon_{LY}$, which as a consequence assumes the value 0.828. This is a considerably higher value than our previous estimates. A summary of 42 estimates of this elasticity in the United States yields an average of 0.828, exactly the same as our estimate (Hamermesh 1993). For other countries, Hamermesh reports a mean of 0.767.

Note that these estimates have high standard errors, and hence estimates are less precise than in previous cases. Again, this arises from the fact that data on actual costs are not available for Argentina. As can be seen in equation (12), the estimation of elasticities based on translog technology requires information on total cost, and consequently on the stock of capital. As in the case of the generalized Leontief technology, the resulting estimates are sensitive to the specific indexes of capital and labor used and total costs of production. Without national accounts on payments to factors, the best we could do was to use the "estimated" shares of labor, and reindex the data on capital and labor to obtain those shares for 1974. Another reason for exercising caution in interpreting these numbers is that there is substantial variation in these elasticities over time. ε_{CY} fluctuates between –0.626 and 1.408. During 1974–90 it has an average value of 1.1. During 1991–95 it has an average value of –0.469. A negative value for this elasticity is worrisome, since it would imply that total costs fell with the level of output, and that returns to scale are low for low output levels, and very high for higher levels of output.

Translog Estimations Incorporating Nonneutral Technical Change

This finding points to the possibility of technical change, which we have ignored so far. Technical change implies that the cost function may have shifted down over time. Indeed, Hamermesh (1993) notes that the presence of increasing returns (or economies of scale) may be due to the fact that econometricians cannot distinguish between the effects of labor-saving technical change and increasing returns. To address this issue, we estimated a translog system adjusting for the effects of biased technical change and total factor productivity growth (TFP). Since we have already rejected the nonhomotheticity restriction and do not have enough degrees of freedom to estimate the full model with technical progress, we estimate only two models: the first with homotheticity imposed, and the second which is further restricted to be linearly homogeneous.

The results are presented in Table 5-7. We cannot reject the hypothesis that technical change is relatively labor saving and, by homogeneity, capital using. Berndt and Khaled (1979) obtain the same result for the United States, but of a smaller magnitude. This points to the fact that labor-saving technical change is strong in Argentina, which in turn is likely to

TABLE 5-7
Translog Technology, Nonneutral Technical Change

	Homothetic	Linear Homogenous
ln a_0	11.548	−5.3204
	(1.66)	(10.46)
a_1	0.374	0.351
	(13.76)	(13.57)
a_2	0.153	0.099
	(2.41)	(1.70)
b_3	−5.25	
	(1.75)	
b_5	1.170	
	(1.82)	
b_6	0.042	0.131
	(10.38)	(1.93)
b_7	−0.006	−0.004
	(2.86)	(1.99)
b_8	−0.001	−0.004
	(7.76)	(1.98)
Restrictions	1	3
Mean of ε_{LL}	−0.183	−0.368
Mean of ε_{KK}	−0.008	−0.159
Mean of ε_{LK}	0.264	
Mean of ee	0.839	0
Mean of ε_{CY}	0.009	0.001

Note: Three-stage least squares estimates, 1974–95. Absolute value of t-ratios in parentheses.

be the result of an increasing price of labor relative to capital. Concerning estimates of elasticities, we find that ε_{LL}, ε_{KK}, and ε_{LK} decrease in value when technical change is allowed for. Still, they remain greater than zero in absolute value. Finally, we again compute our measure of returns to scale ee and find that the degree of increasing returns to scale is large. With an estimate of ε_{CY} of 0.161, the measure of returns to scale ee equals 0.839. Note that this estimate of the output elasticity of demand ε_{CY} is not far from previous estimates with less-structured models. However, for the final part of the sample period (1990–95), the estimated ε_{CY} amounts to 0.29.[11]

Delfino (1984) estimated a translog KLEM model for the manufacturing sector in Argentina for 1950–73, for which National Accounts data were available, estimating the shares of labor, capital, and materials. He finds a labor demand elasticity of –0.40 and a capital elasticity of –0.45 resulted. These elasticities are basically in accord with our previous results. However, Delfino (1984) obtains a relatively low estimate of ε_{KL} of about 0.24.

Policy Implications

In this chapter we provide evidence on the own-wage elasticity and the output elasticity of aggregate employment in Argentina. The own-wage elasticity measures the effect of a change in wages on employment, holding output constant. At the risk of oversimplification, its estimate can be used to quantify the effects of labor policy reforms on employment growth, and hence on unemployment. The output-elasticity provides evidence on the effect of a change in output on employment, holding the wage or unit labor costs constant. It allows us to obtain numerical estimates of employment growth that would occur due solely to GDP growth, that is, without any labor policy reform, which raises or lowers labor costs. The main findings using the different series, technological specifications, and econometric techniques are summarized below.

Estimates of Wage Elasticity of Labor Demand

The results show that the constant-output wage elasticity of labor demand is significantly different from zero. In the preferred models estimated, it ranges from –0.3 to –0.8, giving a "best-guess" estimate of about –0.5. This would mean that if labor costs are reduced by 10 percent, all else remaining the same, employment would increase by 5 percent. With an employment and about 4 million people in Greater Buenos Aires, this would amount to an increase in employment of 200,000. As can be seen in

TABLE 5-8
Estimated Elasticities: Own-Price, Output, and Substitution

Technology assumption	Wage elasticity	Output elasticity	Elasticity of substitution
Cobb-Douglas	–0.60	1.00 (Restricted)	1.00 (Restricted)
Single factor demand	–0.45	0 to 0.10	—
CES	–0.35	0.40	0.50
Generalized Leontief	–0.75	1.00 (Restricted)	1.05
Translog	–0.30	0.30	0.50

Chapter 4, this is greater than the "normal" or trend increase in labor supply, and is likely to lead to a significant and sustainable decrease in the unemployment rate in a relatively short period.

If we assume at the outset a Cobb-Douglas specification, we obtain an elasticity of –0.6, given that the share of labor is approximately 0.4 as indicated by available national accounts (for the 1970s). This lies not far from the results of our estimations. Compared to other findings, our estimates of the own-price elasticity are somewhat higher than those reported on average for the United States, where Hamermesh (1993) places his "best guess" based on aggregate data at –0.3 for the constant-output demand elasticity of labor.

Estimates of Output Elasticity of Labor Demand

The output elasticity is restricted to equal 1 under the Cobb-Douglas, CES, and generalized Leontief functions. Using the CES formulation and relaxing the restriction that the elasticity equals 1, the elasticity of output is estimated to be between 0 and 0.5. The estimate depends on the employment and output series used, whether autocorrelation is corrected for, and whether an instrumental variables approach is applied. Using the single factor demand formulation, the output elasticity is estimated to be 0.2, but is not significant. The best guess, based on these results, would be an output elasticity of about 0.25.

This estimate of the output elasticity is somewhat lower than estimates in other countries. Hamermesh (1993) finds an average elasticity of 0.83 for the United States, while for other countries it is about 0.75. Revenga and Bentolila (1994) obtain lower long-term output elasticities of the employment rate for 11 OECD countries, ranging from 0.21 for Japan to 0.49 for Germany. The estimate for Argentina implies that a 10 percent growth rate in GDP results in a 2.5 percent increase in employment. Table 4.9 sheds light on the years needed to reduce the unemployment rate from 16 percent to 8 percent for different levels of labor force and employment growth. Given an unemployment rate of about 18 percent of a total labor force of about 500,000 in Greater Buenos Aires, and assuming no net growth in the labor supply and an unrealistically high GDP growth rate of 10 percent, it would take about six years to bring the unemployment rate to 8 percent, if the government relies exclusively on output growth. As will be seen in the following chapter, the trend rate of labor force growth actually amounts to 1.5 percent. This implies that pushing the unemployment rate down to 8 percent will take more than 14 years.

TABLE 5-9
Years Needed to Reduce the Unemployment Rate to 8 Percent
(simulations using alternative rates of labor force and employment growth)

		Labor Force Growth (percent)					
		0.0	0.5	1.0	1.5	2.0	2.5
	0.5	28.0					
Employment	1.0	14.0	28.2				
Growth	1.5	9.4	14.1	28.3			
(percent)	2.0	7.1	9.4	14.2	28.4		
	2.5	5.7	7.1	9.5	14.3	28.6	
	3.0	4.7	5.7	7.1	9.5	14.3	28.7

Estimates of the Elasticity of Substitution

In the case of Cobb-Douglas technology, the elasticity of substitution between capital and labor is restricted to equal 1. In the CES case, it is restricted to a constant, which is estimated to equal 0.5. In the generalized Leontief case, where it is allowed to vary over time, the average elasticity is calculated to be more than 1. In the translog case, the estimated elasticity of substitution is about 0.5. In any case, it is clear that the elasticity of substitution between labor and capital in Argentina is significantly greater than zero, but less than 1. At the margin, changes in the price of labor relative to capital will be met by proportional changes in the employment of these two factors.

Summary of Findings

Our analyses in this chapter produce the following findings. First, own-wage elasticities range from –0.3 to –0.8 for the preferred specifications. Based on these results, the own-wage elasticity of employment—as a simple mean at the aggregate level—can reasonably be regarded as about –0.5, implying that a 10 percent decline in labor costs will, all else remaining the same, raise employment by 5 percent. Second, output elasticities range from 0.1 to 0.4 for the preferred specifications. Based on these results and those from an enterprise survey by FIEL (see World Bank 1996), the output elasticity of employment can reasonably be regarded as about 0.25. This implies that a 10 percent growth rate of GDP will result in a 2.5 percent increase in employment. Third, better data are required to narrow these ranges, but these estimates are in the general neighborhood of elasticity estimates for the United States. Our estimates of wage elasticity provide strong evidence that policy reform that lowers the cost of labor relative to capital is urgently needed. To increase labor demand and employment, it is not enough in Argentina to rely exclusively on faster output growth. To reduce unemployment, Argentina has little choice but to accelerate the process of labor market reform.

Notes

1. For example, the "employment encouragement" contract applied to registered unemployed persons. It was limited to a period of 6 to 18 months and allowed an exemption from 50 percent of employers' contributions and a 50 percent reduction in severance payments. Full severance payments had to be paid if the contract was terminated early.

2. The policy reforms discussed in World Bank (1996) are reduction of the payroll tax–related distortions, reform of collective bargaining laws, and a realignment of severance legislation.

3. Elasticity of substitution measures the ease at which a firm can relax the relative use of the two input factors in response to a change in relative prices, without changing the level of output.

4. Self-employment increased by about 19 percent from October 1985 to October 1991, which compares to an increase of 11 percent in total employment. From 1989 to 1991 the number of self-employed decreased by about 4 percent. This trend was reversed after the introduction of the Convertibility Plan, implying an increase in self-employment of 1.5 percent between October 1991 and May 1994. During the same period total employment increased by about 2.3 percent (see Pessino 1997).

5. Alternatively, total employment hours worked may be used to capture labor demand. Using employment instead of work-hours may raise problems when using cross-section data if there is substantial heterogeneity among hours in different firms or industries. Because we use time series data and are interested in estimating long-term elasticities, this issue does not arise due to the fact that worker-hours are highly correlated with variations in employment over the long term.

6. Our analysis does not differentiate between human capital and labor. Pessino (1997) shows that from 1990 onward supply and real wages of individuals with higher education increased, leading to increased differences in returns to education. Demand for less-skilled workers decreased during this period. This is likely to distort our results. A lower real exchange rate also means that imported goods are cheaper. Among other things, Argentina imports capital goods. A lower price of capital goods with respect to the higher price of labor implies a strong substitution effect toward capital and against labor if production processes allow

such adjustments. But here we find evidence of moderate elasticities of substitution between labor and capital.

7. Note that in the above approach, we calculated ε_{LL} using the estimate of σ and the assumption that $s_L = 0.6$.

8. This is identical to the SURE procedure, but with the fitted values of the endogenous variables regressed on all the instruments and exogenous variables. The disturbance covariance matrix is estimated using the original variables, not the fitted ones. A detailed description of the estimation procedure and the assumptions imposed can be found in technical annex B at the end of the book.

9. Notice, however, that the parameter a_4 is only marginally significant. However, we cannot reject the null hypothesis of $a_4 = 0$, when we compare its asymptotic standard error with the critical value of an χ^2 distribution with 1 degree of freedom, which assumes 6.63 at the 1 percent level.

10. Returns to scale μ are computed as the inverse of the elasticity of cost with respect to output $(1/\varepsilon_{CY})$ and equal 1.208.

11. TFP results are interpreted as follows. In the context of a production function, it has been traditional to measure TFP by the residual method, that is, the growth of output minus the growth in inputs. Berndt and Jorgenson (1975) related such a measure to biased technical change and to total factor cost diminution, the dual of TFP. They showed that under the assumption of constant returns to scale, the rate of TFP growth equals $-(\partial \ln C)/\partial t$, which represents the one-period reduction in costs due to disembodied technical progress given that prices and output are fixed. In the more general case of nonconstant returns to scale and nonhomotheticity, Berndt and Khaled (1979) show that $\varepsilon_{Yt} = -\varepsilon_{Ct}/\varepsilon_{CY}$. The value of ε_{Ct} turns out to be positive, meaning that, on average, TFP decreased. This is not surprising if the decrease is concentrated in the 1970s and 1980s, when Argentina underwent a decrease in GDP and investment and collapsed into hyperinflation. Indeed, the data show that the negative values for TFP are concentrated in the first 10 years until 1984. It then becomes less than 4 percent until the late 1980s, increasing monotonically until reaching almost 9 percent in 1995, which is surprisingly high. With the homothetic model, the behavior of TFP is more in line with our priors: negative values until 1988, zero in 1989, and monotonically increasing after that, reaching 3 percent in 1995.

References

Berndt, Ernst. 1991. *The Practice of Econometrics: Classic and Contemporary.* Reading, Mass. Addison-Wesley Publishing Co.

Berndt, Ernst R., and D. W. Jorgenson. 1975. "Energy, Intermediate Goods and Production in an Inter-Industry Econometric Model of the U.S., 1947–71." Paper presented at the World Congress of the Econometric Society, Toronto, August.

Berndt, Ernst R., and Mohamed S. Khaled. 1979. "Parametric Productivity Measurement and Choice Among Flexible Functional Forms." *Journal of Political Economy* 87 (6): 1220–45.

Bour, Juan L. 1995. "Mercado de Trabajo y Productividad en la Argentina." Final version. FIEL, Buenos Aires.

Delfino, José A. 1984. "Analisis economico de la tecnologia del sector manufacturero Argentino." ("Economic Analysis of Argentina's Manufacturing Technology," with English summary). *Economica* 30 (2–3): 149–202.

Elias, Victor. 1988. "Productividad en el sector industrial argentino: 1935–1985." ("Productivity in the Industrial Sector of Argentina, 1935–1985," with English summary). *Economica* 34 (2): 185–202.

Hamermesh, Daniel. 1993. *Labor Demand*. Princeton, N.J.: Princeton University Press.

Hopenhayn, Hugo. 2001. "Labor Market Policies and Employment Duration: The Effects of Labor Market Reform in Argentina." Research Network WP No. R_407. Inter-American Development Bank, Washington, D.C.

Ministry of Economy. 1995. *Informe Economico*. Various issues. Argentina.

Mondino, Guillermo, and Silvia Montoya. 2000. "The Effects of Labor Market Regulations on Employment Decisions by Firms: Empirical Evidence for Argentina." Research Network WP No. R_391. Inter-American Development Bank, Washington, D.C.

Pessino, Carola. 1997. "Argentina: The Labor Market during the Economic Transition." Chapter VI in Sebastian Edwards and Nora Lustig, eds., *Labor Markets in Latin America: Combining Social Protection with Market Flexibility*. Washington, D.C.: The Brookings Institution.

Revenga, Ana, and Samuel Bentolila. 1994. "What Affects the Employment Rate Intensity of Growth?" Draft.

Varian, Hal. 1992. *Microeconomic Analysis*. Third Edition. New York and London: W.W. Norton and Co.

World Bank. 1996. "Argentina Employment Study." Report No. 15643-AR. Washington, D.C.

PART

III

Earnings and Employment Outcomes in Chile

CHAPTERS 6 AND 7 ANALYZE trends in earnings distribution and employment insecurity in Chile between 1970 and 1996. While the chapters do not study the effects of the economic slowdown during 1998–99 and the subsequent recovery in 2000, the analysis remains useful for providing a long-term perspective on the effects of labor market liberalization and growth on labor-related outcomes.

Chapter 6 uses quantitative techniques to analyze whether the rewards to human capital differ by quantile and socioeconomic status, and to quantify the effects of policies to improve access to and quality of education for poorer sections of society. During 1987–92, average labor earnings increased by about 30 percent for the top and bottom quintile groups in Chile, and by about 20 percent for the middle classes. During 1992–94, average earnings fell for the top and bottom quintile groups, but rose modestly for the middle groups. Wage inequality, as measured by the Gini coefficient and the spread between the 90th and 10th percentile groups, rose between 1960 and 1987–88, but declined significantly until the mid-1990s. The authors argue that the change in direction has been missed or underemphasized by earlier studies. Rates of return to education behave in a similar way, rising from 1960 until 1987–88, and then declining until 1996.

These findings suggest that the Chilean government's emphasis on education as an instrument for combating inequality in recent years is appropriate, though this is tempered by the finding that rates of return to education are lower for poorer groups. Simple simulations suggest that further improvements in access to schooling by the poor will have relatively modest effects on earnings inequality, and this only at higher levels of education (grade 9 and above). Improvements in the quality of education appear to be twice as effective as improvements in access to schooling, and the returns to improvements in education quality are obtained largely at lower levels of schooling (0 to 8 years).

Chapter 7 takes up the question of whether Chile's economic reforms (principally a reduced role of government as an employer combined with trade liberalization) have resulted in greater "precariousness" of employment or job instability. This chapter uses a labor flows model to convert reported data into magnitudes that are better suited for addressing this question of precariousness, or volatility, of employment and earnings. The results appear to undermine the claims that employment and labor earnings have become more precarious in Chile. During 1990–97, the Chilean labor market became an increasingly reliable source of income: expected job tenure increased, unemployment rates and duration fell significantly, and long-term unemployment became practically nonexistent. The approach followed in the 1980s and early 1990s paid dividends: poverty and wage inequality fell impressively since 1987, and direct interventions in the labor market (such as restrictions on firing or stringent prohibition of temporary contracts) to reduce poverty or inequality did not appear to be necessary.

These findings have several important implications for labor market policies. Given the average tenure and unemployment duration prevailing during 1990–96, the mandated severance payment system seemed adequate to provide support for most formal sector workers if they become unemployed, though perhaps not suitable for a modern economy that is globally well integrated. Changes in labor legislation that make dismissals harder are likely to prove counterproductive. Additionally, using international experience as a guide—since Chile's programs have not been rigorously evaluated—the authors reason that public training programs are not likely to have a significant effect on earnings inequality of employed workers but, if these programs are well targeted, training programs and job search assistance might help some unemployed workers find jobs.

The declining rates of return to education computed in Chapter 6 were for the first half of the 1990s. Since 1995–96, these rates appear to have risen somewhat. The economic slowdown in Chile at the end of the decade provided a reminder that mechanisms to provide income support during unemployment spells were still needed, since unemployment rates doubled from 5 to 6 percent in 1997 to about 11 to 12 percent by 2000.

The Chilean government has since decided that the appropriate income support program for the formal sector unemployed is a system of individualized severance accounts, along the lines of the much-debated system of mandatory pension funds that Chile pioneered in the 1980s. Proposals to make dismissals more difficult and costly were opposed by private employers, but public sector labor unions appeared to emerge from the decade stronger than before. Chile entered the new decade dealing with proposals to strengthen labor regulations that were initiated during a period of low unemployment and falling earnings inequality, many of which, however, must be resolved in a time of moderate to high unemployment rates and with signs of rising earnings inequality.

6 Responding to Earnings Differentials in Chile

Indermit S. Gill
and Claudio E. Montenegro

Since 1990, Chile's GDP per capita has grown by about 5 percent annually, and reached almost $4,200 in 1996. Open unemployment rates fell from more than 20 percent in the early 1980s to less than 6 percent in 2001. Between 1984 and 1994, average real wages grew by 28 percent. By 1995, aided by a system of targeted transfers, headcount poverty had fallen to about half of what it was in the early 1980s (Haindl 1996). Chile's performance in improving the most basic labor market indicators and in reducing poverty is stellar and—outside of East Asia—unfortunately rare.

Chile's reliance on market-friendly, outward-oriented economic policies has been credited with these successes. But these successes have also invited closer scrutiny of other outcomes of these policies. In particular, observers have questioned whether economic success as measured by average magnitudes such as per capita income, average labor earnings, and job creation mask important socioeconomic failures, as indicated by growing inequality in the distribution of income and earnings and in the quality of social services such as education and health. In fact, some observers "see a real and frightening possibility of [Chile] in 20 years with a booming economy atop a sea of unskilled, underpaid citizens" (Atwood 1996).

Ferreira and Litchfield (1998) provide systematic evidence that the distribution of income did not worsen between 1987 and 1994, so these concerns appear to be either misplaced or to have arisen as a result of developments in the late 1990s. Their findings indicate, however, that Chile remains a highly unequal economy, despite government efforts to provide targeted assistance to the poorest households. In this chapter, we investigate the extent to which the functioning of Chile's labor market is responsible for the persistently high inequality in household income.

It is believed that in Chile, as in other parts of Latin America, greater openness to trade has led to wider wage differentials between skilled and unskilled workers. Wood (1997), for example, argues that this has happened in Latin America since the mid-1980s, and attributes it to the entry of China into the world market and to the adoption of new technology that is biased against unskilled workers. These trends seem to contradict both theory and the stylized facts from East Asia's experience with openness.

The combination of an open economy and a flexible labor market is believed to be the cause of many growing socioeconomic ills, including income inequality. It is argued that international trade has led to widening differentials in earnings between Chile's poor and rich. Leiva (1996) writes that "savage deregulation" of labor markets under Pinochet was followed by a period of "legalized flexibility" since 1987 during which "the new jobs created tended to be low-paying, low-quality, short-term jobs concentrated in agriculture, trade, services and construction, precisely those sectors characterized by greater instability in employment." Leiva suggests that "Chile's flexible labor market not only deepens income inequality, but also acts as a mechanism for reproducing poverty as employment expansion takes place in low-paid, low-quality jobs."

Increasing or high inequality of earnings can slow growth and might induce reversal of earlier reforms, especially the reform of labor legislation. To assist policymakers in identifying when corrective policy actions might be needed, and what the likely payoff to some policies being contemplated might be, we address three sets of issues:

- First, we try to disentangle the links between labor markets, poverty, and inequality—that is, to understand to what extent the labor market is responsible for progress, or the lack of it, in fighting poverty and inequality.
- Second, we analyze the labor market structure as we try to answer whether the labor market changed so that those with human capital (for example, high levels of education) are being rewarded proportionately more, and whether the structure of Chile's labor market implies that returns to human capital are lower for poorer workers.

- Third, we analyze labor-related policy issues. Here we try to answer questions such as: Do recent developments warrant significant policy changes? Does the structure of the labor market in Chile warrant direct interventions? What are the likely consequences of the principal policies being considered to reduce inequality (for example, introduction of unemployment insurance, increases in mandated minimum wages, and initiatives to improve the access to and quality of education and training)?

We use the latest available data and reliable econometric techniques to deal with these issues. University of Chile Household Surveys from June 1960 to June 1996 in Greater Santiago are used to provide a long-term perspective on labor market trends, and Encuesta de Caracterización Socioeconomica Nacional (CASEN) household surveys for 1987, 1990, 1992, and 1994 are used to confirm these findings for the country as a whole, and to further investigate these developments. The principal econometric techniques used are quantile regressions, which allow us to analyze returns to education at different points of the conditional wage distribution, and Oaxaca decompositions, used to quantify the effects of policies to improve access to and quality of education for poorer sections of society.

Labor Market Issues, Methodology, and Data

To keep our task manageable, we analyze only the labor market issues that are critical for explaining earnings inequality, and for evaluating the effects of policies being contemplated to address the concerns regarding income inequality.

Main Labor Market Issues

In principle, these topics relate directly to actual or perceived increases in inequality of access to employment and to earnings conditional upon being employed. While Chapter 7 addresses the question of whether employment has become more precarious, this chapter deals with the following topics:

- *Earnings Inequality Trends.* Have earnings become more unequal over time, especially since 1987?
- *Returns to Education.* To what extent have changes in the distribution of earnings been reflected in changes in the returns to education?

- *Levels of Education.* Do the poor receive less and lower-quality education?
- *Policy Implications.* Given the structure of the Chilean labor market, what is the likely result of the government's decision to rely on improving access to human capital? What would be the result of increasing the quality of education as a means of reducing income inequality?

The Model and the Methodology

The usual empirical human capital earnings function has the following empirical form:

$$\ln y_i = \beta_o + \beta_1 S_i + \beta_2 E_i + \beta_3 E_i^2 + u_i \qquad (1)$$

where $\ln y_i$ is the log of earnings or wages for individual i; E_i is the level of experience, E_i^2 is the square of the level of experience (included to account for the commonly observed effect of a declining age earning profile for a given level of experience), β_1 is the rate of return of one additional year of schooling and u_i is a random disturbance term that reflects unobserved characteristics.[1]

In this specification, we expect β_1 and β_2 to be positive since the level of schooling and level of experience are positively correlated to wages for an individual. As educational attainment increases, wages should increase. As level of experience increases, wages should increase as well. We expect β_3 to be negative since the return to experience after a certain level is negatively correlated to wages for an individual. Equation (1) is based on some restrictive assumptions. It assumes individuals have equal abilities and equal opportunities,[2] overlooks direct costs of schooling, neglects earnings while attending school, and presumes a constant return per year of schooling. We usually refer the estimate of β_1 as the return to schooling. However, looking closely at equation (1) we find that the parameter β_1 is an estimate of the impact of schooling on wages rather than an internal rate of return on investment. If it *were* an internal rate of return it would be a private one, since this specification disregards school subsidies and omits any positive or negative externalities to schooling.

An area of concern with equation (1) is the omission of the relevant variable, ability. Since ability is likely to be positively correlated with schooling, omitting this variable from the regression equation will bias the estimated returns to schooling upward. Regardless of this problem we choose to ignore measuring ability in our estimations because of the difficulty of conceptualizing and measuring it. There is also no consensus as to whether it is significant enough to differentiate earnings.

Traditionally, mean regression has been used to estimate equation (1). However, this method gives disproportional weights to large deviations and thus biases estimations. Hence, the method is not accurate when disturbances are abnormal and when there is a relatively large proportion of outliers. Furthermore, this method provides only a limited aspect when analyzing changes in returns to education with heterogeneous populations because these changes may involve the entire conditional distribution. As a result of these reasons, study of the so-called l-estimators has become widespread. The traditional mean regression method minimizes the squared sum of errors and therefore allows one to identify the value of the parameters. The minimization implies that the fitted curve is the prediction of the mean of Y (the dependent variable) given the values of a certain vector of independent variables X. However, instead of squaring the sum of errors, it is possible to take their absolute value and to minimize their sum. In this case the minimization implies that the fitted curve is the prediction of the median of Y given the values of a certain vector of independent variables X. Similarly, this can be regarded as fitting a curve with the implication that half of the errors will be positive and half negative. Consequently, this concept can be extended to the fitting of a curve that implies that θ percent of the errors will be negative and $(100-\theta)$ percent will be positive, and thus giving rise the quantile regression estimation method. In this context, when we refer to returns to schooling we mean the effect of schooling on the respective quantile of the conditional earnings distribution.

The Data

Two sources of data were used. Data for the Santiago metropolitan area were obtained from the University of Chile Household Surveys. These are comparable and representative annual surveys for Santiago. Each survey includes between 10,000 and 16,000 people, and between 3,700 and 5,400 active labor force participants. During this period, Santiago represented about one-third of Chile's total population,[3] and a higher proportion of GDP. Data at the national level was obtained from the CASEN for the years 1987, 1990, 1992, and 1994. The CASEN is a national and regional representative survey carried out by the Ministry of Planning, with the objective of generating a reliable portrait of social and economic conditions across the country. Each survey includes between 94,000 and 170,000 people and between 32,000 and 61,000 active labor force participants.[4] Computing the same estimations for both data sets has two important payoffs: the University of Chile surveys allow us to distinguish short- from longer-term trends, and the CASEN allows us to extend this analysis to the entire country.

For both surveys the samples include only male workers who worked at least 35 hours per week, which were either *empleados* (white-collar workers) or *obreros* (blue-collar workers). This implies that self-employed workers, domestic servants, and military personnel were eliminated from the sample. Self-employed workers were eliminated because the database did not allow the separation of income into returns to labor and returns to capital; domestic servants were eliminated because they are likely to misreport labor income due to the fact that live-in domestic servants do not properly report the value of room and board, which is part of their labor income; and military personnel were eliminated because their salaries do not correspond to market productivity criteria. We do not include women in our sample because this would require accounting for their labor participation decision, which requires a different econometric model. For similar reasons, the unemployed and people who work in voluntary services are also excluded. The same definitions of variables and samples were used throughout the entire period. This gives us comparable year-to-year (and sample-to-sample) results. The dependent variable is defined as the log of the hourly wage.

Are Labor Earnings Becoming More Unequal?

To address the question of whether labor earnings are becoming more unequal, we first reveal trends and changes of average labor earnings from 1987 to 1994 for different decile groups. In a second step, we use two different measures—one unconditioned and the other conditioned on education and other factors—of earnings distribution to determine whether the distribution of earnings has become more unequal. Finally, we provide evidence on levels of and returns to education at different points of the wage distributions and how they evolved over time.

Patterns and Trends in Labor Earnings

Using decile groups by household per capita income, we first examine the trends in average labor earnings per employed worker. These are reported in Table 6-1. The trends in average earnings conform closely to those found for household income per capita and income per equivalent adult by Ferreira and Litchfield (1998). Between 1987 and 1990, real earnings rose by about 25 percent for the entire sample. Labor earnings for each decile group increased: by approximately 30 percent for the poorest 10 percent of households, by about 20 percent for the median class, and by

TABLE 6-1
Average Labor Earnings and Changes, in Percent Workers Aged 14–65
(1994 prices)

Decile Group	Average Labor Earnings (thousands of pesos)				Change in Labor Earnings (percent)			
	1987	1990	1992	1994	1987–90	1990–92	1992–94	1987–94
1	22.57	29.09	37.12	35.57	28.87	27.60	-4.17	64.43
2	33.80	44.49	52.11	51.27	31.64	17.13	-1.63	54.19
3	38.21	52.68	59.45	58.85	37.87	12.84	-1.00	55.58
4	48.55	59.12	64.93	66.32	21.77	9.83	2.14	33.75
5	52.21	64.51	72.08	72.22	23.57	11.73	0.19	38.07
6	61.64	70.78	79.73	82.42	14.84	12.63	3.38	29.35
7	68.89	80.80	93.35	94.63	17.29	15.54	1.36	35.51
8	87.17	101.78	117.84	119.20	16.76	15.78	1.15	35.18
9	123.02	141.51	170.32	173.32	15.03	20.36	1.76	38.45
10	322.25	422.84	516.21	494.26*	31.22	22.08	-4.25	60.19
Average	99.73	124.65	144.89	142.32*	24.99	16.24	-1.77	45.28
Ratio of 10:1	14.3	14.5	13.9	13.9				

* Indicates that the three households with the highest incomes are excluded.
Note: Decile groups are calculated using household per capita income.
Source: Authors' calculations using CASEN surveys.

about 30 percent for the richest 10 percent. The ratio of earnings of the richest to the poorest groups rose marginally to 14.5 in 1990. During 1990–92, real earnings rose at about the same annual rate; that is, by about 16 percent over the two years. Real earnings rose by 28 percent for the poorest group, by about 12 percent for the median group, and by 22 percent for the richest 10 percent. The ratio of earnings of the richest to the poorest groups fell to below 14 in 1992.

Average labor earnings for all workers fell by 1.8 percent between 1992 and 1994. Earnings for the lowest three decile groups fell between 2 and 4 percent. The subsequent six decile groups enjoyed modest gains. Following the suggestion of Ferreira and Litchfield (1998), we exclude the three households with the highest income.[5] Our findings suggest that average earnings of the richest 10 percent of households fell by about 5 percent and the ratio of earnings of the richest remained about 14 times higher than the earnings of the poorest group. This is the main difference between the patterns for labor earnings and the trends found for household income per capita by Ferreira and Litchfield (1998), who find that average household incomes fell only for the poorest decile group.

In summary, these findings indicate that inequality in earnings remained roughly constant, with some redistribution toward the richest 10 percent and poorest 30 percent of households between 1987 and 1992, and toward the middle and upper-middle classes between 1992 and 1994.[6] These changes are reflected in a decrease of the earnings ratio of the richest relative to the poorest groups from 1987 to 1994.

Measures of Inequality of Labor Earnings

The impression obtained from Table 6-1, that inequality did not increase from the mid-1980s to mid-1990s, is also confirmed when we look at other measures of inequality. In what follows we provide evidence on changes in inequality by means of the Gini coefficient and another measure, which Montenegro (1998) called the spread.

The Gini coefficient measures inequality as the ratio to the mean of half the average over all pairs of the absolute deviations between people; there are $N(N-1)/2$ distinct pairs in all, so that the Gini is:

$$G = \frac{1}{\mu N(N-1)} \sum_{i<j} \sum_i \left| x_i - x_j \right|$$

$$(2)$$

Note that when everyone has the same, μ, the Gini coefficient is zero, while if one person has $N\mu$, and everyone else zero, there are $N-1$ distinct nonzero absolute values differences, each of which is Nμ, so that the Gini is 1.

A natural measure of dispersion is the difference between two quantiles of the wage distribution, as for example the ratio 10:1 presented in Table 6-1. Following this idea and using the results from the quantile regression, we construct our second measure, the spread. The spread is defined as the difference between the 90th and the 10th quantile for given values of the covariates. Hence, in contrast to the 10:1 ratio presented in Table 6-1 and the Gini coefficient, we control for the observed characteristics of the individuals. As mentioned in the section on methodology, the covariates in our specification refer to schooling, experience, and experience squared. We estimate the coefficients on these variable for the 10th and 90th quantiles and calculate the respective predicted wages, evaluated at the mean value of the covariates. The precise definition of the inequality index used here is

$$S_p = anti \log(\hat{w}_{.90} - \hat{w}_{.10}) - 1 \tag{3}$$

This measure tells us that the "representative" agent will earn $(S_p+1)^*$ wage if he or she were in the upper tail of the distribution instead of being in the lower tail (that is, $S_p=2$ means that the representative agent would earn three times as much in the upper tail as he or she would earn in the lower tail).

Table 6-2 lists the two measures of wage inequality that are calculated using the data of the University of Chile. It shows that the Gini coefficient increases from 43 in 1960 to 58 in 1987–88, and decreases to 45 until 1996. Similarly, the 0.90–0.10 spread rises from 2.1 in 1960 to a high of 4.6 in 1987–88, and then declines to 3.3. Both measures, but especially the Gini, exhibit shorter-term sensitivity; for example, the Gini drops sharply during "bad times" (for example, in 1974–75 and 1982). The Gini coefficient and spread clearly show that 1987 marks a break from the past in both direction and association with the economy's health: wage inequality begins to fall during a period of healthy economic growth. By 1996, the Gini coefficient for wage inequality was the same as during the years of the Allende administration, while the 0.90–0.10 spread was only marginally higher. Hence, we can conclude that wage inequality among male workers in Santiago has been marked by a significant decline since 1987.[7]

Figure 6-1 illustrates the results of Table 6-2.[8] Montenegro (1998) also finds the same trends for both more- and less-experienced workers, for workers in both the private and public sectors, and for white-collar work-

TABLE 6-2
Measures of Wage Inequality

Year	Gini coefficient	Spread
1960	42.5	2.1
1962	45.5	2.5
1969	48.9	2.9
1975	41.1	3.1
1980	49.1	3.3
1982	51.2	3.8
1985	51.5	3.3
1987	57.6	4.6
1990	53.9	4.2
1991	52.4	3.7
1992	47.4	3.8
1993	45.4	3.4
1994	45.9	3.3
1995	46.3	3.2
1996	45.4	3.3

Note: For males working 35 hours or more. Spread is the relative difference between the predicted values of the 0.90 and 0.10 percentile wage, evaluated at the mean of schooling, experience, and experience squared.
Source: Montenegro (1998) using University of Chile Household Surveys.

ers. As can be seen in Figures 6-2 and 6-3, the difference in the level of the two measures relative to the normalization for the entire sample is low for white-collar workers, but high for blue-collar workers. However, when we compare the evolution of the two inequality measures, it is easy to see that the trends in the Gini coefficient and spread are very similar for blue-collar worker. This is true to a much lesser extent for white-collar workers.

To check whether our results are robust, we calculate CASEN estimates of wage inequality for 1992 and 1994 and find that they are very similar to University of Chile estimates for the same years.[9] Gini coefficients computed from the two sources for 1990 differ somewhat: the CASEN estimate is about 0.46, while the University of Chile surveys yield a coefficient of 0.53. Although different, this result is not surprising given the fact that the University of Chile survey is basically an urban survey and thus does not include rural areas. This implies that some economic activities, including agriculture, mining, fishing, and forestry, are excluded from the sample.

FIGURE 6-1
Trends in Wage Inequality: Whole Sample

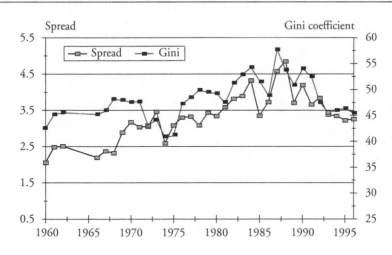

Source: Montenegro (1998); University of Chile Household Surveys for Greater Santiago.

Levels of and Returns to Education

Returns to education have been a topic of considerable interest in Chile. It is believed that the rates of return to education have increased because of structural changes in the economy (see for example, Riveros 1990) and because international trade has rewarded educated workers relatively more. We do not attempt to summarize the literature here, but concentrate instead on the issue of whether returns to education differ across income groups, and whether these differences have increased or decreased over time. Here, we pay special attention to the returns to education because it is an important part of the government's strategy to address concerns regarding income inequality. We start by providing some descriptive statistics on the level of education, and then present our estimates on returns to education.

Table 6-3 reports the mean years of schooling by decile group (by household per capita income). Not surprisingly, workers from poorer households also have lower levels of education. On average, poorer labor force participants have no more than secondary schooling (about 6 to 7 years), which is a little more than half the level for the richest group (11 to 12 years). Roughly speaking, this implies that while the average labor force partici-

FIGURE 6-2
Trends in Wage Inequality: White-Collar Workers

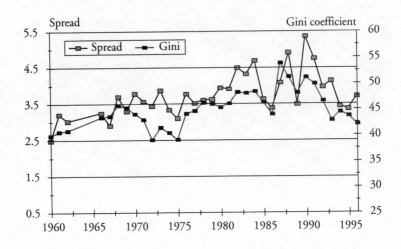

Source: Montenegro (1998); University of Chile Household Surveys for Greater Santiago.

FIGURE 6-3
Trends in Wage Inequality: Blue-Collar Workers

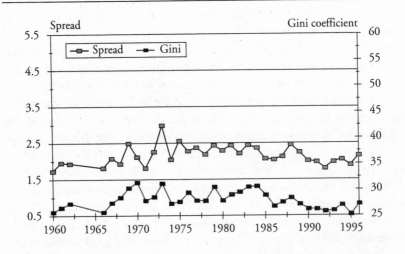

Source: Montenegro (1998); University of Chile Household Surveys for Greater Santiago.

TABLE 6-3
Mean Years of Completed Schooling, Population Aged 14 to 65

Decile Group	1987	1990	1992	1994
1	6.23	6.65	7.10	7.08
2	6.51	7.01	7.36	7.38
3	6.75	7.17	7.53	7.85
4	6.88	7.51	7.75	8.11
5	7.09	7.55	8.06	8.30
6	7.51	7.95	8.46	8.71
7	7.82	8.51	8.95	9.30
8	8.44	9.28	9.56	10.22
9	9.76	10.36	10.57	11.20
10	11.19	11.75	12.10	12.46
Average	7.93	8.57	8.87	9.19
Difference 10:1	4.96	5.10	5.00	5.38

Note: Decile groups are calculated using household per capita income.
Source: Authors' calculations using CASEN surveys.

pant from the bottom third of the household income distribution has at most some secondary education, the average labor force participant from the top third has completed at least a few years of postsecondary education.

Concerning the evolution of years of education from 1987 to 1994, Table 6-4 shows that schooling levels have increased across the board. Average schooling levels increased by a remarkable 1.25 years in the 8 years between 1987 and 1994, and the education levels increased for all groups in every survey year, except for the poorest 10 percent of households between 1992 and 1994. Absolute differences in schooling across groups did not narrow between 1987 and 1994. For example, the difference between the 10th and the 1st quantile increased from 5.0 in 1987 to 5.4 in 1994. However, when we take into consideration that the average increased at the same time, we find that the 10th and the 1st quantiles, as a percentage of the average, have decreased slightly from 0.63 to 0.59.

Figure 6-4 shows the results of mean and median regression for Greater Santiago (reported in Montenegro [1998] and reproduced here).[10] It can be seen that changes in the rate of returns to education for full-time working males closely correspond to changes in wage inequality measures discussed above. That is, the long-term trend is that rates of return rise from 1960 to 1986–87 (from about 11 percent to about 17 percent). They then

TABLE 6-4

Returns to Education by Schooling Level at Different Points of the
Conditional Wage Distribution, Full-Time Male Earners

(percent)

Level	1987			1990		
	0.1 decile	0.5 decile	0.9 decile	0.1 decile	0.5 decile	0.9 decile
All Spline:	9.8	13.0	15.4	7.3	9.5	14.0
0–4 yrs.	2.8	2.7	0.0	3.0	3.4	6.6
5–8 yrs.	4.0	7.3	10.5	4.7	3.7	5.6
9–12 yrs.	9.3	12.7	15.6	6.6	8.8	15.9
13+ yrs.	17.9	21.6	24.5	15.9	23.5	25.2
Level	1992			1994		
	0.1 decile	0.5 decile	0.9 decile	0.1 decile	0.5 decile	0.9 decile
All Spline:	7.2	10.2	14.7	8.5	10.7	14.8
0–4 yrs.	3.6	3.0	4.9	4.6	4.0	7.0
5–8 yrs.	4.3	5.1	6.3	5.4	5.4	9.0
9–12 yrs.	7.3	9.8	14.5	7.9	10.2	13.6
13+ yrs.	15.3	24.4	28.7	16.6	23.4	26.3

Note: Results for 1987 are calculated using monthly earnings; regressions for all other
years use hourly earnings.

Source: Authors' calculations using CASEN surveys.

decline to about 13 percent in 1996. Cyclical patterns are also similar for
wage inequality measures: rates of return fall during bad times (for example, during 1975–76 and 1981–82) and rise during periods of economic
prosperity. Once again, 1987 marks a break from this pattern. This finding, combined with the close conformity of trends in the distribution of
household income and labor earnings discussed in the above section, appears to validate the government's strategy of concentrating on education
as the instrument for reducing income inequality.

To shed some light on changes affecting the entire distribution, we
compute rates of return to education at different points of the conditional
wage distribution. The main results of quantile regressions from both University of Chile and CASEN data can be summarized as follows:

- The rates of return to education are systematically higher for higher
  quantiles: in Greater Santiago, the rates of returns for males are about
  10 percent for the 0.10 quantile, about 12 percent for the 0.25 quantile, about 15 percent for the 0.75 quantile, and about 18 percent for
  the 0.90 quantile regressions (see Figure 6-5). As can be seen in Table

FIGURE 6-4
Return to Education: Mean and Median Estimates, Whole Sample

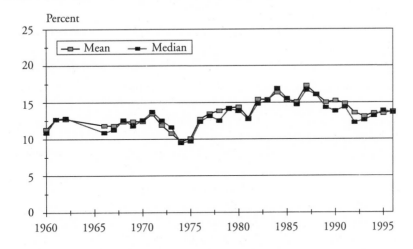

Source: Montenegro (1998); University of Chile Household Surveys for Greater Santiago.

6-4, these patterns are confirmed using CASEN data, though rates of
return are somewhat lower when the sample is extended to the entire
country. In another study, Montenegro (2001) also found very similar
patterns in the Chilean case, not only for men, but also for women,
with one very important difference: the returns to education at the
lower quantiles of the conditional wage distribution are significantly
higher for women than for men, but relatively similar in the higher
quantiles.

- For all quantiles, rates of return are higher for higher education levels: CASEN data indicate that rates of returns for 0 to 4 years of education are about 3 to 5 percent, rising to 5 to 8 percent, 8 to 15 percent, and 15 to 25 percent for groups with 5 to 8, 9 to 12, and 13 or
  more years of schooling, respectively.
- As can be seen in Figures 6-6 and 6-7, the level of returns to education for blue-collar workers are lower than those of white-collar
  workers at all quantiles. Furthermore, differences among quantiles
  are smaller for blue-collar workers. This hints at the fact that white-
  collar workers constitute a more heterogeneous group than blue-
  collar workers. Furthermore, the rates of return to education for
  blue-collar workers reveal a downward trend, while the opposite is
  true for white-collar workers at all quantiles. Under the assumption
  that usually people with low levels of education choose blue-collar

FIGURE 6-5
Return to Education: Quantile Estimates, Whole Sample

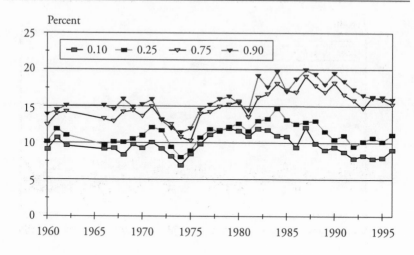

Source: Montenegro (1998); University of Chile Household Surveys for Greater Santiago.

FIGURE 6-6
Return to Education: Quantile Estimates, White-Collar Workers

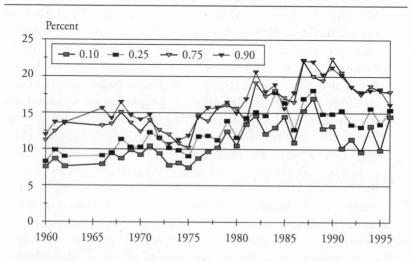

Source: Montenegro (1998); University of Chile Household Surveys for Greater Santiago.

FIGURE 6-7

Return to Education: Quantile Estimates, Blue-Collar Workers

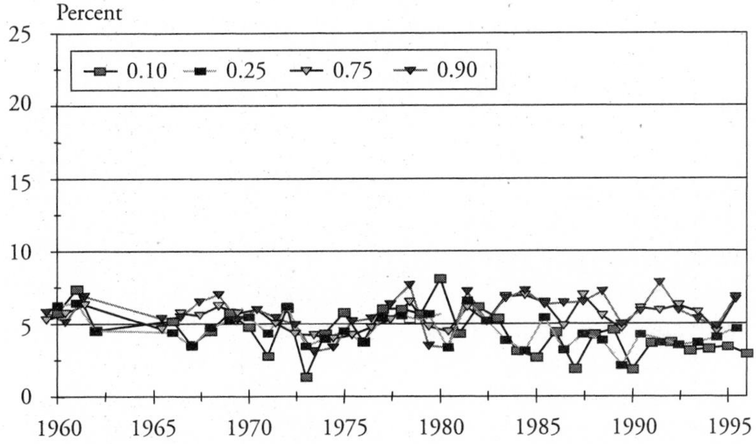

Source: Montenegro (1998); University of Chile Household Surveys for Greater Santiago.

jobs, this indicates that returns to low levels of education decreased from 1960 to 1995.

- Finally, as can be seen in Table 6-4, rates of return to education rise with the level of schooling at the first, fifth, and ninth percentiles. While the returns to up to four years of education ranged from 2.8 to zero percent in 1987, those of more than 13 years of schooling ranged from 18 to 25 percent. Similarly, in 1994, returns to education for the highest education groups were between 3.6 and 5.9 times higher than those of the lowest education group. Differences among returns to education for the highest and the lowest level of education did not increase between 1987 and 1994.

Do Children from Poor Families Obtain Less and Lower-Quality Education?

In the previous section, we found that poorer worker have lower levels of education and that returns to education are lower in the lower part of the conditional wage distribution. This raises the question of whether workers are poor because they have low levels of schooling, or whether they have low levels of schooling because they come from poor families.

This section discusses whether children from poor families obtain less and lower-quality education.

Concerning the quality of primary education, evidence exists that for any level of schooling up to grade 8, schooling outcomes are lower for children from poorer households. While the poor attend municipal or government-subsidized schools, richer children are more likely to attend private schools. Private school students have significantly higher scores in national *Sistema de Medición de la Calidad de la Educación* (Educational Quality Measurement System—SIMCE) tests administered in grades 4 and 8, indicating either that they attend better primary schools or that their socioeconomic status makes them more likely to do better. Lower achievement scores reduce the probability of going on to higher levels of schooling. This means that children from municipal or government-subsidized schools are less likely to continue their education.

Even if they go on to secondary school and higher levels of education, students from poorer households are more likely to enroll in vocational-technical education at the secondary level (see Cox Edwards and Dar 1995). However, returns to vocational-technical education—when estimated rigorously—are lower over the working life than returns to humanistic-scientific education (see, for example, Butelmann and Romaguera 1993). Again, this hints at the fact that workers from poorer households receive education with lower returns to education.

Table 6-5 shows that the parents of students in private humanistic-scientific secondary schools are about twice as schooled as those of students in vocational-technical schools. Parent education level is highest for students in unsubsidized private schools and lowest in municipal schools. Among the students who attend vocational-technical schools, those who go to corporation schools have relatively better-educated parents. At the same time, evidence on the labor market performance of students from corporation schools suggests the quality of education in corporation schools is better. The fact that parent education level is highly correlated with family income provides evidence that children from poorer families attend lower-quality schools. As for access to and type of tertiary education, children from poorer families are less likely to continue with postsecondary education, or at least to opt for cheaper programs, due to budget constraints.

Policy Implications: Reducing Earnings Inequality Through Labor Market and Education Policies

Given the importance of labor earnings in household income, and the importance of education in determining labor earnings, the link between ed-

TABLE 6-5
Education Level of Parents by Type of School Attended by the Child
(years of education)

Type	General	Vocational-technical		
		Commerce	Industry	Agriculture
Males				
Private				
Unsubsidized	14.2			
Subsidized	11.3	7.9	7.6	7.2
Corporation		9.3	7.9	7.3
Municipal	9.9	8.4	6.6	4.5
Females				
Private				
Unsubsidized	14.2			
Subsidized	11.3	7.3	7.2	4.2
Corporation		8.2	8.3	
Municipal	9.2	7.8	7.2	

Source: Cox Edwards and Dar (1995).

ucational attainment and income inequality is obvious. This link has been explicitly tested by researchers in Chile for an explanation of differences in regional poverty and inequality trends using rate of returns to education. Furthermore, it is also the fundamental reason for the government's belief that education and training are likely to be the best instruments for reducing poverty and inequality. In this section we quantify the effectiveness of investments in education in addressing the problem of inequality. Given that even effective education policies will take time to yield results, we discuss which steps could be taken that yield more immediate results. Finally, we address medium- and long-term solutions.

Quantifying the Likely Impact of Policy Measures

For policy purposes, it is important to disentangle the effects on labor earnings of education-related factors such as education level and education quality. Here, we attempt to do this using a standard technique employed in labor economics that decomposes the earnings differential between rich and poor workers into two parts: (a) the component accounted for by education levels, and (b) the component due to differences in rates of return to richer and poorer workers. We provide quantitative estimates of the likely payoff—in terms of lower earnings inequality—of the government's initiatives to improve access to secondary education and training for poorer households. Moreover, we shed light on measures that increase returns to education for poorer workers, such as improvement in the quality of education.

To obtain these estimates, we divide a sample drawn from the 1994 CASEN survey into the poor and nonpoor. The sample consists of about 43,000 male workers who reported labor earnings and worked at least 35 hours per week. We use a standard Mincerian human capital earnings function to characterize labor earnings; that is, one that uses completed schooling—split into splines of 0 to 4, 5 to 8, 9 to 12, and 13 or more years—and potential experience (age minus schooling minus 6 years) as the human capital variables. In the next step we decompose the mean earnings differences between the nonpoor and the poor into the component due to different "endowments" of human capital, and the component due to different rewards in the labor market given the same level of human capital.

Table 6-6 lists the estimated coefficients and variable means. The main findings are the following. First, the difference in log labor earnings between the poor and nonpoor is about 0.86 pesos, which corresponds to a difference in mean wages between nonpoor and poor (relative to the poor) of 1.38. This difference is reflected in lower levels of education and lower returns to education for any schooling level. Second, providing the poor with the same education levels as the nonpoor, while leaving unchanged the structure of rewards to education and experience faced by the poor, increases logwages of the poor by 0.30. Hence, under the assumption that the constant remains unchanged for the poor, their earnings would increase to 11.06. Consequently, increasing the education level of the poor would reduce the wage gap between the poor and nonpoor by about one-third. Third, providing the poor with the same labor market rewards to education and experience as the nonpoor, while leaving unchanged the education levels and years of potential experience of the poor, increases logwages of the poor by 0.41, and implies a reduction in the wage gap of about 50 percent.

These results imply that policies that increase education levels of the poor, and policies that increase returns to education, will help reduce the earnings gap between the poor and the nonpoor to a large extent. However, ensuring that the rewards to a year of schooling are the same for the poor and the nonpoor will have nearly twice the effect. Furthermore, much of the gains from improving access to schooling accrue at relatively high levels (9 or more years). In contrast, most of the gains from quality- and labor-related policy accrue at lower levels of schooling (0 to 8 years). Based on in-

TABLE 6-6

Decomposing the Poor and Nonpoor Earnings Gap
and Simulating Payoffs to Alternative Policies

	Returns		Means		Policy simulations	
Variable	Poor	Nonpoor	Poor	Nonpoor	Education access[a]	Quality & labor[b]
Schooling Splines:						
0–4 years	0.021	0.047	3.60	3.79	0.004	0.094
5–8 years	0.049	0.068	2.58	3.16	0.028	0.049
9–12 years	0.070	0.096	1.11	2.05	0.066	0.029
13+ years	0.025	0.187	0.07	0.59	0.013	0.011
Experience	0.042	0.056	20.93	20.64	–0.012	0.293
Experience Sq.* 100	–0.068	–0.078	665.0	678.4	–0.001	–0.067
Constant	10.052	10.279				
Log (earnings)			10.800	11.668	11.06[c]	11.17[c]
Earnings (pesos)			49,050	116,750	63,720	70,950

Note: All coefficients are significant at the 99 percent confidence level. The independent variable is the log of labor earnings. The sample consists of male workers aged 14 to 65.

a. Education access policy payoffs refer to the gains to the poor if the poor are given the same years of schooling as the nonpoor, but the labor market reward structure is left unchanged. Technically, the equivalent of the payoff is the product of poor coefficients and the difference in mean endowments between the nonpoor and the poor.

b. Quality and labor policy payoffs refer to the gains to the poor if the labor market reward structure faced by the nonpoor is now available to the poor, but their education endowments are left unchanged. The technical equivalent is the product of the endowments of the poor and the difference in coefficients between the nonpoor and the poor.

c. For education access, numbers refer to the constant of the poor plus the sum over the products of the poor coefficients and the respective mean endowment of the nonpoor. For quality and labor, the numbers refer to the constant of the poor plus the sum over the products of the nonpoor coefficients and the respective mean endowment of the poor.

Source: Authors' calculations using CASEN 1994 data.

ternational experience, improving the quality of primary and secondary schools is generally regarded as the best way to increase access to higher secondary and university education (see Ziderman and Albrecht 1995). Consequently, our results lead to the straightforward conclusion that education-related measures to reduce inequality are best focused on improving the quality of schooling at the primary and (junior) secondary levels.

The findings of Riveros (1995) also confirm our results. Using data from CASEN 1992, Riveros imputes that for the poor, the predicted income gain by giving the poor the same quality of secondary education as the nonpoor results in a 50 percent increase in their earnings. For the rich, the increase in earnings was less than 25 percent, which clearly hints at the fact that poorer students benefit more from improvements in school quality.

Differences in the quality of education obtained by the poor and the nonpoor may be only one reason why returns to education are low. Another reason may be labor market discrimination against jobseekers from poorer households. While discrimination against less-privileged jobseekers occurs in every country, its extent is difficult to quantify. It would be best (but not precisely) measured by the residual differences in rewards to human capital after differences in schooling levels and quality between the poor and nonpoor have been accounted for. In countries such as Brazil, India, South Africa, and the United States, observable characteristics such as race, caste, or ethnic origin are normally associated with discrimination. Chile is a relatively homogeneous country, so the extent of discrimination may be statistically difficult to determine. However, anecdotal evidence exists that appears to indicate that discrimination generally takes the form of restricted access—conditional on skill levels—to high-wage jobs for workers from poor households. This differential in access to better jobs would, for any given education level, increase earnings differences. Given that discrimination exists, poor-nonpoor differentials in rewards to education can be lowered by reducing labor market discrimination against poorer workers. The first best policy to achieve this goal is to outlaw discrimination through equal employment opportunity legislation. But these laws are difficult to enforce. Second-best policies, such as affirmative hiring practices and minimum wage legislation, may also be considered.

Immediate Solutions: Interventions in the Labor Market

Measures to improve the quality and accessibility of education, even if implemented immediately, will help only those in the school cycle. For most workers, help must come in the workplace. Potential measures to change the distribution of earnings in the immediate to short term include minimum wage increases, public training programs, and introduction of an unemployment compensation system. We examine the likely effects of the first two here. Chapter 7 addresses issues relating to severance benefits and the unemployment compensation system.

Lopez (1998) estimates that using reasonable values for the relevant parameters such as wage elasticity of labor demand, the impact of the 44 percent rise of the real minimum wage between 1989 and 1994 was a reduction in poverty of about 4.4 percent, or about one-eighth of total poverty reduction.[11] However, he cautions that this estimate is for a period when the real minimum wage was relatively low; that is, less than 30 percent of per capita GDP.

The effectiveness of the minimum wage as an instrument to reduce poverty declines as its level increases, because it may lead to an increase in unemployment, and hence may even become counterproductive—that is, it may increase poverty. This concern is strengthened by the strong correlation between unemployment rates of workers and the probability of their being in the lowest two decile groups. Lopez (1998) also finds, however, that during 1987–94, increases in minimum wages did not have any discernible effect on the distribution of per capita income, as measured by the Theil Index. These results cast doubts on the usefulness—given current levels—of increases in minimum wages as a device to reduce income inequality. Combined with the finding that wage inequality has been decreasing since the late 1980s, and that this can largely be attributed to economic growth combined with investments in human capital, these results form a strong case for not using minimum wage legislation as an inequality-reducing device. Furthermore, using the University of Chile's surveys, Montenegro and Pagés (2001) show that "unskilled workers in general—and the young unskilled in particular—see their probabilities of employment reduced in relation to prime-male skilled workers" when the minimum wage increases. Given that the unskilled workers are usually the workers in poverty, this result casts additional doubts on the usefulness of the minimum wage as a device for reducing income inequality.

Medium- and Long-Term Solutions: Postprimary Education Access and Quality

The results of our policy simulation suggest that improvements in education access and quality are likely to result in improved income distribution. Consequently, this paper supports the government's strategy of relying on education as a main device for reducing income inequality. Still, there are reasons to be cautious. On the one hand, returns from investment in education access and quality will take some time to accrue. Given that earnings inequality has been falling since 1990, reducing inequality is not as urgent as portrayed in the press and by some researchers. On the other hand, our results suggest that the payoff of improving education quality is nearly twice as high as the payoff of increasing access to education. Improvement in education quality, however, is more difficult to achieve than improvement in access to education.

At the secondary school level, perhaps the most direct impact of improvements in education on poorer segments of the population will come through improved quality of vocational-technical education. Poorer groups constitute a large share of this stream of education, and this is unlikely to change in the near future. As can be seen in Table 6-5, all vocational-technical schools are subsidized, (while some general schools do not receive subsidies), which is encouraging from an equity point of view. Among subsidized schools, vocational-technical schools receive larger per student subsidies, a pattern that is equity enhancing. Improvements in vocational education are therefore likely to benefit poorer households more than general secondary education.

In this regard, it is important to note that the *Estatuto Docente*[12] of 1991 is perceived as having slowed education reforms (see, for example, Cox Edwards 1997). For example, the statute assures tenure to teachers as long as their school is managed by the municipality. Consequently, teachers try to prevent municipal schools from being taken over by corporations, and since 1991 fewer corporation schools have been created. In the meantime, it is believed that the quality of education in municipal schools continues to decline, and the gap in quality between private, unsubsidized and municipal schools remains high. In late 1996 the government conceded sizable wage increases to teachers. The effectiveness of this measure in improving the quality of primary and secondary schools—without accompanying reforms to improve school management—is doubtful. Therefore, while all the evidence points to improvements in education quality at the primary and secondary level as necessary for sustainable reductions in wage inequality, the government faces serious institutional obstacles in making this happen. Given the government's obvious commitment to giving a higher priority to education and training, the remaining barriers are institutional rather than fiscal. And the *Estatuto Docente* is likely to be the main institutional barrier to improving educational outcomes and, through it, the distribution of earnings.

Conclusion

Between 1987 and 1992, average labor earnings increased by about 30 percent for the top and bottom quintile groups, and by about 20 percent for the middle classes. Between 1992 and 1994, average earnings fell for the top and bottom quintile groups, but rose modestly for the middle groups. Wage inequality, as measured by the Gini coefficient and the spread between the 90th and 10th percentile groups, rose between 1960 and 1987–88, but has declined significantly since then. This change of direction—first pointed out by Montenegro (1998) and confirmed by Ruiz-Tagle (1999)—has been missed or underemphasized by earlier studies.

These findings suggest that the government's emphasis on education as an instrument for combating inequality is appropriate, though this is tempered by the finding—based on quantile regression techniques—that rates of return to education have decreased slightly since 1987. Simple simulations using Oaxaca-type decomposition techniques suggest that further improvements in access to schooling by the poor will have relatively modest effects on earnings inequality, and this only at higher levels of education (grade 9 and above). Improvements in the quality of education appear to be twice as effective as improvements in access to schooling, and these returns to improvements in education quality are obtained largely at lower levels of schooling (0 to 8 years).

Using international experience as a guide, public training programs are not likely to have a significant effect on earnings inequality of employed workers. However, if these programs are well targeted, training programs and job search assistance may help some unemployed workers find jobs. This subject is taken up again in Chapter 7.

Notes

1. This correspond to the standard Mincer (1974) wage equation. Refinements and revisions of the assumptions can be found in Willis (1986) and Polachek and Siebert (1993).

2. Equation (2) assumes perfect capital and labor markets, which allows us to take earnings as a proxy for marginal productivity.

3. According to the censuses of 1960, 1970, 1982, and 1992, Santiago accounts, respectively, for 32, 35, 38, and 39 percent of the total population in each year.

4. A detailed description of the CASEN can be found in Ferreira and Litchfield (1998).

5. Ferreira and Litchfield (1998) claim that the incomes of the three richest households in the 1994 sample are true outliers.

6. It also appears that autonomous transfers prevented household per capita income from falling for decile groups 2 and 3, despite falls in real earnings per worker.

7. Using the same survey but different measures of income and several other measures of income inequality, Ruiz-Tagle (1999) arrives at the same conclusions—that is, that inequality declined significantly since 1987.

8. Annex Table 6.A.1 at the end of this chapter presents the same results for the whole available period and its breakdown by white- and blue-collar workers.

9. Hourly earnings are not available in the 1987 CASEN survey.

10. Annex Table 6.A.2 presents the returns to education by year, subsample, OLS, and QRM estimates.

11. During this period, average salaries rose by 22 percent, or half the rate of increase of minimum wages (Bravo and Vial 1997).

12. *Estatuto Docente* refers to the Law No. 19.070 (1991), which constitutes the labor regulation for the teaching staff and is a supplement to the Labor Code.

References

Atwood, Roger. 1996. "Clouds Mar Chile's Sunny Economic Horizon." *Business World Update* October 19–25: 12.

Bravo, D., and J. Vial. 1997. "La Fijación del Salario Mínimo en Chile: Elementospara una Discusión." *Colección de Estudios.* CIEPLAN, 45: 117–51.

Butelmann, Andrea, and Pilar Romaguera. 1993. "Educación media general vs. técnica: retorno económico y deserción." *Colección Estudios Cieplan* (38): 5–26.

Cox Edwards, Alejandra. 1997. In Indermit Gill, Fred Fluitman, and Amit Dar, eds., *Vocational Education and Training Reform: Matching Skills to Markets and Budgets*, Chapter 10. Washington, D.C.: Oxford University Press for the World Bank.

Cox Edwards, Alejandra, and Amit Dar. 1995. "Technical-Vocational Education in Competition: Evidence from the Chilean Reform of the Early 1980s." Poverty and Social Policy Department. World Bank, Washington, D.C. Draft.

Ferreira, Francisco, and Julie Litchfield. 1998. "Calm After the Storms: Income Distribution in Chile, 1987–1994." Draft.

Haindl, Erik. 1996. "Poverty and Income Distribution in Chile: A Survey." World Bank, Washington, D.C. Draft.

Leiva, Fernando. 1996. "Flexible Labor Markets, Poverty and Social Disintegration in Chile, 1990–1994: The Limitations of World Bank Policies." Paper presented at the World Bank, OXFAM draft.

Lopez, Ramon. 1998. "Poverty in Chile: Analyzing the Role of Minimum Wages and Other Factors Using Regional Evidence." *Economic Journal.*

Mincer, Jacob. 1974. "Schooling, Experience and Earnings." National Bureau of Economic Research, New York.

Montenegro, Claudio E. 1998. "The Structure of Wages in Chile 1960–1996: An Application of Quantile Regression." *Estudios de Economía* 25 (1): 71–98.

_____. 2001. "Wage Distribution in Chile: Does Gender Matter? A Quantile Regression Approach." Policy Research Report on Gender and Development No. 20, World Bank Development Research Group. World Bank, Washington, D.C. Processed. Available at www.worldbank.org/gender/prr/wp.htm.

Montenegro, Claudio E., and Carmen Pagés. 2001. "Who Benefits from Labor Market Regulations and Institutions? Chile 1960–1998." World Bank and the Inter-American Development Bank. Washington, D.C. Processed.

Polachek, S., and W. S. Siebert. 1993. *The Economics of Earnings.* Cambridge: Cambridge University Press.

Riveros, Luis. 1990. "The Economic Return to Schooling in Chile. An Analysis of its Long-Term Fluctuations." *Economics of Education Review* 9 (2): 111–121.

_____. 1995. "The Economic Impact of Improving the Quality of Secondary Education in Chile." Report prepared for the World Bank. University of Chile, Santiago.

Ruiz-Tagle, Jaime A. 1999. "Chile: 40 Años de Desigualdad de Ingresos." Departamento de Economía, Documento de Trabajo No. 165. Universidad de Chile, Santiago.

Willis, R. 1986. "Wage Determinants, A Survey and Reinterpretation of Human Capital Earnings Functions." In Orley Ashenfelter and Richard Layard, (eds.), *The Handbook of Labor Economics* 1: 525–602. Amsterdam: North Holland- Elsevier Science Publishers.

Wood, Adrian, 1997. "Openness and Wage Inequality in Developing Countries: The Latin American Challenge to East Asian Conventional Wisdom." *World Bank Economic Review* 11 (1): 33–57.

Ziderman, Adrian, and Douglas Albrecht. 1995. *Financing Universities in Developing Countries.* Washington, D.C: The Falmer Press.

ANNEX TABLE 6A-1
Trends in Hourly Wage Inequality

	Spread			Gini coefficient		
Year	Total sample	White collar	Blue collar	Total sample	White collar	Blue collar
1960	2.066	2.495	1.734	42.517	39.875	25.776
1961	2.492	3.205	1.959	45.158	40.612	26.619
1962	2.511	3.025	1.940	45.539	40.847	27.413
1966	2.200	3.251	1.822	45.188	43.392	25.738
1967	2.381	2.910	2.080	45.775	43.613	27.526
1968	2.323	3.702	1.938	48.145	45.695	28.541
1969	2.894	3.297	2.499	47.980	45.268	30.369
1970	3.174	3.786	2.119	47.542	44.069	31.436
1971	3.041	3.578	1.809	47.741	42.979	27.968
1972	3.048	3.443	2.262	43.088	39.059	28.640
1973	3.463	3.878	2.989	44.122	41.425	31.200
1974	2.595	3.341	2.044	40.743	40.428	27.354
1975	3.083	3.109	2.566	41.099	39.111	27.726
1976	3.299	3.783	2.278	47.162	44.100	29.495
1977	3.328	3.521	2.378	48.372	44.663	27.956
1978	3.084	3.616	2.186	49.789	46.233	27.885
1979	3.434	3.628	2.436	49.408	45.999	30.543
1980	3.341	3.954	2.293	49.133	45.358	27.948
1981	3.588	3.917	2.435	47.285	46.102	29.057
1982	3.821	4.496	2.207	51.163	48.243	29.582
1983	3.899	4.317	2.446	52.744	48.053	30.555
1984	4.329	4.689	2.367	54.159	48.456	30.686
1985	3.347	3.635	2.066	51.516	46.323	28.994
1986	3.732	3.384	2.039	48.695	44.001	26.855
1987	4.584	4.087	2.125	57.568	53.880	27.630
1988	4.852	4.911	2.453	53.660	51.180	28.499
1989	3.711	3.493	2.243	50.752	48.164	27.240
1990	4.199	5.358	2.014	53.916	51.145	26.294
1991	3.667	4.747	1.975	52.394	49.913	26.260
1992	3.843	3.970	1.804	47.369	46.620	25.820
1993	3.379	4.137	1.981	45.437	42.871	26.027
1994	3.346	3.436	2.043	45.886	44.472	27.078
1995	3.222	3.364	1.890	46.268	43.743	25.235
1996	3.256	3.716	2.152	45.362	42.136	27.305

Source: Unpublished data, Montenegro (1998).

ANNEX TABLE 6A-2
Returns to Education

Year			Total sample			
	OLS	Q=0.10	Q=0.25	Q=0.50	Q=0.75	Q=0.90
1960	0.114	0.091	0.101	0.109	0.124	0.138
1961	0.127	0.107	0.119	0.127	0.139	0.145
1962	0.127	0.096	0.111	0.129	0.142	0.151
1966	0.118	0.092	0.098	0.109	0.132	0.151
1967	0.118	0.093	0.102	0.113	0.129	0.146
1968	0.124	0.083	0.101	0.126	0.142	0.160
1969	0.124	0.098	0.106	0.118	0.144	0.149
1970	0.124	0.093	0.110	0.126	0.136	0.152
1971	0.134	0.101	0.121	0.137	0.150	0.159
1972	0.119	0.092	0.117	0.125	0.132	0.131
1973	0.108	0.082	0.095	0.116	0.125	0.120
1974	0.097	0.069	0.081	0.095	0.107	0.114
1975	0.101	0.085	0.089	0.097	0.103	0.120
1976	0.127	0.098	0.107	0.124	0.139	0.145
1977	0.135	0.111	0.119	0.132	0.142	0.152
1978	0.138	0.117	0.116	0.125	0.149	0.160
1979	0.142	0.120	0.122	0.141	0.152	0.163
1980	0.144	0.116	0.126	0.139	0.157	0.154
1981	0.128	0.109	0.116	0.127	0.135	0.144
1982	0.154	0.119	0.130	0.148	0.162	0.191
1983	0.154	0.117	0.132	0.153	0.167	0.176
1984	0.164	0.110	0.147	0.169	0.181	0.197
1985	0.153	0.109	0.131	0.155	0.172	0.170
1986	0.151	0.094	0.126	0.147	0.169	0.187
1987	0.173	0.121	0.128	0.167	0.191	0.200
1988	0.161	0.099	0.130	0.161	0.178	0.193
1989	0.150	0.090	0.115	0.143	0.169	0.179
1990	0.152	0.094	0.104	0.138	0.182	0.195
1991	0.149	0.088	0.110	0.144	0.166	0.184
1992	0.136	0.079	0.095	0.122	0.158	0.173
1993	0.131	0.083	0.102	0.126	0.147	0.165
1994	0.135	0.078	0.107	0.132	0.163	0.161
1995	0.135	0.080	0.101	0.139	0.159	0.162
1996	0.137	0.090	0.111	0.136	0.152	0.159

(Table continues on the following page.)

ANNEX TABLE 6A-2 (continued)

Year		White-collar workers				
	OLS	Q=0.10	Q=0.25	Q=0.50	Q=0.75	Q=0.90
1960	0.097	0.076	0.083	0.093	0.112	0.119
1961	0.111	0.087	0.099	0.120	0.124	0.136
1962	0.110	0.076	0.090	0.115	0.136	0.137
1966	0.117	0.079	0.091	0.119	0.132	0.156
1967	0.118	0.095	0.095	0.117	0.134	0.142
1968	0.127	0.087	0.114	0.130	0.151	0.164
1969	0.120	0.099	0.103	0.116	0.136	0.146
1970	0.117	0.093	0.103	0.122	0.124	0.140
1971	0.126	0.105	0.123	0.125	0.139	0.147
1972	0.113	0.094	0.116	0.123	0.126	0.114
1973	0.106	0.078	0.102	0.116	0.120	0.107
1974	0.103	0.081	0.099	0.103	0.108	0.112
1975	0.096	0.075	0.090	0.090	0.102	0.118
1976	0.127	0.087	0.118	0.128	0.146	0.143
1977	0.128	0.097	0.119	0.122	0.138	0.156
1978	0.137	0.103	0.113	0.135	0.157	0.156
1979	0.153	0.125	0.139	0.152	0.160	0.164
1980	0.140	0.105	0.116	0.149	0.156	0.149
1981	0.145	0.134	0.143	0.148	0.138	0.169
1982	0.168	0.146	0.151	0.165	0.191	0.206
1983	0.162	0.121	0.146	0.171	0.172	0.178
1984	0.174	0.130	0.178	0.170	0.180	0.188
1985	0.158	0.145	0.164	0.172	0.170	0.155
1986	0.143	0.110	0.127	0.156	0.164	0.177
1987	0.199	0.153	0.170	0.211	0.221	0.222
1988	0.187	0.170	0.181	0.186	0.200	0.220
1989	0.170	0.129	0.149	0.176	0.194	0.202
1990	0.187	0.132	0.149	0.201	0.224	0.212
1991	0.173	0.102	0.153	0.187	0.205	0.201
1992	0.160	0.114	0.134	0.171	0.185	0.185
1993	0.153	0.097	0.131	0.163	0.175	0.178
1994	0.165	0.132	0.156	0.176	0.186	0.180
1995	0.162	0.099	0.135	0.174	0.180	0.182
1996	0.160	0.145	0.154	0.174	0.178	0.161

ANNEX TABLE 6A-2

Year		Blue-collar workers				
	OLS	Q=0.10	Q=0.25	Q=0.50	Q=0.75	Q=0.90
1960	0.057	0.058	0.063	0.054	0.052	0.058
1961	0.058	0.074	0.065	0.053	0.057	0.051
1962	0.056	0.045	0.045	0.062	0.063	0.069
1966	0.049	0.052	0.044	0.050	0.046	0.054
1967	0.046	0.036	0.035	0.051	0.057	0.055
1968	0.050	0.045	0.047	0.048	0.056	0.065
1969	0.054	0.058	0.052	0.053	0.062	0.070
1970	0.054	0.048	0.055	0.063	0.057	0.052
1971	0.049	0.028	0.043	0.051	0.059	0.059
1972	0.058	0.061	0.062	0.065	0.050	0.054
1973	0.037	0.013	0.035	0.047	0.043	0.049
1974	0.038	0.043	0.040	0.034	0.042	0.031
1975	0.043	0.058	0.045	0.038	0.040	0.033
1976	0.045	0.038	0.037	0.045	0.042	0.051
1977	0.053	0.060	0.054	0.052	0.047	0.053
1978	0.057	0.060	0.056	0.060	0.053	0.063
1979	0.057	0.057	0.053	0.049	0.065	0.076
1980	0.057	0.081	0.056	0.037	0.047	0.034
1981	0.039	0.043	0.033	0.048	0.044	0.033
1982	0.057	0.062	0.065	0.056	0.061	0.072
1983	0.059	0.054	0.052	0.061	0.051	0.051
1984	0.047	0.031	0.038	0.066	0.068	0.067
1985	0.051	0.027	0.031	0.062	0.069	0.072
1986	0.056	0.044	0.054	0.061	0.064	0.063
1987	0.041	0.019	0.032	0.041	0.048	0.064
1988	0.054	0.042	0.042	0.053	0.069	0.064
1989	0.051	0.046	0.038	0.043	0.055	0.071
1990	0.033	0.018	0.021	0.039	0.046	0.049
1991	0.049	0.037	0.042	0.042	0.060	0.058
1992	0.052	0.037	0.039	0.051	0.059	0.078
1993	0.043	0.031	0.035	0.037	0.062	0.058
1994	0.048	0.033	0.036	0.057	0.057	0.052
1995	0.042	0.034	0.040	0.038	0.044	0.047
1996	0.054	0.029	0.046	0.051	0.066	0.068

Source: Unpublished data, Montenegro (1998).

7 Dealing with Employment Instability in Chile

Indermit S. Gill, Erik Haindl,
Claudio E. Montenegro,
and Claudio N. Sapelli

This chapter addresses the question of whether the combination of an open economy and a flexible labor market increased uncertainty in employment and earnings in Chile. Some authors, such as Leiva (1996), argue that since 1987 "the new jobs created tended to be low-paying, low-quality, short-term jobs concentrated in agriculture, trade, services and construction, precisely those sectors characterized by greater instability in employment." Concerns about increased precariousness of employment were commonplace even before the Asian and Russian financial crises, and are likely to gain even more attention today.

Although earnings inequality in Chile did not become worse in the 1990s, and indeed improved over the last decade (see Chapter 6), employment may nevertheless have become more precarious. That is, while workers enjoy higher earnings across-the-board, these earnings are believed to be more unreliable. Indeed, it is common to hear that Chilean workers are more likely to lose their jobs—and related benefits—now than at any point in Chile's history. Moreover, if employment in low-paying jobs became more precarious, this change might largely affect poor people. These concerns have fueled the debate over both the need for greater mandated job security and an unemployment insurance system (see, for example, Sapelli 1996; and Coloma 1996), and have even been used as an argument for erecting trade barriers.

In this chapter we provide evidence on the evolution of expected tenure and unemployment duration from 1962 to 1995. We use data from the University of Chile Households Survey and a model developed by Haindl (1985), which converts reported labor market stock data into flows. We will present basic issues and describe the methodology and the data used, discuss changes in expected tenure and unemployment duration and the relation evolution of unemployment rates across different income quantiles, and conclude with a discussion of policy implications.

Issues, Methodology, and Data

To assess whether employment has become more precarious in recent years, we use data from the University of Chile Household Surveys from 1962 to 1995. These are comparable annual surveys for Santiago. Each survey covers between 7,000 and 16,000 people, and between 3,700 and 5,400 active labor force participants. The sample is periodically updated to reflect the growth of the Greater Santiago Area, and the questionnaire has been modified in only minor aspects, making it possible to rely on fairly comparable information. The survey is conducted in June each year, and contains information on labor force participation (LFP) and employment during the week preceding the survey. It does not provide information on worker tenure. Consequently, the data set reveals direct evidence on stocks, such as the number of people employed or unemployed, but not on flows into and out of unemployment.[1]

Employment becomes more precarious if the probability of an employed worker losing his or her job increases, or if the probability of an unemployed worker finding a job decreases. The first translates into a reduction of the expected tenure on the current job (that is, the stability of employment). Accordingly, a decrease in the probability of finding a job corresponds to an increase in unemployment duration. Thus, the question of precariousness of employment refers to a *change* in employment status and, consequently, the *relevant labor indicators measuring precariousness are flows, not stocks*. Because our data set does not contain information on the relevant flows, we use a labor flows model, which converts data on current period stocks (for example, employment and unemployment) into current period flows. Furthermore, it allows us to calculate the probability of losing one's job when employed, and finding a job when unemployed, and the relevant prospective indicators, such as expected tenure and unemployment duration. The model was developed by and explained in Haindl (1985). See Technical Annex D for a summary.

To understand the functioning of a labor market, looking at flows is much more instructive than looking at stocks. For example, a 5 percent unemployment level is consistent with 200,000 people (out of a population of 4 million) unemployed during one year; but it is also consistent with 3.2 million people working during the whole year and 800,000 people that are unemployed for an average of three months; and is also consistent with the 4 million workers unemployed for an average of 18 days a year. Obviously, the implications for the unemployed people are different in each case. Hence, to see how difficult it is to find a job in a given period, we need to complement the information given by the unemployment rate with the expected time that people will spend unemployed, or with the probability of finding a job in a given period.

The labor market is usually characterized by large flows of workers into or out of employment. Those unemployed consist of workers who either quit their job or were fired. When the flow of people entering employment exceeds the flow of people leaving employment, the employment level increases. In addition, the people who are unemployed are not the same throughout the year. On the contrary, people are continuously entering and leaving the pool of unemployed. Hence, unemployment increases if the flow of the number of people into unemployment exceeds the flow of people out of unemployment. Furthermore, there is also a continuous flow of people who are entering or leaving the labor force. The interaction of these flows drives the patterns of the unemployment and employment levels, and hence the unemployment rate. In mathematical terms we can describe the evolution pattern in terms of a difference equation that relates the change in the stock variables to the relevant flows. Solving the system of equations in finite differences, we obtain flows from the stock variables.

The interrelations among the flow variables and the stock variables in the labor market can be presented in a schematic diagram. Figure 7-1 shows that the employment level at the end of a period is equal to the stock of the people employed at the beginning of the period, plus the number of people hired during the period, minus the number of people leaving employment. In the same way, the unemployment level at the end of a period is equal to the number of unemployed people at the beginning of the period, plus the number of people that entered the unemployment pool minus the number of people that left unemployment. People who enter the unemployment pool are either people who quit their jobs or were fired, or people who entered the labor force but have not yet found employment. People who leave unemployment may either have found a job or have left the labor force.

FIGURE 7-1
Labor Force Flows

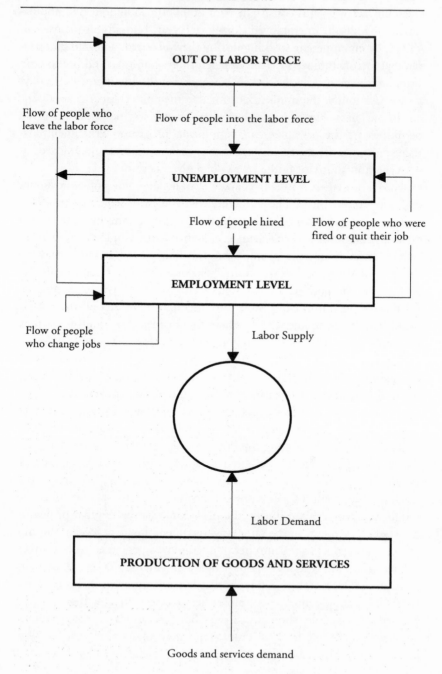

Has Chile's Employment Grown More Precarious?

Precariousness of employment may be estimated by expected tenure on current job and unemployment duration. Expected tenure captures the stability of employment, which critically depends on the incidence of unemployment, that is, the probability of losing one's job. Unemployment duration, that is the time a worker is likely to be without work, depends on the probability of a worker exiting unemployment. This is estimated as the probability of finding a job in a fixed period of time, using the sample of unemployed jobseekers.

Is Expected Tenure Decreasing?

To give a first insight about the evolution of tenure from 1962 to 1995, Figure 7-2 plots the expected tenure (in months).[2] A first glance reveals that expected tenure increased until 1969, followed by a large downward trend, which was reversed at the end of the 1980s. Expected job tenure declined from more than seven years in 1969 to less than three years in the early 1980s. It increased to more than six years in 1992, and remained over four years in the following years. On average, expected tenure seems not to have decreased during the last years.

Often concerns about increased precariousness of employment are based on statistics that show falling average tenure (on current job), which is not confirmed in our data. Moreover, it is true that changes in average tenure may be driven by structural and legislative changes in the economy, such as less restrictive firing laws or an increased creation of low-quality, short-term jobs. But this is only one part of the story. Business cycle fluctuations and changes in the composition of the labor force by age and gender may matter as well. Additional information on employment flows and labor force entrants is displayed in Table 7-1. Table 7-2 sheds light on the changes in the LFP of women.

Recessions usually lead to a decrease in employment. This arises from the fact that although during recessions the number of quits decreases, layoffs usually increase by a much higher amount. Furthermore, flow into employment decreases as fewer new jobs are created. Blanchard and Diamond (1990) show that for the United States, recessions are associated with large increases in job destruction, but small decreases in job creation. This suggests that we expect tenure to decrease during recessions. Chile faced two major recessions in 1975 and 1982–83, which reduced GDP growth significantly below its long-term trend. As can be seen in Table 7-1,

FIGURE 7-2
Expected Job Tenure

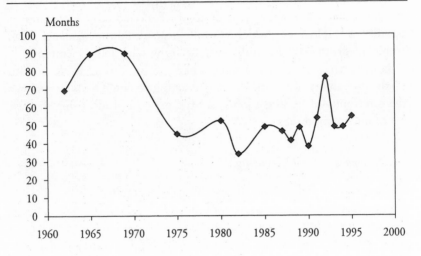

Source: Authors' calculations using University of Chile Household Surveys for Greater Santiago.

employment decreased during the two recession years by more then 7 percent. These changes were largely driven by an increase in the flows out of employment. Tenure fell from 7.5 years in 1969 to 3.8 years in 1975, and reached its lowest point during the 1982 recessions, at 2.8 years.

Changes in labor force composition may also affect expected tenure. For example, it is reasonable to expect that mean tenure of women is lower than that of men. Consequently, an increase in the participation of women in work is likely to decrease average tenure. As can be seen in Table 7-2, women's LFP rate increased from 26.4 in 1987 to 33.7 in 1994.

The trend decline in expected tenure until 1985 may in part be explained by a steady increase in first-time job seekers, which rose from about 25,000 to 100,000. Furthermore, the age composition of the labor force mattered. Pagés and Montenegro (1999) show that in 1987 about 70 percent of male workers aged 15 to 25 had been on the job less than two years. The same was true for only 35 percent among male workers aged 26 to 50, and to 20 percent among male workers aged 51 to 65. This indicates that for men there exists a strong link between tenure and age. In 1996 the percentage of low-tenure workers was slightly higher among all age groups. From 1987 to 1990 mean tenure decreased, especially for older workers. This is likely to have negatively influenced average tenure.

TABLE 7-1

Estimates of Labor Force Entrants and Employment Flows, 1962–95

	Labor force entrants			Employment flows			
Year	First time ('000)	Reentrant ('000)	Total (% of LF[a]) (%)[a]	Outflow ('000)	Inflow ('000)	Net (% of total[a]) (%)[b]	Expected Tenure (months)
1962	26	5	4.0	128	159	4.2	69.3
1965	30	20	6.2	104	152	6.2	89.3
1969	45	0	4.6	123	166	4.6	89.7
1975	73	–39	3.0	273	199	–7.2	45.1
1980	91	11	6.0	267	365	8.4	52.3
1982	70	–46	1.6	452	356	–7.5	34.0
1985	99	–10	2.0	324	433	8.2	49.0
1987	76	–22	3.2	389	438	3.2	46.6
1988	88	–39	2.8	451	525	4.8	41.5
1989	78	21	5.5	404	490	5.4	48.7
1990	74	–15	3.1	540	590	2.9	38.2
1991	62	–17	2.3	395	497	5.8	53.8
1992	94	44	6.9	293	432	7.4	76.6
1993	79	–51	1.3	491	512	1.0	49.1
1994	105	–19	4.0	496	556	2.9	49.1
1995	85	5	4.0	—	—	—	54.8

— Not available.

Note: Calculated using Haindl (1985) labor flow model.

a. As percentage of last year's labor force.

b. As percentage of last year's employment.

Source: Authors' calculations using University of Chile Household Surveys for Greater Santiago.

However, from 1985 onward, employment rates for all age groups increased due to a period of sustained growth, but employment rates for older and middle-age groups increased at a faster rate. This should have had a positive affect on expected tenure. In another paper, Montenegro and Pagés (2001) show that the gender composition of the working labor force also matters: women tend to have, on average, less tenure than men. This fact, plus the fact that female participation in the working labor force has been steadily increasing over time (Montenegro 1998), should have had a negative effect on expected tenure.

To summarize, we find that expected tenure does not appear to be falling anymore. While expected tenure did fall until 1982, it has exhib-

TABLE 7-2

Labor Force Participation Rates, Females Aged 14 to 65

Decile Group	1987	1990	1992	1994
1	12.3	14.7	12.8	15.3
2	13.1	16.3	15.7	18.7
3	14.4	16.2	18.8	21.9
4	17.1	20.7	24.8	25.1
5	20.1	24.5	27.9	29.4
6	24.1	30.0	33.3	33.8
7	28.9	33.1	37.2	39.6
8	31.9	35.1	40.0	41.8
9	37.2	41.5	44.2	46.6
10	54.0	53.1	57.9	57.0
Average	26.4	29.3	32.2	33.7
Ratio 10:1	4.4	3.6	4.5	3.7

Note: Decile groups are calculated using household per capita income.
Source: CASEN surveys.

ited an upward trend since then. This is true even though female LFP increased during this period and the percentage of low-tenure workers was slightly higher among young, prime-aged, and older workers, which is likely to have affected expected tenure negatively. While it is legitimate for workers, policymakers, and nongovernmental organizations to be concerned about job permanency, these findings provide a compelling argument that changes in labor legislation to reduce involuntary turnover may not be necessary. Proponents of reform of labor laws may thus be trying to fix a problem through government mandates that the market appears to have already fixed in the decade of economic prosperity since 1987.

Is Unemployment Duration Increasing?

Employment does not only become more precarious if expected tenure on a current job decreases, but also if unemployment duration, that is the time a worker is likely to be without work, increases. Frequent job changes do not necessarily imply unstable labor earnings, given that workers who change jobs may not enter the unemployment pool. Instability in earnings hence is determined by the probability of becoming unemployed, and the probability of exiting unemployment. To examine whether Chilean workers have experienced increases in instability of earnings, we analyze the changes in average (expected) unemployment duration and the probability of exiting unemployment. The results are reported in Table 7-3 and plotted in Figures 7-3 and 7-4.

The main findings are:

- Unemployment rates—plotted in Figure 7-3—rose steadily from 5 percent in 1962 to about 16 percent during 1974–75, fell until 1980, and peaked again at about 22 percent during 1982–83. Since then, unemployment rates have fallen sharply, and appear to have stabilized at about 7 percent. If unemployment rates were a guide to the precariousness of labor earnings, the last 15 years have seen a sizable decline in precariousness. CASEN surveys since 1987 show that while unemployment rates are higher for workers from poorer households (see Table 7-4), trends in unemployment appear to be the same for all workers.

TABLE 7-3

Estimates of Unemployment Rates and Duration, 1962–95

		Probability of Finding Job in:				Expected
Year	Rate (%)	1 mo. (%)	3 mos. (%)	6 mos. (%)	1 yr. (%)	Length (months)
1962	5.1	26.7	60.6	84.4	97.6	2.7
1969	6.2	20.1	48.9	73.9	93.2	4.0
1975	16.1	9.6	26.2	45.5	70.3	9.4
1980	11.8	16.7	42.2	66.6	88.9	5.0
1982	22.1	8.9	24.5	43.0	67.5	10.2
1985	16.4	12.7	33.6	55.9	80.5	6.8
1987	12.2	15.6	39.8	63.8	86.9	5.4
1988	10.9	19.8	48.4	73.4	92.9	4.0
1989	9.1	21.3	51.3	76.2	94.4	3.7
1990	9.6	23.1	54.6	79.4	95.7	3.3
1991	7.4	23.4	55.0	79.8	95.9	3.3
1992	6.0	25.0	57.9	82.3	96.9	3.0
1993	6.3	26.8	60.9	84.7	97.7	2.7
1994	6.8	26.2	59.8	83.8	97.4	2.8
1995	6.8	26.1	59.7	83.8	97.4	2.8

Note: Calculated using Haindl's labor flow model. Unemployment rate is averaged for March, June, September, and December.

Source: Authors' calculations using University of Chile surveys for Greater Santiago.

FIGURE 7-3
Unemployment Rate and Duration, Greater Santiago

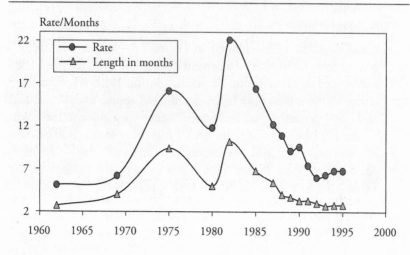

Source: Authors' calculations using University of Chile Household Surveys for Greater Santiago.

FIGURE 7-4
Probability of Finding a Job, Greater Santiago

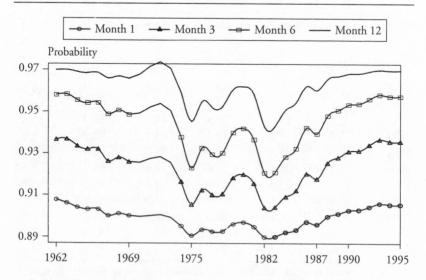

Source: Authors' calculations using University of Chile Household Surveys for Greater Santiago.

- Since 1962, unemployment duration has risen from less than three months, and it reached its highest level of 10.2 months during the recession of 1982–83. Since then it has declined steadily, reaching 2.8 months in 1995. As can be seen in Figure 7-3, unemployment duration closely tracks the pattern of unemployment rates. This hints at the fact that changes in unemployment rates are due rather to fluctuations in the time needed to find employment (that is, unemployment duration), and to a lesser extent to changes in the likelihood of losing one's job in the first place (that is, unemployment incidence).[3]
- Table 7-3 and Figure 7-4 also provide evidence on the probability of finding employment within a certain time period. A first glance at Figure 7-4 reveals that the probability of finding a job dropped largely during the recession years. From 1982 the probability of finding a job increased continuously and came to a halt in 1993. For example, the probability of exiting unemployment in three months or less (that is, an average duration of about 1.5 months) was about 6 percent in 1962, falling to about 30 percent during 1982–83 and rising to about 60 percent again.
- The probability of a worker joining the ranks of the long-term unemployed (defined as being unemployed for more than one year) was negligible in 1962, and after rising significantly in the 1970s and early 1980s, declined to close to zero in 1995. These findings provide strong evidence that the labor market has become an increasingly reliable source of earnings for labor force participants.

Precariousness and the Poor

An important question for policy reasons is whether unemployment is a phenomenon largely experienced by the relatively rich. But unemployment of workers—especially primary earners—may be an important determinant of a household's relative position in the per capita income distribution. Marcel and Solimano (1994) suggest that changes in unemployment rates are important in explaining short-term fluctuations in the income distribution through losses in the share of the poorest households. Cowan and de Gregorio (1996) point out that, almost tautologically, unemployment is highest among those with lowest incomes. Even for the employed, a rise in informal work during bad times leads to a deterioration of work conditions.

Therefore, before discussing the policy implications of any findings on the problem of precarious employment, we briefly examine whether un-

employment rates differ for rich and poor households, and whether fluctuations in unemployment rates differ significantly for wealthy and poorer
households. A person is considered unemployed if he or she did not work
last week and looked for a job. Hence, we are not able to distinguish between short-term and long-term unemployed. Unemployment rates are
calculated using the microdata sets of the *Caracterización Socioeconómica
Nacional* (CASEN) for the years 1987, 1990, 1992, and 1994.[4]

Tables 7-4 and 7-5 report unemployment rates for men and women.
During 1987–92, average male unemployment rates fell steadily from almost 9 percent to 4.7 percent, and then rose to about 6 percent in 1994.
Female unemployment rates are higher, but exhibit similar trends. They
amounted to 10.5 in 1987 and decreased to 7.1 in 1992. Furthermore, Tables 7-4 and 7-5 shed light on unemployment rates for different decile
groups of household income. As expected, unemployment is significantly
correlated with being in a poorer household for both men and women:
workers in the poorest 10 percent of households are almost four times
more likely to be unemployed than the average worker. This ratio does not

TABLE 7-4
Average Unemployment Rates, Men Aged 14 to 65
(percent)

Decile Group	1987	1990	1992	1994	Change[a]
1	33.0	26.3	16.9	21.1	−36.1
2	13.9	11.3	7.7	8.1	−41.7
3	10.8	9.7	6.8	7.4	−31.5
4	9.6	8.6	4.2	6.7	−30.2
5	7.4	6.3	3.8	6.0	−18.9
6	7.5	6.2	4.3	4.5	−40.0
7	6.4	3.5	2.9	3.7	−42.2
8	5.3	3.8	2.8	3.3	−37.7
9	3.5	2.8	2.1	1.9	−45.7
10	1.4	1.9	0.7	1.9	35.7
Average	8.9	7.1	4.7	5.9	−33.7
Ratio 1: Average	3.7	3.7	3.6	3.6	

Note: Unemployment is defined as, "Did not work last week and looked for a job."
Decile groups are calculated using household per capita income.

a. Change from 1987 to 1994 is 80 percent with respect to 1990, but 500 percent with
respect to 1987.

Source: CASEN surveys.

TABLE 7-5
Average Unemployment Rates, Women Aged 14 to 65
(percent)

Decile Group	1987	1990	1992	1994	Change[a]
1	38.7	35.2	28.1	36.8	−4.9
2	27.3	25.7	19.5	26.0	−4.8
3	22.0	16.9	16.6	20.3	−7.7
4	16.0	12.5	13.6	13.9	−13.1
5	14.5	10.8	7.3	10.3	−29.0
6	10.0	12.5	7.6	9.4	−6.0
7	6.2	7.2	6.1	7.4	19.4
8	7.9	5.2	3.9	7.0	−11.4
9	6.1	4.4	3.7	4.1	−32.8
10	3.8	1.2	0.1	1.8	−52.6
Average	10.5	9.2	7.1	9.7	−7.6
Ratio 1: Average	3.7	3.8	4.0	3.8	

Note: Unemployment is defined as, "Did not work last week and looked for a job." Decile groups are calculated using household per capita income.

a. Change refers to percent change from 1987 to 1994 with respect to 1987.

Source: CASEN surveys.

change much over the years, which may indicate that unemployment is always critical in determining household income—the variable used to classify households into decile groups.

From 1987 to 1994 the average unemployment rate for men decreased by 33.7 percent, and for women by 7.6 percent. Looking at the different income deciles it can be seen that the change in unemployment ranged from 30 to 46 percent for most decile groups. For the highest decile group the unemployment rate increased, mainly driven by the change from 1992 to 1994. The median decile group realized a relatively low decrease in unemployment rate of only 18.9 percent. For women, the upper three and the fourth and fifth decile groups faced the highest decrease in unemployment rates. The lowest three decile groups also faced a reduction in unemployment rates, but to a lower extent: among these groups percentage changes in unemployment rates range from 4.8 to 7.7 percent.

Short-term fluctuations in unemployment rates by decile group defy simple characterizations, however. For men, unemployment rates decreased from 1987 to 1992 among all decile groups. Changes in unemployment rates range from 37 percent for the third decile group to 56 percent for the fourth decile group. Women faced a negative change in unemployment rates throughout this period. However, the range of changes among decile groups is much larger among women. It extends from a 1.6 percent decrease for the sixth decile group to a 97 percent decline for the highest decile group. The bottom three decile groups faced a decline in their unemployment rates of approximately 26 percent.

The overall decrease in unemployment rates was reversed from 1992 to 1994. Unemployment rates increased for all decile groups, with the only exception being the eighth decile group of men. For men, the increase in unemployment rates was lowest for the sixth decile group (4.6 percent) and highest for the ninth decile group (171.1 percent), while women faced increases ranging from 2.2 percent (fourth decile group) to 795 percent (sixth decile group).[5]

During the entire time period, no clear relation is visible between decile group and change in unemployment rate. However, the overall increase in unemployment rates from 1992 to 1994 may well have given rise to concerns. The question that needs to be answered is whether this requires changes in labor legislation related either to dismissals or unemployment compensation.

Policy Implications: Reducing Precariousness Through Labor Market and Education Policies

Since the early 1980s, expected tenure has increased, while unemployment rates have declined steadily, and duration of unemployment has fallen significantly. Long-term unemployment—defined as being unemployed for more than one year—has declined to negligible levels. Future labor market reforms may require introducing unemployment insurance schemes and improving the education system for those who have difficulties finding jobs.

Is an Unemployment Insurance System Needed?

Concerns regarding the precariousness of employment have fueled a debate over whether an unemployment insurance system is needed in Chile. From the evidence on labor flows presented above, it appears that these concerns are largely unfounded. The probability of a worker being without earnings is low: the unemployment rate was less than 6 percent in 1997. For the average worker, unemployment duration was less than three months in 1995, and has been falling over the last five years. Long-term unemployment was not pervasive: more than 60 percent of job seekers find employment in less than three months, and almost all find work within a year. These results are consistent with the findings of Edwards and Cox Edwards (2000), who show that Chile experienced both a reduction in persistence and in the natural rate of unemployment. In cases of unjustified dismissal, the labor code ensures that workers get a severance payment of one monthly wage for each year of tenure, with a maximum of 11 months. With expected tenure at 4.5 years and the expected duration of unemployment at three months, at least on average, therefore, this severance payment seems to be adequate in helping job seekers maintain their standard of living while looking for work.

But there is a demand for income support during unemployment even in labor markets where unemployment rates are low, and Chile's unemployment rates climbed into the double digits in 1999. As pointed out in Chapter 1, severance payments may be a rather inefficient and inequity-enhancing means of providing financial support to the unemployed. Transforming severance payments into a deferred compensation scheme would increase efficiency of the labor market. In 1990, the Aylwin government introduced the option of an unemployment fund for workers with tenure above six years, as an alternative to the job security protection. If the workers chose the unemployment fund the employer made a monthly contribution of 4.11 percent of taxable monthly wages to a savings account bearing the worker's name. While employees have no access to a severance package if dismissed with just cause, they can always withdraw the money accumulated in the unemployment fund independent of the reason for dismissal. In 2001, Chile replaced the traditional severance pay arrangements with individual severance accounts, essentially mandating self-insurance (with little pooling of risk), thus eschewing alternatives that involve substantial pooling of risk, such as conventional unemployment insurance programs like those in all OECD countries.

But for countries like Chile that have relatively balanced labor laws, the strong prejudice against insurance schemes that involve pooling of unemployment risk among formal sector workers should be reconsidered. The economic rationale for this is that pooling makes sense when the unemployment risk faced by the median worker is low and noncovariate. This appears to have been the case in Chile until the late 1990s (unemployment rates rose from 6.1 percent in 1998 to 9.7 percent in 1999, before falling to about 9.0 in 2001). In our view, there are few strong theoretical reasons to think that Chile would be wrong to consider some pooling of unemployment risks, given its strong insurance fundamentals, that is, comprehensive macroeconomic reforms, generally balanced labor legislation, and strong administrative capacity. (See de Ferranti and others 2000 for a discussion of these concepts.) If a private market for insuring against unemployment were to arise under the circumstances generally prevailing in Chile (low long-term unemployment, low to moderate incidence of unemployment), it would probably offer an instrument of the pooled type. So there is an argument that the government should correct this market failure with a similar instrument (the alternative being mandatory self-insurance such as individual accounts). See Table 7-6 for a summary.

We could still justify arguments against such schemes for practical reasons, one of them being administrative capacity concerns. But administrative capacity can always be built, and it is generally built while—not before—implementing a public intervention. Besides, the Chilean government has shown that it can competently set up and manage social assistance schemes that, by most accounts, are more administratively demanding than social insurance programs.

Another argument against conventional unemployment insurance programs is moral hazard—that is, the possibility that an employee might engineer a job separation to gain access to unemployment benefits. Two points are relevant here. First, any insurance scheme runs the risk of moral hazard that reduces labor market efficiency, but policymakers deal with this problem all the time because their public policy objective is welfare, not efficiency, maximization. Second, moral hazard can be minimized by keeping benefit levels low or by making insurance premia reflect risk levels by, for example, experience-rating.[6]

The presence of a large number of informal workers creates a problem for any formal unemployment insurance (UI) scheme. The most obvious one is that it becomes difficult for the UI administrator to determine whether a claimant is in fact unemployed, or simply working in an unregistered job. This is not strictly a moral hazard problem because it is not legally abusing the system. But it is a legitimate concern. Countries such as Argentina have tried to deal with this problem by making collecting these benefits costly in terms of time (for example, claimants have to collect payments in person, during peak business hours, and face long queues). The other problem may be one of adverse selection, where the low-unemployment-risk workers may choose to be informal, while high-risk workers choose to be formal. What is likely to be a more serious issue is that a formal UI system could discourage informal UI mechanisms.

Guasch (1999) recommends combining individual savings accounts and conventional unemployment insurance with a part of worker contri-

TABLE 7-6

Income Support Programs for the Unemployed: Findings and Policy Implications

Measure	Nature of instrument	Advantages and disadvantages	Policy implication
Individual saving accounts	Self-insurance—no pooling of risk	Low labor market efficiency costs, but welfare reduction especially for poorer workers.	Should be considered by countries that have high unemployment, especially where labor reforms are only a distant possibility.
Severance pay	Pooling over small group—globalization makes group even smaller	Almost no advantage. Little pooling of risk, entails labor market inefficiency, makes labor relations contentious, and is administratively challenging.	Possibly the worst form of unemployment support in a globalized economy.
Public works and training programs	Market-type insurance elements—implicit pooling of risk	Can reach informal sector workers and the poor, but can entail high leakages in the form of nonlabor costs when investment element is made a priority. Training programs show less leakage but also lower coverage potential.	Should be considered for a part of workforce, but not a universal scheme. Permanent schemes allow for better balance between consumption smoothing and investment over the economic cycle.
Unemployment insurance	Market-type insurance—explicit pooling of risks	Most pooling of risk can be used to address both idiosyncratic and aggregate risk, and hence serve as automatic fiscal stabilizer, generally politically popular. May be administratively demanding.	Should be considered by governments that have carried out comprehensive economic reforms; labor market disincentive effects can be reduced by keeping benefits frugal and mimicking the market as much as possible in design.

Source: de Ferranti and others (2000).

butions going toward a general fund to complement individual accounts of workers who have not reached levels of saving that would allow minimum unemployment benefits when dismissed from work. It appears that Chile has adopted precisely such a system.

Since it is unlikely that even the strongest administrative efforts will considerably reduce informality in Chile, and so a good fraction of the workers will not be covered by the contributory insurance system, the government should also think of other insurance mechanisms for such workers. Public works programs are the main candidates, but there may be others (such as transfers conditioned on participating in job search assistance programs or training programs). Obviously, these schemes will be noncontributory and hence financed through general taxation, but perhaps the government should be encouraged to think of such programs as social insurance and not assistance (the main difference being that one tends to think of the latter as temporary—for example, existing in bad times—and the former as more permanent—that is, existing in both good and bad times). There is, of course, a significant antipoverty element in these programs: de Ferranti and others (2000) report that Argentina's work-conditioned transfers and Mexico's training-conditioned transfers appear to help mainly labor force participants from the poorest 40 percent of households.

There is also the option of providing cash or in-kind transfers to people below the poverty line: since unemployment appears to be particularly pernicious for the lowest two decile groups (see Tables 7-4 and 7-5), this would help the poorest among the unemployed. Another approach used in the past that proved to be quite successful was to provide low-wage work for the poor through, for example, the *Programa de Empleo Minimo* (Minimum Employment Program) and the *Programa Ocupacional para Jefe de Hogar* (Occupational Program for Households Heads), rather than to subsidize unemployment. Finally, the most disadvantaged job seekers, especially those who have been unemployed for long periods, may lack marketable skills or may require assistance with a job search. This provides an argument for helping job seekers acquire relevant skills through public retraining programs, and assisting them with job placement.

Are Government-Sponsored Training Programs Helping the Poor?

The Ministry of Labor's *Servicio Nacional de Capacitación y Empleo* (SENCE) is cited worldwide as an example of good practice in encouraging in-service training and in helping unemployed workers find jobs (see Gill, Fluitman, and Dar 1999). SENCE regulates the tax credit for training, and also plays an active role in funding training courses for target groups (Cox Edwards and Dar 1995). In 1995, 430,000 people were trained under the tax credit scheme at a cost of $35 million ($24 million public, and $11 million private). The redistributive aspects of SENCE's activities are:

- *Tax Credit System.* The higher the salary of the trainee, the lower the tax credit to firms for training. For salaries below 10 minimum wages, the tax credit is for 100 percent of the training cost. For salaries above this, the tax credit is only 50 percent of the cost, and this ratio falls further as the salary increases.
- *Scholarships System.* SENCE provides training scholarships for specific groups, such as youth aged 15 to 24, ex-convicts, and rural women. These programs appear to help the relatively disadvantaged segments, but it is not clear that the participants are the worst off. In 1996, for example, about 55 percent of those participating in the training program for youth, *Chile Joven,* had completed at least 12 years of schooling, and another 27 percent had completed 9 to 11 years of schooling.
- *Apprenticeship Schemes.* Since 1994, SENCE has subsidized about 10,000 apprenticeships for disadvantaged job seekers in firms. Initially, the government provided 100 percent of the wages during the apprenticeship period, which was about 8 to 10 months. Since 1995, SENCE has provided 40 percent of wages for the apprentices, with the firms paying the remainder.

In general, SENCE's programs appear to be well designed and efficiently administered. However, none of them has been rigorously evaluated. The tax credit system is likely to be equality enhancing, but we are not aware of any systematic evaluation of the incidence of these expenditures. Similarly, it is difficult to determine whether the scholarship system is effective. Based on a survey of *Chile Joven,* Paredes (1996) recommends that the program be evaluated to resolve the tension between targeting the most vulnerable and ensuring high effectiveness. The same is true for the apprenticeship system. The program is quite new, and as a consequence no systematic evaluation exists yet.

Rigorous evaluation of training programs and other similar labor market interventions is seldom found—not only in Chile, but across the world. Even in OECD countries, almost half of all evaluations are nonscientific and few contain a rigorous analysis of costs (Dar and Gill 1998). This is surprising because public retraining schemes are usually an important component of the total package of assistance for those laid off due to plant closure or restructuring. Furthermore, they include programs to assist other unemployed people. The main benefit of rigorous evaluations is that they are critical in resolving the contradiction between equity and efficiency objectives. (See Gill and Dar [1995] for an illustration using evaluations of public training programs in Hungary.)

Scientific evaluations, when they are conducted, show poor results for retraining programs. Some programs resulted in modest gains in reemployment probabilities, but wage changes are generally insignificant. Evaluations indicate that retraining programs are generally no more effective than job search assistance (JSA) in increasing either reemployment probabilities or earnings. Finally, retraining programs appear to be two to four times more expensive than JSA. Since JSA yields outcomes in terms of earnings and reemployment probabilities that are not worse than those of retraining programs and is also cheaper, it is more cost-effective than retraining in assisting displaced workers to get jobs.

To illustrate the importance of doing rigorous analysis, we use Hungary's experience with retraining programs. A nonrigorous evaluation of Hungarian public training programs would have led to increased support for programs that recruited young and educated job seekers from better-off regions that have high placement rates and earnings. Rigorous evaluation yielded a different result. In Hungary, public training programs appear to be substitutes for attributes that lead to higher reemployment probabilities in the absence of any intervention—for example, being younger, more educated, and from more dynamic regions. That is, the program's value added (in terms of improving labor market outcomes) is greater for relatively disadvantaged job seekers, such as older, less-educated workers from worst-off regions. Consequently, targeting job seekers who are relatively disadvantaged in terms of age and education, or who come from relatively backward regions, would appear to better serve *both* equity and efficiency objectives than simply ensuring support for programs whose retrainees have high reemployment probabilities and earnings gains.[7] Concerning the effect of public training programs on earnings, aggregate results of the evaluation of Hungarian public training programs show that when differences in characteristics of program participants and control groups (such as age, sex, education, and skills) are controlled for, retraining is at best marginally successful. This leads to the conclusion that public training programs do not increase earnings. However, because retraining programs might increase reemployment probabilities, they might marginally reduce volatility of earnings.

In summary, experience in both OECD and middle-income countries does not appear to justify large-scale training programs for the unemployed. Rather, it indicates that retraining programs are more beneficial for some groups of job seekers than others, and hence should be carefully targeted to specific types of job seekers. However, it is difficult to predict who will benefit most from retraining. Since public training programs are expensive, modest pilot programs might be implemented first, and then rigorously evaluated. Retraining can then be tightly targeted to those for whom it is found most cost-effective. For both equity and efficiency reasons, Chile would do well to institute rigorous evaluation mechanisms for SENCE's training programs.

Summary and Conclusions

Concerning the evolution of expected tenure the main results are, first, expected job tenure declined from about seven years in the 1960s to three years in the mid-1980s; since 1987, however, expected tenure has risen to 4.5 years and appears to be increasing. Thus while concerns of declining expected job tenure (increased precariousness) appeared to be well founded between 1960 and 1982–83, they are unwarranted since 1982–83. Second, in part, the trend decline in expected tenure until 1985 can be explained by a steady increase in first-time job seekers, the number of which rose from about 25,000 to 100,000. First time job seekers can reasonably be expected to be more likely than reentrants to change jobs. With a decline in the absolute number of labor force entrants, it is likely that expected tenure will continue to rise. Third, cyclical fluctuations in labor demand may result in shorter-term fluctuations in expected tenure. Thus, for example, expected tenure fell during the recession years of 1975–76 and 1982–83. Years of economic prosperity are associated with increases in expected tenure, and this basic relationship has not changed over the years.

Analyzing the changes in expected unemployment duration and the probability of exiting unemployment, we find that:

a. Unemployment rates rose from 5 percent in 1962 to about 16 percent during 1974–75, and peaked at about 22 percent during 1982–83; since then, unemployment rates have fallen sharply to less than 7 percent by 1997, before rising to about 10 percent in 2000.

b. Unemployment duration rose from less than 3 months to about 10 months in the two decades since 1962, and has since fallen to below 3 months. The duration of unemployment tracks unemployment rates closely, implying that there have not been significant long-term changes in the *incidence* of unemployment.

c. The probability of exiting unemployment in 3 months or less (that is, an average duration of about 1.5 months) was about 60 percent in 1962, falling to about 30 percent during the 1982–83 recession, and rising to about 60 percent again.

d. The probability of a worker joining the ranks of the long-term unemployed (defined as being unemployed for more than a year) was negligible in 1962, rose significantly in the 1970s and early 1980s, but declined to almost zero by 1995.

These findings indicate that the Chilean labor market has become an increasingly reliable source of earnings for labor force participants, and while expected tenure fell until 1982–83, it has exhibited an upward trend since then. The duration of unemployment rose until the late 1980s, but has fallen sizably since then. Unemployment rates decreased from 1982–83 on, increased from 1992 to 1994, fell again between 1995 and 1998, and spiked upward due to the global economic crisis in late 1998. These findings provide a compelling argument that government initiatives to address the problem of earnings instability for individual workers may be needed, but these should be instead of, and not in addition to, the mandated severance payments system that existed until 2000. A welfare-enhancing action by the government might be to provide facilities to insure against unemployment. In 2001, the Chilean government introduced an unemployment insurance program, which largely relies on mandated self-insurance.

Notes

1. For more information on the data set see Chapter 6.

2. Even though it would be very interesting to see the tenure calculations conditional on labor force characteristics such as gender or age, this was impossible to achieve given the small size of the sample. Using a different Chilean survey, Pagés and Montenegro (1999) and Montenegro and Pagés (2001) look at this topic in more detail.

3. The expected unemployment duration is different from the one reported in Edwards and Cox Edwards (2000) due to the different methodologies used (Edwards and Cox Edwards used a duration model instead of a flow model).

4. The first CASEN survey was conducted in 1985, but it is widely reported to be less reliable; that is, it is of inferior quality than and less comparable with subsequent surveys.

5. The increase in the 10th percent decile group of women exceeds 795 percent; however, it is not mentioned here because it is very susceptible to outliers.

6. Experience-rating means that unemployment tax rates vary according to the frequency with which an employer's workers have filed for unemployment benefits. This transfers the problem of determining unemployment risk onto the employer, but makes employees who have frequently filed unemployment insurance benefits less attractive to future employers.

7. Generally, training programs should not be targeted to a specific group. Which group or groups should benefit from training programs might depend on such factors as the country and its educational system. For example, in Mexico training programs appeared to help educated workers more than other groups.

References

Blanchard, Oliver Jean, and Peter Diamond. 1990. "The Cyclical Behavior of the Gross Flows of U.S. Workers." *Brookings Papers on Economic Activity* 2:85–142.

Coloma, Fernando. 1996. "Seguro de desempleo: teoria, evidencia y una propuesta." *Cuadernos de Economía* 33 (99): 295–320.

Cowan, Kevin, and Jose de Gregorio. 1996. "Distribution and Poverty in Chile Today: Have We Gained or Lost Ground?" Ministry of Finance, Chile. Draft.

Cox Edwards, Alejandra, and Amit Dar. 1995. "Technical-Vocational Education in Competition: Evidence From the Chilean Reform of the Early 1980s." Poverty and Social Policy Department, World Bank, Washington, D.C. Draft.

Dar, Amit, and Indermit Gill. 1998. "Evaluating Retraining Programs in OECD Countries: Lessons Learned." *The World Bank Research Observer* 13 (1): 79–101.

de Ferranti, David, Guillermo Perry, Indermit Gill, and Luis Serven. 2000. *Securing our Future in a Global Economy.* Washington, D.C.: World Bank.

Edwards, Sebastian, and Alejandra Cox Edwards. 2000. "Economic Reforms and Labour Markets: Policy Issues and Lessons from Chile." *Economic Policy: A European Forum* 0 (30):181–217.

Gill, Indermit, and Amit Dar. 1995. "Costs and Effectiveness of Retraining in Hungary." Report No. IDP-155, Internal Discussion Paper, Europe and Central Asia Region. World Bank, Washington, D.C.

Gill, Indermit, Fred Fluitman, and Amit Dar, eds. 1999. *Skills and Change: Constraints and Innovation in Reform of Vocational Education and Training.* Washington, D.C.: World Bank.

Guasch, José Luis, 1999. "An Alternative to Traditional Unemployment Insurance Programs: A Liquidity-Based Approach Against the Risk of Earnings Losses." Unpublished note. World Bank, Washington D.C.

Haindl, Erik. 1985. "Un modelo para la determinación de flujos y parámetros dinámicos en el mercado del trabajo." *Estudios de Economia* 12, Marzo. Universidad de Chile.

Leiva, Fernando. 1996. "Flexible Labor Markets, Poverty and Social Disintegration in Chile, 1990–1994: The Limitations of World Bank Policies." Paper presented at the World Bank, OXFAM draft.

Marcel, Mario, and Andres Solimano. 1994. "The Distribution of Income and Economic Adjustment." In Barry P. Bosworth, Rudiger Dornbusch, and Raul Laban, eds. *The Chilean Economy: Policy Lessons and Challenges.* "Washington, D.C.: The Brookings Institution.

Montenegro, Claudio E. 1998. "The Structure of Wages in Chile 1960–1996: An Application of Quantile Regression." *Estudios de Economia* 25 (1): 71–98.

Montenegro, Claudio E., and Carmen Pagés. 2001. "Who Benefits from Labor Market Regulations and Institutions? Chile 1960–1998." World Bank and the Inter-American Development Bank, Washington, D.C. Processed.

Pagés, Carmen, and Claudio E. Montenegro. 1999. "Job Security and the Age-Composition of Employment: Evidence from Chile." Office of the Chief Economist, Working Paper No. 398. Inter-American Development Bank, Washington, D.C.

Paredes, Ricardo. 1996. "Evaluación Programa Chile Joven." Universidad de Chile, Santiago.

Sapelli, Claudio. 1996. "Modelos para pensar el mercado de trabajo: Una revisión de la literatura chilena." *Cuadernos de Economia* 33 (99): 251–276.

8 Some Guidelines for the New Decade: Summary and Conclusions

INDERMIT S. GILL
AND CLAUDIO E. MONTENEGRO

IN THE LAST DECADE, many Latin American countries have undertaken far-reaching economic reforms. In many countries the direct role of government in production has been scaled back through privatization of state enterprises and functions. The region has led the world in reforming social security. Almost all countries have eased restrictions on capital flows within and across countries. Even land reform, while not widespread, has been carried out in some countries. Largely absent from this litany of achievements is far-reaching labor reform to match the changes in how product and factor markets now operate.

The lack of far-reaching or comprehensive labor reform should not be viewed as arising from a judgment by Latin Americans that labor reform is relatively unimportant for economic outcomes, though that claim, too, is sometimes made. There are few things that affect the welfare of individuals and households as directly and deeply as efforts to obey and avoid labor market rules and regulations. The apparent lack of success at the policy level in vigorously addressing labor issues is accompanied by widely expressed concerns about labor market outcomes: opinion polls in the region reveal, for example, that 3 out of every 10 Latin Americans regard poor employment and wage prospects as the most important problem facing them. Many important labor market indicators, such as unemployment rate, informal sector size, and wage differentials, worsened

215

during the 1990s. The coexistence of widely expressed concern with policy inaction appears to stem from disagreement on what changes would help, and the particularly difficult political economy of reform in this area.

To narrow the divergence of views somewhat and move the debate from fiery rhetoric to cooler calculations of the payoffs and tradeoffs involved in labor reform, this book advocates a quantitative approach to some of the main labor market concerns facing countries in the region. Two points deserve mention here. First, while neither quantitative labor economics nor its application to analysis of developing countries is new, this book breaks some new ground in applying such analysis to a wide range of labor policy issues in developing countries. Second, while this book examines labor policies in only three countries in Latin America (Argentina, Brazil, and Chile), and hence provides policy recommendations for just the problems faced by these countries, the policies illustrate techniques and approaches that might be applicable in other countries in the region, for other times and, indeed, even in other parts of the developing world.

Argentina, Brazil, and Chile in the Regional Context

Following are some of the principal labor policy issues faced by Argentina, Brazil, and Chile in the 1990s, and their prospects as they entered the new decade.

- Argentina faced a high level of unemployment—about 15 percent—for which both labor demand and supply factors could be responsible. Under the macroeconomic constraints facing the country, labor legislation is identified as a major policy area for reform.
- Brazil confronted high costs of public employment that have led to large government deficits and public debt. Onerous levels of taxation, combined with problems of labor legislation, are central to the phenomenon of widespread and growing informality, which—by one measure—accounted for more than 50 percent of employment.
- At the time of the study, Chile had policies that led to a decade of wage and employment growth, but which a large number of Chileans believe have led to growing income inequality and uncertainty of employment. For those not content with high average wages and low unemployment, labor reform held high promise as an effective remedy. At the end of 1999 high unemployment rates of about 10 percent had compounded these concerns.

Readers familiar with other countries in the region and around the world will recognize some or all of these phenomena—high unemployment, public-private labor market segmentation, informality of employment, growing earnings inequality accompanying economic growth, and increased uncertainty of employment even when accompanied by low levels of unemployment.[1]

Data compiled by the Economic Commission for Latin America and the Caribbean (ECLAC), ILO, IDB, and the World Bank suggest that these three countries are not unusual within the region in terms of broad labor market indicators in the 1990s:

- Real wage growth during 1990–97 in the sample countries spans the full range in the region from the lowest (Brazil with almost –6 percent) to the highest (Chile with 32 percent).
- In terms of employment growth, the sample countries have both relatively low employment growth (Argentina with 0.4 percent) and relatively high employment growth (Chile at 3 percent).
- In terms of labor force growth, the sample countries are in the low range in the region: Brazil with 1.7 percent and Argentina and Chile with 2.1 percent.
- In terms of unemployment and female participation rates, the sample countries are again not different from the rest of Latin America.

The particular labor market issues facing the three countries studied here during the 1990s are closely related to their general economic conditions. First, all three have reduced annual inflation rates from above 1,000 percent to less than 10 percent, shifting the focus from just macro imbalances to a mix of micro and macro concerns. This shift results in heightened concerns about factor markets, including labor. Second, as countries move beyond stabilization and through fiscal adjustment, the nature of the concerns becomes predominantly microeconomic. Third, as fiscal adjustment is completed and the economies hit a period of sustained growth, the concerns are almost exclusively related to micro imbalances. This shift in focus from macro to micro is illustrated in this book by examining three countries at different macroeconomic stages.

The three countries studied faced different macroeconomic challenges in the 1990s. Brazil was studied during a stage of stabilization initiated in 1994, while it was still struggling to begin a serious fiscal adjustment. Argentina was midway through fiscal adjustment, having undergone stabilization in the early 1990s. Chile was studied during a stage of sustained growth, having completed its stabilization and fiscal adjustment in the

1980s. These countries therefore span a broad spectrum in terms of their macroeconomic performance:

- In the early and mid-1990s, Chile had experienced sustained and high gross domestic product (GDP) growth rates of more than 8 percent per year, Argentina had more variable but still impressive growth rates of about 6 percent, but Brazil had experienced wildly oscillating growth rates averaging less than 3 percent.
- Chile and Brazil faced income inequality levels that were among the highest in the world, while Argentina had inequality levels that are average by Latin American standards but are high relative to OECD countries.
- Brazil had averaged a high fiscal deficit of about 5 percent of GDP, Argentina's government accounts were relatively balanced, and Chile's completion of fiscal adjustment by the late 1980s shows up in consistent surpluses in the 1990s, rare among Latin American countries.
- Chile enjoyed relatively low rates of inflation, having consolidated its stabilization through fiscal adjustment in the 1980s; Argentina had reduced its rate of inflation from triple to single digits during the early 1990s through some fiscal restraint, but mainly through monetary discipline imposed by adopting currency convertibility; and Brazil had just begun the process of consolidating the stabilization achieved by the adoption of a new currency and a tight monetary stance, by beginning a fiscal adjustment that threatened to be difficult and protracted.
- In terms of external sector performance, Argentina, Brazil, and Chile represented the middle ground in Latin America, with current account deficits averaging 1.4, 0.4, and 2.8 percent of GDP respectively during 1990–97.

It should be reemphasized that evidence that the countries and problems studied here are representative of other countries in the region should not be interpreted as a claim that the policy solutions proposed here can be applied without additional analysis in, say, Mexico or Colombia, simply because they face general economic conditions that seem similar to those in Argentina, Brazil, or Chile. In fact, we have made precisely the opposite point in this book. On the question of whether labor laws affect employment and earnings outcomes, for example, the general message of the book is that a country's economic and political history are critical determinants of the manner in which labor legislation affects wages and employment, so that labor markets must be studied and understood country by country to arrive at policy recommendations that have any chance of being implemented.

Stabilization, Public Employment, and Informality in Brazil

The two chapters on Brazil examine the public and private sector labor market during a period of stabilization and attempt to initiate fiscal adjustment. The Real Plan, adopted in July 1994, brought down annual inflation rates from about 3,000 percent in 1993 to less than 5 percent by 1998. But the currency-based stabilization depended on the government's ability to rein in public sector expenditures, a large part of which is personnel related. Since personnel expenditures have been difficult to cut—due to a combination of constitutional guarantees of generous pensions and tenure for government workers and a lack of political consensus—attempts to control budget deficits have been centered on raising general tax revenues and earmarked contributions. At about 30 percent, the tax-revenue-to-GDP-ratio in Brazil is one of the highest in the developing world. A plethora of earmarked taxes are believed to raise the cost of labor in the formal, regulated sector by two-thirds of wage levels or more. The share of informality—measured as the fraction of workers who paid social security and severance fund contributions—rose from 40 percent in 1980 to almost 60 percent by the end of the 1990s.

Chapter 2 tackles the issue of public employment. Based on the general finding that the ratio of public employment to the total (less than 9 percent in the mid-1990s) is not abnormally high by international standards, but the financial burden of public employment is quite high (more than 12 percent of GDP), the approach adopted is that the problem is not best solved by only cutting employment. A common problem with public employment reform has been the high incidence of reversal of actions a few years after the reforms were undertaken. For public employment reform to be sustainable and to reduce the probability of later reversals, it should be based on the principle of labor market efficiency. The most important rule in this regard is that compensation for government workers should not be vastly out of line with pay and employment conditions in the private sector.

In 1995, the conventional wisdom in Brazil was that government workers received considerably lower compensation than similar workers in the private sector—their pensions were more generous, but this was simply delayed compensation for a lifetime of relatively low pay. Chapter 2 summarizes the first attempt in Brazil to systematically quantify public-private differences in compensation (pay, pensions, and stability of tenure). Quantification of salary differences was the most important, both because the magnitudes were hotly disputed, and because pension benefits are viewed almost as a continuation of salary payments upon completion of active service under the Brazilian pension regime for government workers.[2] Using nationwide household survey data, Chapter 2 provides estimates of human capital earnings functions designed to determine the premia attached to public employment. That is, the empirical analysis examines whether, on average, people with similar observable skills and other characteristics such as education, tenure, age, gender, race, and location obtain significantly different compensation in government and private employment. These earnings functions were estimated for workers at all levels (federal, state, and municipal) and in all branches (public administration, education and health, military, judiciary, legislature, and public enterprises) of government.

Results at this level of aggregation obviously miss many differences that might exist between public and private workers, but the level of detail at which empirical analysis was conducted was purposefully matched to address the questions being raised in the national debate on this subject, and was also constrained by tractability concerns. Pension and job stability differences between government and private sector workers were also estimated at the same level of detail. In qualitative terms the findings surprised some people, but the magnitudes surprised many more. Chapter 2 reports that in the mid-1990s, when Brazil initiated its fiscal adjustment efforts, public-private differentials in salaries and pensions were large:

- Compared with equally qualified workers in the private sector, salaries of public employees were 30 to 50 percent higher for federal administration and judicial and legislative workers, 20 to 35 percent higher for employees in federal and state enterprises, roughly the same for state civil servants, and 5 to 15 percent lower for municipal administration and education and health sector workers.
- Compared with their private sector counterparts, pension levels of civil servants were 25 to 50 percent higher, depending on their salary level, gender, and occupation.

Despite the aggregate nature of the analysis, such findings can help to derive policy actions that explicitly consider labor market efficiency. The results suggested that efforts to reduce government payroll expenses in Brazil should focus on lowering salary and pension levels at the federal level, a mix of salary restraint, reduced pensions, and reduced employment at the state level, and reductions of employment combined with pension restraint and selected pay increases at the municipal level. The focus on relative rather than absolute benefits also implied that, while reductions in public-private salary and pension differences and revocation of tenure rights of civil servants would both reduce the fiscal burden and increase labor market efficiency, so would the reform of selected private sector labor laws that introduce distortions, decrease labor demand, and raise informality in Brazil, which may in turn lower expected job stability, salary, and pension benefits in private employment. Chapter 3 tries to identify the aspects of labor legislation that most urgently require attention.

As one of the contributors to *Custo Brasil*—the abnormally high costs of doing business in Brazil—labor legislation that allegedly both raises labor costs and makes them more uncertain had been a topic of some discussion for the last decade. The introduction of the *real* and the resultant fall in inflation removed an instrument for keeping real wages flexible, increased openness resulted in unemployment rates rising steadily (especially for more experienced industrial sector workers in areas such as São Paulo), and the nature of the stabilization plan left little recourse to devaluation as an alternative to wage flexibility. These factors resulted in a steady buildup of pressure for labor market reforms. A sharp rise in open unemployment rates in early 1998 precipitated by the Asian crisis of October 1997 brought the debate on labor market reforms to the forefront in mid-1998.[3]

Brazil's experience suggests that the economic and political history of a country is a critical determinant of which labor laws influence wages and employment, and which are not binding. Long periods of high inflation, illiteracy of the workforce, and biases in the design and enforcement of labor legislation bred by the country's socioeconomic history are all important in determining the reach of labor laws.[4] Contrary to conventional wisdom, these factors are shown to affect labor market outcomes even in the sector regarded as unregulated or informal.

Following accepted practice in Brazil, Chapter 3 distinguishes regulated from unregulated employment by determining whether or not the contract has been ratified by the Ministry of Labor—that is, whether or not workers have a signed work booklet (carteira de trabalho). It then examines the degree of adherence to labor laws in the formal and informal sectors, and finds "pressure points"—that is, evidence of the law on minimum wage, work-hours, and payment timing being binding on outcomes—in both the formal and informal sectors of the Brazilian labor market. Some of the findings are:

- A significant number of workers are paid exactly the legal minimum wage, and adjustments in this wage are matched by salary adjustments in Brazil's unregulated sector, even in today's low-inflation environment.
- Brazil's labor laws specify that workers are paid within the first week of the month. We provide evidence that this law—which was critical in periods of high inflation—appears to be obeyed by employers in both formal and informal sectors even today.
- High income inequality and a prolonged period of socialist policies have led to labor laws with a prolabor bias, and to labor courts acquiring a similar bias in their verdicts on disputes. Combined with increased ambiguity of labor laws, this prolabor bias of dispute resolution has resulted in the ability of workers who have been dismissed from either formal or informal employment to extract generous severance benefits from their former employers. Large backlogs in labor courts, ambiguities in labor laws, and the manner in which labor legislation is enforced have led to higher and more uncertain labor costs in both regulated and unregulated employment.

The findings of Chapter 3 suggest that in terms of the design of legislation, informality in Brazil is mainly a fiscal, and not strictly a legal, phenomenon, a conclusion also reached by Amadeo and Camargo (1997). But the manner in which these laws have been enforced is also a critical determinant of informality in Brazil: poor record keeping by the government has strengthened the incentives for workers to stay informal that are already built into the design of the main social security programs, and slanted enforcement by labor courts have led to workers effectively being accorded the same labor rights whether or not they have ratified contracts. The incentives to stay informal are naturally higher for workers who are assured of protection under labor legislation regardless of the nature of their contracts, which alters only their financial relationship with the government. The rise of informal self-employment should be of little surprise: such conditions discourage people from employing anyone other than themselves. The chapter concludes that informality in Brazil will remain high as long as labor laws remain ambiguous and enforced with a clear prolabor bias, and social security programs lack tighter benefit-contribution linkages and strong enforcement mechanisms. But the laws often viewed as culprits—minimum wage, severance legislation, collective bargaining mandates, and the level of payroll taxes—are, somewhat surprisingly, not the binding constraints to obtaining better labor market outcomes.[5]

Some recent developments in Brazil deserve mention. In 1998, the combination of slow progress in social security and public employment reform, high levels of public debt, and currency crises in East Asia and Russia tested investor confidence in Brazil. The Brazilian Central Bank raised interest rates to unprecedented levels to defend the real against speculators, slowing economic growth. The slowdown continued after the real was allowed to float in January 1999, underwent a maxidevaluation in January 1999, and settled at levels 40 percent below predevaluation levels by the end of the year. GDP growth slowed from about 3 percent in 1998 to close to zero in 1999, showing some recovery toward the end of 1999. Metropolitan unemployment rates, while low compared with some of Brazil's neighbors such as Argentina, rose to historically high levels of more than 8 percent in mid-1998, but have come down marginally since then despite continued sluggishness in economic growth. In a simple model of the Brazilian economy, high interest rates would lead to a fall in the relative price of labor relative to capital (and to a substitution of labor for capital in response to this change in relative prices), but would also be associated with lower output growth (and a fall in the derived demand for labor). These offsetting substitution and output effects on labor demand could explain both the pattern of high but falling unemployment rates and sluggish wage growth in Brazil in 1999. Chapter 5 develops this approach in more detail for Argentina.

Adjustment, Labor Demand, and Unemployment in Argentina

In the years following the initiation of economic reforms in the late 1980s, Argentina's employment growth has increasingly lagged behind output growth. Despite healthy GDP growth of about 5 percent annually during the 1990s, average yearly employment growth has been less than 2 percent. With labor force participation (LFP) growth of 3 percent per year, the result was high unemployment, which reached almost 20 percent in 1995, and hovers around 15 percent as the country enters the new decade. In the latter half of the decade, there was improvement in measured unemployment, but this appears to have been driven in part by growing underemployment (World Bank 2000). In any case, concerns about high unemployment have dominated labor policy discussions in Argentina for the last five years.

Patterns of unemployment growth do not show much evidence that this is due to a lack of relevant skills; a more likely explanation for the rise in unemployment in the early 1990s is that the costs of labor were high, prompting a shakeout of excess labor and the adoption of capital-intensive methods of production by firms under increased pressure to improve competitiveness. Evidence on the combined effects of the Convertibility Plan, introduction of subsidies for domestic capital, and falling interest rates indicate that the price of capital relative to labor fell between 26 to 40 percent during 1990–94 (Bour 1995). Thus, countering the "output effect" on employment since the Convertibility Plan was initiated was a "substitution effect" of increases in the price of labor relative to capital. Chapter 5 formalizes this approach and quantifies the benefits to labor reforms that lower the price of labor, in contrast to simply relying on economic growth to pull down unemployment rates.

Of course, unemployment rates depend on both labor supply and labor demand, so understanding short-term variations in the supply of labor are crucial to any satisfactory treatment of the issue. With a relatively stable population, this is largely about variations in LFP rates. But more striking are the patterns in LFP, which is countercyclical in Argentina, in contrast to the United Kingdom and the United States, for example, where it is procyclical. This phenomenon has important implications for policy, and Chapter 4 examines the issue of short-term and long-term changes in labor supply in more detail.

Based on an analytical framework that considers output, the relative price of labor, and technology as the main determinants of labor demand, Chapter 5 provides quantitative estimates of the likely payoff (in terms of greater employment) to Argentina's initiatives to improve labor market functioning. The analysis allows for comparisons between strategies that rely only on economic growth to reduce unemployment, and those that combine these strategies with labor policy reforms. The output elasticity of aggregate employment—holding wages or unit labor costs constant, and with an initial condition of high unemployment—helps in obtaining numerical estimates of employment growth that would occur solely due to economic growth; that is, without any labor policy reforms that raise or lower labor costs. The constant-output own-wage elasticity can be used to quantify the effects of labor policy reforms on employment growth.

The authors estimate labor demand functions using a range of assumptions regarding technology, from relatively restrictive to the more flexible characterizations. Estimated wage elasticities range between –0.3 and –0.8 for the preferred specifications. Based on these results, the own-wage elasticity of employment can reasonably be regarded as about –0.5, implying that a 10 percent fall in labor costs will, all things being equal, raise employment by 5 percent. Estimated output elasticities range from 0.1 to 0.4. Based on these results, the output elasticity of employment can be regarded as about 0.25, implying that a 10 percent growth rate of GDP will result in a 2.5 percent increase in employment. These results showed that far-reaching policy reform to lower the cost of labor relative to capital was urgently required in 1996, and Argentina could not rely solely on faster output growth to noticeably increase labor demand and employment. A World Bank study found that the situation had not changed significantly four years later (World Bank 2000).

Women are often blamed when men face new and more serious problems, and labor policy analysts are not immune to launching similar hunts for scapegoats. With Argentine unemployment rates above 15 percent in the mid-1990s, speculation that this rise was due to an abnormally large increase in labor supply of women became common. The quantitative response to this involved decomposing the changes in unemployment into a component related to labor demand or an unexpected slowdown of employment growth, and another related to labor supply, or unexpected increases in LFP especially of women. While such exercises are largely useful only for accounting purposes—since any sensible policy measure for reducing unemployment must rely on stimulating labor demand and not discouraging labor supply—they can be important in determining whether labor reforms are urgent or unimportant. In joining this debate, Chapter 4 contends that common definitions of "unexpected" or "abnormal" fluctuations in labor supply employed ignored a fundamental attribute of the Argentine labor market; that is, that LFP is positively correlated with the unemployment rate over the business cycle. The main contribution of this chapter is to use a model of LFP to explain shorter-term LFP patterns in Argentina, reexamine changes in unemployment using these results, and draw policy implications from these exercises.

Using this approach, Chapter 4 concludes:

- First, during 1974–95, aggregate LFP rose by almost 18 percentage points, fuelled entirely by increases in female participation rates, which registered a sharp rise during 1994–95. Higher income usually brings about a shorter lifetime career through more schooling—delaying the entry into the labor force—and earlier exit (retirement) from the labor force.
- Second, in the first half of the 1990s, an increase in real wages accompanied an increase in the unemployment rate in Argentina. This is the opposite of the experience of countries such as the United States, where increases in unemployment rates are accompanied by falling real wages, so there is both lower expected household income *and* a lower real wage for women during economic slowdowns, and the change in participation rates is ambiguous since the income effect

(the added worker effect) will imply higher participation, but the substitution or wage effect (the discouraged worker effect) will imply lower participation. In the United Kingdom and the United States, the empirical finding is that the discouraged worker effect dominates, resulting in procyclical behavior of labor supply, so that fluctuations in unemployment rates are dampened. In Argentina, on the other hand, both the wealth effect and substitution effect increase participation, and cyclical changes exacerbate the unemployment problem.

- Third, increased female LFP could at best account for less than 6 percentage points of the 14 percentage point increase in unemployment between 1987 and 1995 (from 6 percent to 20 percent). This is largely because of the low initial rates of female participation, so that absolute increases in female workers are not sufficiently large to confirm conjecture that increased supply, not slowing demand, is responsible for the rapid rise in unemployment.

- Finally, analyses that attribute the observed rise in unemployment to abnormally large labor supply increases understate the importance of policy reform to stabilize and increase labor demand. Interpreting departures from a linear trend as abnormal, participation levels for both women and men appear to be about 5 and 2 percentage points, respectively, above their normal levels. But both theory and empirical analysis suggest that using only trend values as expected LFP ignores an important attribute of the Argentine labor market—that is, LFP is systematically influenced by cyclical factors. When cyclical factors are incorporated, the "surprise" component of the increase in labor supply in the 1990s diminishes significantly.

The pattern of unemployment in Argentina indicates that it is a widespread phenomenon, and not restricted to a few clearly identified worker groups. The relatively uniform increase in unemployment rates across worker categories points to falling labor demand as the main cause of growing unemployment, and these patterns do not lend themselves easily to effective labor market interventions by the government. With widespread unemployment, special incentives for hiring workers with certain attributes (for example, relaxed hiring rules for women and younger workers, and incentives adopted by the government to encourage employers to hire certain types of workers) will be less effective than reform of labor market regulations that allow real wages to respond to economic shocks, and growth-enhancing policies that raise the demand for labor. Comprehensive labor reform would allow the government to concentrate on the task of instituting policies for raising long-term employment growth, instead of being distracted by temporary but sharp increases in unemployment, which are politically difficult to ignore.

Growth, Inequality, and Uncertainty in Chile

The combination of an open economy and a flexible labor market is believed by some to be the cause of growing socioeconomic ills in Chile, including income inequality. It is argued that international trade has led to widening differentials in earnings between Chile's rich and poor, and labor market reforms have prevented the disadvantaged from stemming this tide. The deregulation of labor markets under the military regime has been followed by a period of flexibility since 1987 (Cortazar 1997). Some observers have alleged that the new jobs created in the 1990s are "low-paying, low-quality, short-term jobs" (Leiva 1996). "Low quality" is often used to connote work in which job stability is not a norm: concerns of increased precariousness of employment were commonplace even before the Asian and Russian financial crises, and are likely to occupy even more attention today.

Increasing inequality and uncertainty of earnings can slow growth and may induce reversal of earlier reforms, especially the reform of labor legislation. Chapters 6 and 7 address two sets of issues: first, whether the labor market has changed so that those with human capital (for example, high levels of education) are being rewarded proportionately more, and whether the structure of Chile's labor market implies that returns to human capital are lower for poorer workers; and second, whether the combination of a flexible labor market and increased openness has resulted in greater uncertainty of earnings, and whether these recent developments warrant significant policy changes.

Chapter 6 uses quantile regression techniques to analyze whether the rewards to human capital differ for workers in different parts of the wage distribution, and uses simple statistical techniques to quantify the benefits of improved education policies for poorer sections of society. The main findings are:

- During 1987–92, average labor earnings increased by about 30 percent for the top and bottom quintile groups in Chile, and by about 20 percent for the middle groups. During 1992–95, average earnings fell for the top and bottom quintile groups, but rose modestly for the middle classes.

- Wage inequality, as measured by the Gini coefficient and the spread between the 90th and 10th percentile groups, rose between 1960 and 1987–88, but has declined sizably since then. This change in direction has been missed or underemphasized by earlier studies on the subject.
- Rates of return to education behave in a similar way, rising from 1960 until 1987–88 and declining since then.
- These findings suggest that the Chilean government's emphasis on education as an instrument for combating inequality is appropriate, though this is tempered by the finding that rates of return to education are lower for lower quantile groups.
- Simulations suggest that further improvements in access to schooling by the poor will have modest effects on earnings inequality, and this only at higher levels of education (grade 9 and above). Improvements in the quality of education appear to be twice as effective as improvements in access to schooling, and the returns to improvements in education quality are obtained largely at lower levels of schooling (0 to 8 years).

Chapter 7 examines the validity of claims that, although employment growth during 1990–97 outstripped labor force growth, this may have been cold comfort for workers because employment has also grown more precarious in Chile. While precariousness normally refers to the uncertainty surrounding employment, the more meaningful measure of the uncertainty in the labor market is the precariousness of earnings, that is, of a worker being without labor income and related benefits. This depends less on how likely the loss of a job is (the incidence of unemployment), and more on how long a worker is likely to be without work (the duration of unemployment), best estimated as the probability of finding a job. In either case, because precariousness refers to the probability of a change in employment status, the relevant indicators measuring precariousness are flows, not stocks.

The authors use a labor flows model developed by Haindl (1985) to convert reported data into magnitudes that are better suited for addressing the question of precariousness of employment and earnings. The results contradict the belief that employment and labor earnings have become more precarious in Chile:

- In the years since 1987, the Chilean labor market has become an increasingly reliable source of income: expected job tenure has increased, unemployment rates and duration have fallen significantly, and long-term unemployment has become practically nonexistent.

- The approach followed during the last decade has paid dividends: poverty and wage inequality fell impressively since 1987, and direct intervention in the labor market to reduce poverty or inequality is neither necessary nor effective, and may prove counterproductive.
- Given the average tenure and unemployment duration in the economy before the international currency crises slowed growth, the Chilean mandated severance payment system seemed adequate to provide support for most formal sector workers if they become unemployed.
- Changes in labor legislation to make dismissals harder are likely to prove counterproductive, and further increases in minimum wages are as likely to worsen poverty and inequality as to improve them. Improvements in the quality of vocational secondary education are more likely to benefit the poor, but these have proved difficult and expensive to attain in public schools.

Since 1998, unemployment rates have climbed to above 10 percent in Chile, and the clamor for a formal unemployment insurance system has increased. In late 1999 and early 2000, aided by economic recovery, employment growth picked up again and unemployment fell considerably. Changes in labor laws that would have introduced rigidities were aborted in mid-1999 due to pressure from employers, but the new government that took office in 2000 will face pressure to introduce changes that edge labor markets away from competitiveness and toward intermediate-centralized structures.

Lessons Learned

It is difficult to draw general lessons in the area of labor policy by studying the experience of just three countries over less than a decade but, with care, some conclusions are possible.

Labor Policy Issues are Country Specific

The first general lesson is, paradoxically, that generalizations about labor policy are likely to be pointless or misleading. The findings in this book suggest that the economic and political history of a country is a critical determinant of the relative importance of legislation on wages and employment, so that the subset of binding laws is country specific. For example, the book provides evidence that a large number of workers are paid exactly the legal minimum wage even in Brazil's unregulated sector, and adjustments in this wage are matched by salary adjustments. It is possible—and indeed it has been confirmed—that in some other countries minimum wages are not binding even in the regulated sector. It would be foolhardy to assert either that minimum wage legislation is not important for economic outcomes or that it is important for all or most countries. Similarly, it would be misleading to use the demand elasticity results for, say, Argentina, to argue that reductions in labor costs would have the same employment effects in Brazil or Chile or Mexico; at best, these estimates can serve as a guide for policymakers in Argentina. Again, the finding that sustained growth in Chile has not been associated with increasing earnings inequality does not guarantee similar results for other countries; it merely refutes some of the claims by people who question the desirability of growth-oriented labor policies that were instituted by the Chilean government during the 1980s. And the finding that many of Brazil's federal government employees are grossly overcompensated may not necessarily apply to other countries.

Implementable labor policies have to be designed by studying and understanding labor markets country by country, not by compiling and analyzing cross-country data to obtain a policy verdict that is correct on average, or by extrapolating results found for one country to others that happen to share some attributes.[6] This has some obvious implications for what type of research would be most useful in promoting better labor policies in developing countries.

Labor Outcomes Depend Only Partly on Labor Policies

The second general lesson is rather obvious, but bears repeating since it is so often forgotten: Labor reform is neither necessary nor sufficient for improving labor outcomes. As the experience of these countries shows, a successful stabilization unaccompanied by changes in labor policy will in general improve labor outcomes, though it will also unmask microeconomic imbalances (public-private compensation differentials in Brazil, relative prices of labor and capital in Argentina, and the gaps between the rich and poor in Chile). Similarly, fiscal adjustment could also improve employment and earnings outcomes, illustrating that actions such as putting government finances in order can improve outcomes in the private labor market, even if no labor reforms take place. And moving from a period of adjustment to sustained economic growth will improve earnings and employment outcomes, even if there are no accompanying improvements in labor policies. However, this does not rule out that, all things being equal, outcomes would be better still if appropriate labor reforms are made, though it is harder to make this case persuasively.

Making Labor Policies Better Is Difficult During Good Times

The first corollary of the above—that labor outcomes can improve even without labor reform, or worsen after labor reform—is that it is difficult to carry out such reforms during periods of general economic improvement. In Argentina, for example, labor policies did not rise to the top of the reform agenda during 1990–94, even though unemployment was increasing steadily, because of generally improving wage and employment conditions as a result of successful stabilization. When the Tequila Crisis hit Argentina, unemployment skyrocketed and labor reform came to the forefront of discussions, only to recede again when economic growth resumed as fiscal and financial reforms advanced. Again, in Brazil, labor reforms only briefly dominated the political landscape when unemployment rates rose to historic levels in mid-1998 after Brazil was rocked by the Russian financial crisis and the economy slid into a recession. When the economic slowdown proved to be less severe than anticipated and unemployment rates fell marginally, labor policy reform was moved off the Brazilian government's list of priorities. Finally, a decade of sustained growth and improving employment and earnings outcomes in Chile had the perverse effect of prompting the reversal of labor reforms that may have made these outcomes possible in the first place. Unsubstantiated (but vocal) allegations that the improvements in average earnings and employment had masked deteriorated distribution and increased uncertainty of labor earnings have made the Chilean government seriously consider reversing some of the policies adopted in the 1980s.

Quantifying Key Magnitudes Can Facilitate Labor Reform

The second corollary of the finding that labor outcomes depend only partly on labor policies is that quantification of the likely effects of policy reform can help to advance the agenda. Rhetoric on labor policy is as abundant as relevant numbers are rare. Labor reform is always difficult and, when attempted—reforms are usually piecemeal. In every country, there are well-entrenched labor interests such as labor unions, political risks for reformers are high, and proponents of reform—generally employers or economists—are often ineffective in convincing policymakers of the benefits of taking these risks. Under these circumstances, to help policymakers focus their efforts and explain them to the electorate, it helps to know whether labor policy changes are necessary and, if so, which aspects of labor policy are binding and which are relatively irrelevant, and what are the likely benefits of such reforms in terms of improved labor market outcomes.

Drazen (2000) discusses "stage one" reforms such as stabilization, the benefits of which are widely distributed, but also refers to "stage two" reforms such as labor market restructuring, where there are obvious winners and losers. Drazen notes that one reason for delay or nonadoption of reform may be the inability of policymakers to communicate the benefits of reforms to the electorate, and suggests that convincing "left-wing" policymakers about the benefits of "right-wing" reforms such as labor market restructuring may be a good reform strategy since they may be more likely to achieve success than right-wing policymakers. This line of reasoning suggests that quantification of the benefits of reform may be even more crucial for such stage two reforms than for macroeconomic reforms, which is one of the themes of this book.

In this book, we quantify the growth in employment that labor policy reform in Argentina could have generated. For Brazil, again using a quantitative approach, the book illustrates an approach to determine aspects of labor legislation—both design and implementation related—that are the most important for outcomes and those that may be relatively nonbinding. Quantifying the concept of precariousness leads to the recommendation that Chile may be better off leaving labor policies unaltered, and looking to other policy measures such as improved education quality to narrow the income gap between the rich and the poor.

Optimism for the Next Decade

In the early 1990s it would not have been an exaggeration to characterize the reform of labor policies as a "forgotten reform" (Edwards and Lustig 1997). Most countries had by then put in place successful macroeconomic stabilization programs, and many had already launched financial sector reforms. By the middle of the decade labor policy changes could reasonably be upgraded from forgotten to the "unfinished agenda" (Guasch 1999). We are optimistic that labor reform will continue during the next decade, and even be upgraded from largely unfinished to merely tardy in some countries of the region. Recall that the 1980s saw much of Latin America attempting macroeconomic reform with little success. We think that some of these experiments bore fruit in the 1990s, because most countries in the region stabilized, so the decade of the 1980s was not as much of a loss as many believe. Being microeconomic in nature, labor reform will be even more difficult because it generates clearly identifiable winners and losers. But we hope that a decade from now, the 1990s will be regarded as the time when the seeds of durable labor reform were sown in Latin America.

Notes

1. Together, the population of Argentina, Brazil, and Chile is about 215 million, or about 40 percent of the regional total of 500 million; Argentina had 36 million, Brazil 164 million, and Chile 15 million. Of a total labor force of 206 million in Latin America in 1997, the sample countries had about 94 million, or 45 percent of the total (Argentina with 14 million, Brazil with 74 million, and Chile with 6 million). In 1998, these countries had US$1,150 billion—or more than 50 percent—of the regional GDP of about US$2,000 billion; Argentina had US$300 billion, Brazil US$775 billion, and Chile US$75 billion. Naturally, therefore, the income levels in these countries were somewhat atypical of the region: in 1998, Argentina (with US$8,600), Brazil (with US$4,700), and Chile (with US$5,000) each had a GNP per capita higher than the regional average of US$3,900.

2. Under the Brazilian Constitution, upon eligibility government workers get 100 percent of their final salary as pensions; contribution rates average about 10 percent, but eligibility rules are notoriously generous and are often applied in a lax manner. It is not an exaggeration to describe pensions as a continuation of salary payments upon retirement. The rules for determining pensions in the private sector are somewhat more in line with international standards for pay-as-you-go social security, but again are considerably more generous because of easy eligibility and the absence of a minimum age at which social security benefits commence. Brazil has been engaged in pension reform for the last three years (see World Bank 2001 for details).

3. As it turned out, few reforms were actually implemented.

4. For example, Chapter 3 reasons that, even in the unregulated sector, changes in mandated minimum wages were used by workers as a signal for revising nominal wages during a period of high inflation rates, and continue to be used in this manner even in today's low-inflation conditions.

5. See Maloney (1998) for an analysis of informality using data from Mexico.

6. Cross-country analysis such as that in Forteza and Rama (2000), where the authors use data for more than 100 countries to conjecture that minimum wages and mandatory benefits have a marginal impact only, but the size and strength of

organized labor appear to be crucial for outcomes, should therefore be no more than a starting point for policy discussions.

References

Amadeo, Edward J., and Jose Marcio Camargo. 1997. "Brazil: Regulation and Flexibility in the Labor Market." In S. Edwards and N. Lustig, eds., *Labor Markets in Latin America: Combining Social Protection with Market Flexibility.* Washington, D.C.: The Brookings Institution Press.

Bour, Juan Luis. 1995. "Mercado de trabajo y Productividad en la Argentina." Draft. Latin American Economic Research Foundation. Buenos Aires.

Cortazar, Rene. 1997. "Chile: The Evolution and Reform of the Labor Market." In S. Edwards and N. Lustig, eds., *Labor Markets in Latin America: Combining Social Protection with Market Flexibility.* Washington, D.C.: The Brookings Institution Press.

Drazen, Allan. 2000. *Political Economy in Macroeconomics.* Princeton, N.J.: Princeton University Press.

Edwards, Sebastian, and Nora Lustig, eds. 1997. *Labor Markets in Latin America: Combining Social Protection with Market Flexibility.* Washington, D.C.: The Brookings Institution Press.

Forteza, Alvaro, and Martín Rama. 2000. "Labor Market 'Rigidity' and the Success of Economic Reforms Across More than One Hundred Countries." Paper prepared for the research project on *The Impact of Labor Market Policies and Institutions on Economic Performance.* World Bank, RPO 680-96. Washington, D.C.

Guasch, José Luis. 1999. "Labor Market Reform and Job Creation: The Unfinished Agenda in Latin American and Caribbean Countries." Directions in Development Series. Washington, D.C.: World Bank.

Haindl, Erik. 1985. "Un modelo para la determinación de flujos y parámetros dinámicas en el mercado de trabajo." *Estudios de Economia* 12 (1) (primer trimestre).

Leiva, Fernando. 1996. "Flexible Labor Markets, Poverty and Social Disintegration in Chile, 1990–1994: The Limitations of World Bank Policies." Paper presented at the World Bank, OXFAM draft. Washington, D.C.

Maloney, William F. 1998. *Efficiency Wages, Unions, and the Structure of the Mexican Labor Market—Three Essays.* Latin America and Caribbean Region, Poverty Reduction and Economic Management Department. World Bank, Washington, D.C.

World Bank. 2000. *Argentina—Labor Market in the New Millenium.* Confidential Report No. 19996-AR. Washington, D.C.

_____. 2001. "Brazil: Critical Issues in Social Security." A World Bank Country Study. Washington, D.C.

Technical Annexes

A Technical Annex to Chapter 2: The Public-Private Wage Gap

This Annex presents a brief methodological discussion of how both the wage gap between the public and private sectors, and the controlled wage gap, are measured in Chapter 2.

Wage Gap Concepts

In the empirical analysis of wage differentials, the use of wages, logwages, arithmetic means, and geometric means is common. In this section we briefly review the relationships between these concepts and how they are used to obtain measures for the public-private earnings and wage gap.

We begin by reviewing the advantages and disadvantages of using differences in logwages compared with absolute or relative differences in wages. Let w_a and w_b be the average wages in the public and private sectors, respectively. Using this notation, we can define the absolute wage difference (G_0), two alternative versions for the relative wage difference $(G_{1a}$ and $G_{1b})$, and the logwage difference (G_2) as follows:

$$G_0 = w_a - w_b \tag{A-1}$$

$$G_{1a} = \frac{w_a - w_b}{w_a} \tag{A-2}$$

$$G_{1b} = \frac{w_a - w_b}{w_b} \tag{A-3}$$

$$G_2 = \ln(w_a) - \ln(w_b) = \ln(w_a / w_b) \qquad\qquad\text{(A-4)}$$

The absolute wage difference, G_0, has the disadvantage compared to the relative difference in wages, G_{1a} and G_{1b}, and the difference in log-wages, G_2, that it is sensitive to the unit of measurement. The relative differences in wages, G_{1a} and G_{1b}, have the major disadvantage relative to differences in logwages, G_2, that their calculation requires selection of a baseline wage as reference and that the measure is sensitive to this choice. Consequently, one has to constantly refer to the chosen baseline wage, which makes the use of relative wage differences cumbersome in a detailed analysis of wage differentials. For example, if the average wage in the public and private sectors is 50 and 20 monetary units, respectively, then the wage gap can be expressed in relative terms as 150 percent of the private sector average wage or 60 percent of the public sector average wage. The logwage difference G_2 overcomes this issue and hence eliminates the need to keep track of the wage used as reference. In our example above, the log-wage difference between the public and private sectors is 0.92.

The major disadvantage of G_2 can be seen in the fact that it is more difficult to interpret. One way to facilitate its interpretation is to notice that, for small variations, the logwage difference is an approximation for the relative change in the level of wages. For example, if the wages are 50 and 51, the relative wage variations using 50 or 51 as the baseline references are 0.0200 and 0.0196, respectively. In this case the logwage difference is 0.0198. In the general case, if $w_a > w_b$ then

$$\frac{w_a - w_b}{w_a} \geq \ln\left(\frac{w_a}{w_b}\right) \geq \frac{w_a - w_b}{w_b}$$

or

$$G_{1a} \geq G_2 \geq G_{1b}$$

Calculation of Controlled Wage Gap

Let w denote the wage and let p be an indicator for the public sector, which assumes 0 for the private sector and 1 for the public sector. Denote by h the regression function of logwages on gender (g), race (r), schooling (e), age (a), tenure (t), and p, then

$$E[\ln(w)/g, r, e, a, t, p] = h(g, r, e, a, t, p) \qquad\qquad\text{(A-5)}$$

Now, the specification of our regressions can be seen as a series of hypotheses about the functional form of h. Our basic assumption is that the regression function is separable on gender, race, schooling, age, and tenure, but not necessary on the indicator for the public sector, that is,

$$h(g, r, e, a, t, p) = f_1(g, p) + f_2(r, p) + f_3(e, p) + f_4(a, p) + f_5(t, p) \quad \text{(A-6)}$$

Nonseparability in p implies that the wage advantage of workers in the public sector varies with their characteristics. If the regression function is separable in p, then the wage advantage is the same for all public sector workers independent of their individual characteristics.

To simplify our empirical analysis, we assume that the dependency on gender, race, schooling, and tenure is linear, and that the dependency on age is quadratic. This allows us to express the logwage regression function as

$$h(g, r, e, a, t, p) = a_0(p) + a_1(p).g + a_2(p).r + a_3(p).e \quad \text{(A-7)}$$
$$+ a_4(p).a + b_4(p).a^2 + a_5(p).t$$

We will refer to this expression as the "general model." To estimate the "general model" we regress logwages on gender, race, schooling, age, and tenure for the public and private sectors, separately.

In addition, we estimate and analyze a simplified version of this model, which we will refer to as the "basic model." It is given by

$$h(g, r, e, a, t, p) = \alpha + a_0.p + a_1.g + a_2.r + a_3.e + a_4.a + b_4.a^2 + a_5.t \quad \text{(A-8)}$$

The basic model imposes separability of p, which, given the above assumption, implies that all coefficients except the intercept are common to both sectors. It is estimated by regressing logwages on gender, race, schooling, age, tenure, and an indicator for public employment in a sample pooling together the public and private labor force.

In the case of the "general model," the average logwage in the public sector is

$$a_0(1) + a_1(1).\mu(g/1) + a_2(1).\mu(r/1) + a_3(1).\mu(e/1) + a_4(1).\mu(a/1)$$
$$+ b_4(1).\mu(a^2/1) + a_5(1).\mu(t/1)$$

where, $\mu(x/1)$ denotes the average of the characteristic x in the public sector. Based on the same model the average logwage that would prevail in the private sector if the labor force in the sector had the same characteristics as those of the public sector is given by

$$a_0(0) + a_1(0).\mu(g/1) + a_2(0).\mu(r/1) + a_3(0).\mu(e/1) + a_4(0).\mu(a/1)$$
$$+ b_4(0).\mu(a^2/1) + a_5(0).\mu(t/1)$$

Therefore, the estimate of the logwage gap between workers with identical observed characteristics is given by

$$(a_0(1)-a_0(0)) + [a_1(1)-a_1(0)].\mu(g/1) + [a_2(1)-a_2(0)].\mu(r/1)$$
$$+ [a_3(1)-a_3(0)].\mu(e/1) + [a_4(1)-a_4(0)].\mu(a/1) + [b_4(1)-b_4(0)].\mu(a^2/1)$$
$$+ [a_5(1)-a_5(0)].\mu(t/1)$$

In the case of the "basic model" the average logwage in the public sector is given by

$$\alpha + a_0 + a_1.\mu(g/1) + a_2.\mu(r/1) + a_3.\mu(e/1) + a_4.\mu(a/1)$$
$$+ b_4.\mu(a^2/1) + a_5.\mu(t/1)$$

and the average logwage that would prevail in the private sector if the labor force in the sector had the same characteristics as those of the public sector labor force is given by

$$\alpha + a_1.\mu(g/1) + a_2.\mu(r/1) + a_3.\mu(e/1) + a_4.\mu(a/1) + b_4.\mu(a^2/1) + a_5.\mu(t/1)$$

Consequently, the logwage gap between workers with identical observed characteristics is given simply by a_0.

B Technical Annex to Chapter 5: Wage and Output Elasticities of Labor Demand

Cobb-Douglas Technology

The Cobb-Douglas production function is

$$Y = A. K^\beta. L^{1-\beta} \qquad \text{(B-1)}$$

where Y denotes output, K capital, and L labor. β is the share of capital. A indicates the level of technology.

Using B.1, through cost minimization we can derive the cost function

$$C = C(w, r, Y) = Z. w^{1-\beta}.r^\beta.Y \qquad \text{(B-2)}$$

where Z is a constant, and w and r are the prices of labor and capital.

Using Shephard's lemma, the labor demand equation is obtained:

$$L^d = \alpha^1.w^{(-\beta)}.r^\beta.Y \qquad \text{(B-3)}$$

α^1 is a constant. The Cobb-Douglas technology restricts the elasticity of substitution between L and K, σ, to equal 1. The own-wage elasticity of demand can be estimated in two ways:

(i) Taking logs of B-3

$$\ln L^d = \ln A + (-\beta)\ln w + \beta \ln r + \ln Y \qquad \text{(B-4)}$$

The own-wage elasticity of demand corresponds to the coefficient on lnw, that is $(-\beta)$.

(ii) Estimating the production function directly, using a log-log form of equation B-1:

$$\ln Y = \ln A + \beta \ln K + (1-\beta) \ln L. \tag{B-5}$$

Constant Elasticity of Substitution (CES) Technology

The CES production and cost function are, respectively

$$Y = [\alpha L^\rho + (1-\alpha).K^\rho]^{1/\rho} \tag{B-6}$$

$$C = Y[\alpha^\sigma.w^{1-\sigma} + (1-\alpha)^\sigma.r^{1-\sigma}]^{1/(1-\sigma)} \tag{B-7}$$

where $\sigma = 1/[1-\rho]$; σ is the elasticity of substitution and is a constant, but not necessarily 1. The CES is sufficiently general that σ is free to fluctuate between 0 and ∞, so one can infer its size. Having obtained an estimate of σ, the own-wage elasticity ε_{LL} can then be inferred by using

$$\varepsilon_L = -[1-s_L]\sigma. \tag{B-8}$$

Using Shephard's lemma, the labor demand equation can be derived, and taking logs we obtain

$$\ln L = \alpha'' - \sigma \ln w + \ln Y \tag{B-9}$$

Alternatively, we can estimate σ by using what Hamermesh (1993) calls the estimate of the marginal productivity condition:

$$\ln L = \alpha'' - \sigma_1 \ln w + \varepsilon_{LY} \ln Y \tag{B-10}$$

This produces estimates not only on σ, but also on ε_{LY}. Together with information on s_L, the estimate of σ generates ε_{LL}, as can be seen in B-8.

Estimation of Single Factor Demand Equations

For easy estimation, the Shephard condition can be written in logarithmic form:

$$\ln L = \alpha' + \varepsilon_{LL} \ln w + \varepsilon_{LK} \ln r + \varepsilon_{LY} \ln y \tag{B-11}$$

This yields the own-wage elasticity ε_{LL}, the cross-elasticity of demand for labor ε_{LK}, and the employment-output elasticity.

Generalized Leontief Technology

Input demand functions using well-established forms that are second-order approximations to arbitrary cost or production functions—such as the generalized Leontief and the translog forms—can also be estimated. The advantage of these functional forms in the two-factor case over the CES function lies in the fact that σ and the elasticities are not restricted to be constant, but are allowed to vary with the values of the factor inputs or prices.

Imposing constant returns to scale, the generalized Leontief cost function becomes

$$C = Y[a_{11}w + 2a_{12}w^{0.5}r^{0.5} + a_{22}r] \tag{B-12}$$

Using Shephard's lemma, the labor demand equation is

$$L^d = a_{11}Y + a_{12}Y(w/r)^{-0.5} \tag{B-13}$$

Dividing by Y this yields

$$L/Y = a_{11} + a_{12}(w/r)^{-0.5} \tag{B-14}$$

Proceding similarly for capital provides

$$K/Y = a_{22} + a_{12}(w/r)^{-0.5} \tag{B-15}$$

To estimate this model, we use Zellner's seemingly unrelated estimator (SURE) with the cross-equation restriction imposed. We employ the three-stage least squares estimation procedure to correct for simultaneous equation bias.

Transcendental Logarithmic (Translog) Technology

The translog cost function is written as

$$
\begin{aligned}
\ln C = {} & \ln a_0 + a_1 \ln w + 0.5a_2\,[\ln w]^2 + a_3\,\ln w.\ln r \\
& + 0.5b_1\,[\ln r]^2 + b_2 \ln r + 0.5b_1\,[\ln r]^2 + b_3.\ln Y + b_4\,\ln r.\ln Y \\
& + a_4 \ln w.\ln Y + 0.5b_5\,[\ln Y]^2
\end{aligned} \tag{B-16}
$$

The labor demand function—actually the share equation—derived from the above translog cost function, is given by

$$wL/C = a_1 + a_2\ln w + a_3\ln r + a_4\ln Y \tag{B-17}$$

When the full model and the cross-equation restrictions are specified, there is one redundant equation. In our case, with only two inputs of data available, only one equation, the share of labor, is specified. The translog cost function as specified above is a highly general, nonhomothetic form. In the general case, nonhomotheticity implies that output is not separable from factor prices. Instead, the effect of factor prices depends on the scale of output. This is reflected in the terms $b_4 \ln Y . \ln r$ and $a_4 \ln Y . \ln w$ in B-16. A test for homotheticity is whether a_4 and b_4 are equal to 0. Since the cost function is homogeneous of degree one in prices $a_4 + b_4 = 0$, which implies the case that here we simply have to test that $a_4 = 0$. Homogeneity of a constant degree in output occurs if, in addition to the homotheticity restrictions, $b_5 = 0$; in this case the degree of homogeneity equals $1/b_3$. Constant returns to scale of the dual production function occurs when, in addition to the above restrictions, $b_3 = 1$. Finally, the translog function reduces to the CRS Cobb-Douglas when, in addition to the above restrictions, $a_3 = 0$.

Estimating Returns to Scale

In the presence of scale effects (B.8) becomes

$$\varepsilon_L = -[1 - s_L]\sigma - s\eta \tag{B-18}$$

where η is the elasticity of product demand.

To estimate returns to scale, it is usually necessary to add the translog cost function to the share equation to be estimated, since b_3 and b_5 appear only in the cost function. Christensen and Greene (1976) note that the optimal procedure is to jointly estimate the cost function and the cost share equation as a multivariate regression system. This has the effect of adding additional degrees of freedom and only a few (b_3 and b_5) unrestricted regression coefficients. Following Hanoch (1975), returns to scale μ are computed as the inverse of the elasticity of cost with respect to output. That is

$$\mu = 1/\varepsilon_{CY} = \text{average cost/marginal cost} \tag{B-19}$$

For the translog cost function

$$\varepsilon_{CY} = b_3 + b_4 \ln r + a_4 \ln w + b_3 \ln Y \tag{B-20}$$

Hence, with constant returns to scale, both ε_{CY} and μ are equal to 1. If there are increasing returns ($\mu > 1$), then $\varepsilon_{CY} < 1$. A more natural way to represent returns to scale is to define $ee = (1 - \varepsilon_{CY})$. This results in a positive number for increasing returns to scale, and negative numbers otherwise. Note that unless ε_{CY} is constant for all values of Y and independent of factor prices (that is, homothetic), it will not equal the elasticity of labor demand with respect to output. In the general nonhomothetic case with the cost function C = C(w, r, Y), there is no exact relationship between ε_{CY} and ε_{LY}. With homotheticity, the two are equal.

We estimate the joint system using iterated three-stage least squares imposing both the homogeneity and cross-equation restrictions. This is identical to the SURE procedure, but with the fitted values of the endogenous variables regressed on all the instruments and exogenous variables. The disturbance covariance matrix is estimated using the original variables, not the fitted ones.

References

Hamermesh, Daniel S. 1993. *Labor Demand.* Princeton and Chichester, U.K.: Princeton University Press.

Hanoch, Giora. 1975. "Production and Demand Models with Direct or Indirect Implicit Activity." *Econometrica* 43 (3): 395–419.

C Technical Annex to Chapter 6: The Quantile Regression

The standard econometric tool used to estimate the Mincerian wage equation has been ordinary least squares (OLS). This technique implies the minimization of the sum of the squared errors under the assumptions that (a) the model is the true model, (b) that the expected value of the errors is zero, (c) that the matrix of explanatory variables (x) is a nonstochastic matrix of full column rank, and (iv) that the vector of errors is independent with zero mean. This formulation implies that the predicted value of y given x is equal to the mean of y (conditional on the x values). The representativeness of the predicted value of y given x depends on the variance of y given x. This leads to the fact that when disturbances are not normal, or when there is an important proportion of outliers, the traditional mean regression loses robustness. One robust way to estimate the relationship between two variables is the use of the least absolute deviation (LAD) technique. In this case, instead of minimizing the sum of the squared errors, we minimize the sum of the absolute value of the error. In other words, OLS minimizes

$$\psi_{OLS} = \sum_{i=1}^{n}(y_i - \hat{y}_i)^2 = \sum_{i=1}^{n}(y_i - x_i'\beta)^2 \tag{C-1}$$

and LAD minimizes

$$\psi_{LAD} = \sum_{i=1}^{n}\left|y_i - \hat{y}_i\right| = \sum_{i=1}^{n}\left|y_i - x_i'\beta\right| \tag{C-2}$$

In this case the predicted value of y conditional on x corresponds to the median of y conditional on x; that is, the value that would leave 50 percent of the errors above and 50 percent of the errors below. One obvious extension of this concept is to adjust the different hyperplanes so that θ percent of the errors will be negative and $(1-\theta)$ percent will be positive. Achieving this only requires weighting differently positive and negative errors in equation C-2. This is what gives the origin to the quantile regression method (QRM). Note that with the QRM, in principle, we may have as many fitted curves as we want (just varying θ), but in practice the number of curves is limited by the numbers of observations available. The purpose of the classical least squares estimation is to determine the conditional mean of a random variable y, $E(y|x)$, given some explanatory variables x, usually under some assumptions about the functional form of $E(y|x)$, for instance, linearity. The QRM enables us to pose such a question at any quantile of the conditional distribution. A real-valued random variable y is fully characterized by its distribution function $F(y) = P(Y \leq y)$. Given $F(y)$, we can for any $\theta \in (0,1)$ define θth quantile of Y given by $Q_Y(\theta) = \inf\{y \notin \Re \mid F(y) \geq \theta\}$. The quantile function, $Q_Y(\theta)$ as a function of θ, completely describes the distribution of the random variable y. Hence, the estimation of conditional quantile functions allows us to obtain a more complete picture about the dependence of the conditional distribution of y on x. In other words, this means that we have a possibility of investigating the influence of explanatory variables on the *shape* of the distribution, and we also have a possibility of investigating the conditional impact of the regressors on the dependent variables at different "layers" of the distribution.

To formalize the presentation of the QRM, let us assume that we have a sample of size n on wages (y) and some vector of individual characteristics. Let y_i (i=1,.....,n) be the wage of individual i and let x_i be a known vector of individual characteristics. Let us assume that the θth quantile of the conditional distribution of y_i given x_i is linear, that is

$$y_i = x_i'\beta_\theta + u_{\theta i} \; with \; Q_\theta(y_i|x_i) = x_i'\beta_\theta \; i = 1, 2, ...,n \qquad \text{(C-3)}$$

where x_i' is a k $\times$ 1 vector of covariates with $x_{i1} = 1$, and β_θ for all i, and is an unknown k $\times$ 1 parameter vector whose estimation, for different values of θ [0 < θ < 1] is of interest to us. The term $Q_\theta(y_i|x_i)$ denotes the conditional quantile of y_i given x_i. In this specification $u_{\theta i}$ is defined by $u_{\theta i} = y_i - x_i'\beta_{\theta i}$, from where it follows that $Q_\theta(u_{\theta i}|x_i) = 0$. Therefore, the θth quantile regression based on a sample (y_i, x_i) i = 1, 2, ..., n, is a vector β_θ that minimizes:

$$\psi_{QRM,\theta} = \theta \sum_{i|y_i \geq x_i'\beta_\theta}^{n} \left|y_i - x_i'\beta_\theta\right| + (1-\theta) \sum_{i|y_i \langle x_i'\beta_\theta}^{n} \left|y_i - x_i'\beta_\theta\right| \qquad (C\text{-}4)$$

One typical misconception in the interpretation of the QRM is that comparing different estimates of $\hat{\beta}_\theta$ is equivalent to comparing the returns of the rich (for θ = 0.90) versus the returns for the poor (for instance for θ = 0.10). This is not the case. What we are comparing is the distribution of the residuals after compensating for education and experience. In other words, those individuals who are high in the distribution are those who earn above what would be expected given their individual characteristics, which may include both rich and poor people.

The robustness of the method comes from the fact that the estimates rely only on the sign (positive or negative) of each observation (that is, only on whether the observation is above or below the hyperplane), but the actual magnitude of the error is irrelevant.

The QRM method can be easily explained using graphs. The following figure (taken from Montenegro 1998) shows three different distributions of the errors.

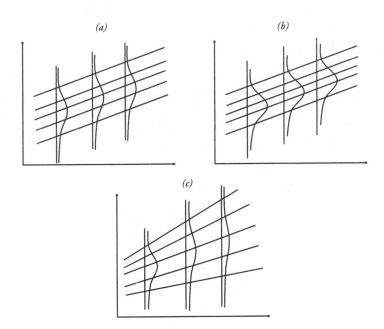

(a)

(b)

(c)

In panel (a) we observe a homoscedastic distribution. In this case the set of QRM estimates is basically a set of parallel lines. Note that the slopes of the different curves adjusted for different θs will be the same, but the position parameters for each curve (that is, the parameter that shows the intersection of the curve with the y-axis will vary). In the panel (b) we again have a homoscedastic distribution, but with a smaller variance. In this case, again, the different slopes of the different curves adjusted for different θs will be the same; the position of the parameters for each curve will vary, however, although less than in the case of panel (a), given that the distribution has a smaller variance (in an extreme case, if the variance of the distribution is zero, all the position parameters estimated will be the same). Finally, panel (c) shows a distribution of y given x that exhibits heteroscedasticity. In this case the slopes of the different curves increase as we move from the lower quantile estimates to the upper quantile estimates.

Note that the estimation of C-4 is not a problem that may be estimated using standard minimization techniques, because those require that the functions involved be of a continuous nature (and the absolute value function is not). Linear programming techniques can be used to find the vector β_θ that minimizes equation C-4, as it is shown in Koenker and Bassett (1978, 1982). The solution does not have an explicit form and does not have some common properties attributed to OLS standard estimation. Nevertheless, it can be shown to fit into the generalized method of moments framework. From this well-developed asymptotic theory we can derive statistical tests and perform statistical analysis on the parameters (Koenker and Bassett 1982).

Using the first-order condition along with the GMM it is possible to demonstrate that the parameters estimated will be consistent and asymptotically normal (Koenker and Bassett 1978, 1982; Powell 1984; Buchinsky 1998). If $\lim[(X'X)/n] \rightarrow V$ with $X_{i1}=1$ for all i, and the error distribution, F, has strictly positive density at the θth quantile [that is, $f(F^{-1}(\theta))>0$], then $\hat{\beta}_\theta$ is asymptotically normal. That is,

$$\sqrt{n}(\hat{\beta}_\theta - \beta_\theta) \xrightarrow{d} N(0, g^2(\theta, F)V^{-1}) \tag{C-5}$$

where $\beta_\theta = \beta + (F^{-1}(\theta), 0, \ldots, 0)'$ and $g^2(\theta, F) = \theta(1-\theta)/f^2(F^{-1}(\theta))$. From this it follows that a natural statistical test for $H_o: M\beta = m$ is

$$\lambda = \hat{g}^{-2}(M\hat{\beta}_\theta - m)'(M(X'X)^{-1}M')(M\hat{\beta}_\theta - m) \tag{C-6}$$

where $\hat{g}$ is a consistent estimator of g.

The bootstrapping method is used to calculate the standard errors in the empirical test. The reason is that when the residuals are heteroscedastic, the formula given in Koenker and Bassett (1982) appears to grossly underestimate the true standard errors. Note that the precision of the parameters estimated depends on the magnitude of the density for each quantile. Therefore, the quantiles at the "border" of the distribution are more difficult to estimate because the density of the "dots" is low, and so the test has less power.

The QRM just discussed is not exempt from criticism. One criticism is related to the arbitrariness in the election of the proportion θ. This criticism is not relevant to our study: our main purpose is to characterize the distribution of the wage structure, so we use several conditional quantiles. Another problem associated with the QRM is that the final solution may not be unique. But uniqueness can always be achieved by selecting an appropriate design or by using an arbitrary rule to select from any set of multiple solutions (this problem is exactly similar to selecting the median among a sample that has an even number of observations).

References

Buchinsky, Moshe. 1998. "Recent Advances in Quantile Regressions Models: A Practical Guideline for Empirical Research." *Journal of Human Resources* 33 (1): 88–126.

Koenker, R., and G. Bassett. 1978. "Regression Quantiles." *Econometrica* 46: 33–50.

———. 1982. "Test of Linear Hypothesis and l_1-Estimation." *Econometrica* 50: 1577–83.

Montenegro, Claudio E. 1998. "The Structure of Wages in Chile 1960–1996: An Application of Quantile Regression." *Estudios de Economia* 25 (1): 71–98.

Powell, James. 1984. "Least Absolute Deviation Estimation of the Censored Regression Model." *Journal of Econometrics* 25: 303–25.

D Technical Annex to Chapter 7: Haindl's Labor Flows Model

The main purpose of Haindl's labor flows model is to derive flow variables from stock variables such as employment, unemployment, and labor force reported in the University of Chile's Household Surveys for Santiago.

Definition of Variables

Let us first define the following variables:

E = Employment level (in thousands of persons)

F = Labor force (in thousands of persons)

D = Unemployment level (in thousands of persons)

D^1 = Unemployed that are first-time job seekers (in thousands of persons)

D^2 = Unemployed persons that have been looking for a job for less than one quarter (in thousands of persons)

D^3 = Unemployed persons that have been looking for a job more than one quarter (in thousands of persons)

d = Number of persons that have been fired, have retired, or have left the labor force (in thousands of persons)

f = Number of persons that have entered the labor force during the period (in thousands of persons per quarter)

f^1 = Number of persons that entered the labor force for the first time (in thousands of persons per quarter)

f^2 = Number of persons that have entered the labor force that have worked before (in thousands of persons per quarter)

c = Number of persons that are hired in the current period (in thousands of persons per quarter)

c^1 = Flow of persons hired among those looking for a job for the first time (in thousands of persons per quarter)

c^2 = Flow of persons hired among those that had a job and have been looking for a new job one quarter or less (in thousands of persons per quarter)

c^3 = Flow of persons hired among those that had a job and have been looking for a new job more than one quarter (in thousands of persons per quarter)

π = Probability of finding a job in a quarter

P = Probability of finding a job in a month and a half

R = Average employment duration (in months)

T = Expected unemployment duration (in months)

We add the subscript "t" to the previous variables to indicate the respective quarter. The previous variables are related in the following ways.

Identities

$$D_t = D_t^1 + D_t^2 + D_t^3 \tag{D-1}$$

$$f_t = f_t^1 + f_t^2 \tag{D-2}$$

$$c_t = c_t^1 + c_t^2 + c_t^3 \tag{D-3}$$

$$D_t = F_t - E_t \tag{D-4}$$

Relationships Between Flows and Stocks

$$F_t = F_{t-1} + f_t \tag{D-5}$$

$$E_t = E_{t-1} + c_t - d_t \tag{D-6}$$

$$D_t = D_{t-1} + f_t + d_t - c_t \tag{D-7}$$

$$D_t^1 = D_{t-1}^1 + f_t^1 - c_t^1 \tag{D-8}$$

$$D_t^2 = f_t^2 + d_t - c_t^2 \tag{D-9}$$

$$D_t^3 = D_{t-1}^2 + D_{t-1}^3 - c_t^3 \tag{D-10}$$

Closing the System

The previous equations represent identities and relationships that determine the movements of the stocks variables based on the flow variables.

These relationships are deterministic and by definition are true in each period. However, they are not sufficient to obtain the flow variables from the stock variables. One way to close the system of equations is to relate the flow of people hired in a period to the probability of finding a job. To do that we assume that the probability of two different people finding a job in a certain period of time is independent of how long they have been looking for a job. The simplification permits closing the system and obtaining the flow variables based on the available information. If we estimate the flow of people hired in a period based on their expected value we have

$$c_t^1 = P_t - f_t^1 + \pi_t D_{t-1}^1 \tag{D-11}$$

$$c_t^2 = P_t(f_t^2 + d_t) \tag{D-12}$$

$$c_t^3 = \pi_t(D_{t-1}^2 + d_{t-1}^3) \tag{D-13}$$

The probability of finding a job for people who were unemployed in the previous period is different from the probability of finding a job for people that are first-time job seekers. If we use a quarter as the period of reference, then the search period of those that were unemployed at the beginning of the period is a quarter. If we assume that the flow of people that are entering the labor force for the first time follow the uniform distribution, the average search period for them is equal to half the period (one and a half months). This permits us to relate both probabilities as follows:

$$(1 - P_t)^2 = \pi_t \tag{D-14}$$

Obtaining Flows from Stocks

We can now solve the system. Using equations (D-10) and (D-13) we get:

$$\pi_t = 1 - \frac{D_t^3}{D_{t-1}^2 + D_{t-1}^3} \tag{D-15}$$

From equation (D-14) we get:

$$P_t = 1 - (1 - \pi_t)^{1/2} \tag{D-16}$$

From equations (D-2) and (D-15) we get:

$$f_t = f_t^1 + f_t^2 = F_t - F_{t-1} \tag{D-17}$$

Now using equations (D-8) and (D-11) we obtain the flow of people entering the labor force for the first time:

$$f_t^1 = \frac{(D_t^1 - D_{t-1}^1(1 - \pi_t))}{(1 - P_t)} \tag{D-18}$$

Using (D-17) and (D-18) we get:

$$f_t^2 = f_t - f_{t-1} \tag{D-19}$$

Combining equations (D-8), (D-9), (D-11), (D-12), (D-18), and (D-19) we can obtain the flow of people that have been fired, that have retired, or that have dropped out of the labor force in the period:

$$d_t = \frac{D_t^2}{1 - P_t} - f_t^2 \tag{D-20}$$

Finally we can obtain the flow of people hired in the period using equations (D-6) and (D-20):

$$c_t = E_t - E_{t-1} + d_t \tag{D-21}$$

The average tenure can be defined as the time it would take to fire all the people that are working at the beginning of the period, based on the assumption that the flow of people that are fired, retired, or just drop out of the labor force does not change and that the flow of newly hired people is zero. This can be expressed in the following equation:

$$R_t = \frac{3E_{t-1}}{d_t} \tag{D-22}$$

The expected time that a person is going to be unemployed can be estimated from the probability of finding a job in a given period. Let P_t^* be the probability that a person finds a job in a particular period t. In this case, the probability that the person will be unemployed for n months before finding a job, P_n, (that is, will find work in time n + 1) is given by:

$$P_n = P_t^*(1 - P_t^*)^n \tag{D-23}$$

The expected unemployment time is then

$$E(n) = \sum_{n=0}^{\infty} n P_n = \sum_{n=0}^{\infty} n P_t^*(1 - P_t^*)^n \tag{D-24}$$

Which implies that

$$T_t = E(n) = \frac{1 - P_t^*}{P_t^*} \qquad \text{(D-25)}$$

In other words, to calculate the expected unemployment time, T_t, it is necessary to estimate the probability that a person would find a job in any given month in quarter t. This can be done relating the probability P_t^*, with the probability of finding a job in period t, π_t. If the period is a quarter, then the relationship is the following:

$$(1 - \pi_t) = (1 - P_t^*)^3 \qquad \text{(D-26)}$$

From this we can get

$$P_t^* = 1 - (1 - \pi_t)^{1/3} \qquad \text{(D-27)}$$

Finally, combining equation (D-25) and (D-27):

$$T_t = \frac{(1 - \pi_t)^{1/3}}{1 - (1 - \pi_t)^{1/3}}. \qquad \text{(D-28)}$$

Contributors

Edward J. Amadeo is the Secretary of Economic Policy in the Ministry of Finance of the government of Brazil. His research has included topics in macroeconomics and labor markets. His contribution to the book was written when he was Professor of Economics in the Pontifical Catholic University of Rio de Janeiro. Since that time, he has served as the Minister of Labor for Brazil. He has a Ph.D. in economics from Harvard University.

Ricardo Paes de Barros is Director for Social Programs at the Brazilian Institute for Applied Economic Research (IPEA) in Rio de Janeiro, and has been a Research Economist for Inequality, Education, Poverty, and Labor Market Issues there since 1979. He has written extensively on issues related to poverty, labor markets, and education in Brazil. He has taught at the University of Chicago and Yale University. He has a Ph.D. in economics from the University of Chicago.

Dörte Dömeland is a doctoral student in Economics at the Universitat Pompeu Fabra in Barcelona, Spain. While contributing to this book, she was a consultant to the World Bank. She has a master's degree in economics from Universitat Pompeu Fabra and a bachelor's degree in economics from Eberhards-Karls-Universität, Tübingen, Germany.

Miguel Nathan Foguel is a Researcher at the Brazilian Institute for Applied Economic Research. Since contributing to this book, he has served as advisor to Brazil's Minister of Labor. He has a master's degree in economics from the Catholic University of Rio de Janeiro, where he has also taught.

Indermit S. Gill is the Lead Economist for Human Development in the World Bank's Latin America and Caribbean Region. This book was written while he was a Senior Economist in the Brazil Country Management Unit based in Brasilia. Before joining the World Bank in 1993, he taught at the State University of New York at Buffalo. He has a Ph.D. in economics from the University of Chicago.

José Luis Guasch is Sector Manager for Private Sector Development in the World Bank's Latin America and Caribbean Region. His recent work includes a book on labor market reform in Latin America. He is Professor of Economics at the University of California at San Diego, on leave since 1998. He has a Ph.D. in economics from Stanford University.

Erik Haindl is Director of the Economics Institute at Gabriela Mistral University in Santiago, Chile. He has written on labor and poverty issues in Latin America. He has a master's degree in economics from the University of Chicago.

Rosane Silva Pinto de Mendonça has been a Researcher at the Brazilian Institute for Applied Economic Research in Rio de Janeiro since 1987, and Assistant Professor in the Economics Department of the Federal University Fluminense. She has a master's degree in economics from the Catholic University of Rio de Janeiro, and a Ph.D. in economics from the Federal University of Rio de Janeiro.

Claudio E. Montenegro is an Economist with the Development Research Group in the World Bank. He worked on this book as a consultant to the Bank. He has held several positions at the University of Chile in Santiago, the Inter-American Development Bank, and the World Bank. He has a masters degree in economics from the University of Maryland at College Park and a masters degree in statistics from The George Washington University.

Marcelo Neri teaches at the Getulio Vargas Foundation in Rio de Janeiro. During the time he contributed to this book, he was a researcher at the Brazilian Institute for Applied Economic Research and Professor of Economics at the Federal University of Rio de Janeiro. He has written extensively on labor issues in Brazil. He has a Ph.D. in economics from Princeton University.

Carola Pessino is Professor of Labor Economics at CEMA in Buenos Aires. Since contributing to this book, she has served as the Secretary for Social and Fiscal Affairs in Argentina's Federal Ministry for Finance and the Economy. She has taught at Duke University and Yale University. She has a Ph.D. in economics from the University of Chicago.

Claudio N. Sapelli is Associate Professor of Economics at the Pontifical Catholic University in Santiago, Chile. His recent research has been in the areas of education and health economics. Before taking up his current appointment, he worked at the World Bank. He has a Ph.D. in economics from the University of Chicago.

Index

Note: *f* indicates figures, *n* indicates notes, and *t* indicates tables.

Economic Commission for Latin
America (ECLAC), 217
Ecuador
compensation funds in, 19
temporary contracts' rules
changes in, 6, 7
unemployment compensation
in, 22
Education
during 1990s, 2
in Chile, for poor children,
175–76
in Chile, impact of policies to
reduce wage inequalities
with, 179t
in Chile, mean and median
estimates of wage inequality
and, 173f
in Chile, mean years of schooling by decile group, 169,
171, 171t
in Chile, of parents by child's
school type, 177t
in Chile, quantile estimates of
wage inequality and, 174f
in Chile, rates of return to,
155–56, 161, 184n10, 187,
228
in Chile, wage inequality and,
169, 171–73, 172t, 175,
227–28
in Chile, wage inequality for
blue-collar workers and,
173, 175, 175f, 189
in Chile, wage inequality for
white-collar workers and,
173, 174f, 188
in Chile, wage inequality patterns and trends and, 164
public-private pensions differences in Brazil and, 59–60
public-private sector compensation differentials in Brazil
and, 38
severance pay mandates and, 13

Edwards, Sebastian, 205, 212n3
Elasticity of substitution
definition of, 152n3
estimates of labor demand in
Argentina, 151
Elías, Victor, 139
Employment Law, Argentina (1991),
130
Employment levels. See also Job
instability
in Argentina, labor force growth
vs. growth in, 129–30
in Argentina, population
growth and, 104
job security legislation and, 4–6
in Latin America during 1990s,
217
Employment precariousness
in Chile, 195–98, 216, 228–29
in Chile, poor workers and,
201–204, 202t, 203t
in Latin America, 217
model for measurement of,
192–93, 194f
Encuesta de Caracteriación Socioeconomica Nacional (CASEN)
household surveys, 161, 163–64,
184n9, 212n4
description of, 183n4
wage inequality analysis using,
168
Equal employment opportunity laws,
in Chile, 180
Estatuto Docente, Chile, 184n12
education reforms and, 182
Exchange rates, in Argentina, 99,
152n6
Experience rating, 206, 213n6

Fallon, Peter R., 28n13
Family workers, severance payments
and, 28n14
Ferreira, Francisco, 159, 164, 166,
183n4, 183n5